Words Matter

History and current affairs show that words matter – and change – because they are woven into our social and political lives. Words are weapons wielded by the powerful; they are also powerful tools for social resistance and for reimagining and reconfiguring social relations. Illustrated with topical examples, from racial slurs and sexual insults to preferred gender pronouns, from ethnic/racial group labels to presidential tweets, this book examines the social contexts which imbue words with potency. Exploring the role of language in three broad categories – establishing social identities, navigating social landscapes, and debating social and linguistic change – Sally McConnell-Ginet invites readers to examine critically their own ideas about language and its complicated connections to social conflict and transformation. Concrete and timely examples vividly illustrate the feedback loop between words and the world, shedding light on how and why words can matter.

Sally McConnell-Ginet is Professor Emerita of Linguistics at Cornell University and a Past President of the Linguistic Society of America.

Words Matter

Meaning and Power

SALLY MCCONNELL-GINET
Cornell University

CAMBRIDGE
UNIVERSITY PRESS

University Printing House, Cambridge CB2 8BS, United Kingdom

One Liberty Plaza, 20th Floor, New York, NY 10006, USA

477 Williamstown Road, Port Melbourne, VIC 3207, Australia

314–321, 3rd Floor, Plot 3, Splendor Forum, Jasola District Centre,
New Delhi – 110025, India

79 Anson Road, #06–04/06, Singapore 079906

Cambridge University Press is part of the University of Cambridge.

It furthers the University's mission by disseminating knowledge in the pursuit of
education, learning, and research at the highest international levels of excellence.

www.cambridge.org
Information on this title: www.cambridge.org/9781108427210
DOI: 10.1017/9781108641302

First published 2020

A catalogue record for this publication is available from the British Library.

Library of Congress Cataloging-in-Publication Data
Names: McConnell-Ginet, Sally, author.
Title: Words matter : meaning and power / Sally McConnell-Ginet, Cornell
University, New York.
Description: Cambridge, UK ; New York : Cambridge University Press, 2020. |
Includes bibliographical references and index.
Identifiers: LCCN 2020009172 | ISBN 9781108427210 (hardback) | ISBN
9781108641302 (ebook)
Subjects: LCSH: Sociolinguistics. | interpersonal communication. | Linguistic change.
| Language and culture.
Classification: LCC P40 .M425 2020 | DDC 306.44–dc23
LC record available at https://lccn.loc.gov/2020009172

ISBN 978-1-108-42721-0 Hardback
ISBN 978-1-108-44590-0 Paperback

Contents

Figures

Acknowledgments

Writing this book has been challenging and rewarding. For more years than I care to admit, I have circled around the topic of the embedding of meaning-making in social life. This book finally brings together some of my thinking on that topic in a way that I hope will engage people who have not thought much about these issues before and will also interest some who have. I could not have done it without a large community of supportive friends and colleagues to whom I am very grateful. Some readers may just want to look for names or skip this section altogether; these acknowledgments situate my gratitude in my intellectual history, and I have not written that for the book's general audience. Inevitably, I will have neglected to mention names of some important contributors to or supporters of my work. I hope my imperfect memory will be forgiven.

My first paper in graduate school was for a semantics course taught by Adrienne Lehrer, whose own work has explored a variety of topics connected to lexical meaning. That paper, which I revised and published a decade later, focused on the abstract and difficult word *good* and the way in which the words it modified (*good dancer* vs *good mother* vs *good wine*) shifted how it was understood. Adrienne graciously agreed to supervise my PhD on the semantics of comparatives, which focused on the map between syntax and semantics rather than on specific meanings of content words.

By happy accident, just as I was beginning my dissertation, I was able to attend an NEH summer program on semantics organized by philosopher Gil Harman. There I heard and learned directly from such people as Gareth Evans, Paul Grice, David Kaplan, Saul Kripke, Barbara Partee, Bob Stalnaker (later a Cornell colleague in philosophy), Rich Thomason, and others. And I was introduced to work by Joan Bresnan, Hans Kamp, Irene Heim, David Lewis, Richard Montague, Hilary Putnam, and more. Their ways of thinking about language resonated for me, so I was 'primed' when

Gennaro Chierchia arrived at Cornell in the 1980s and suggested we coauthor a text to introduce semantics to linguists, which turned out to be a very rewarding collaboration. That collaboration might never have borne fruit without Craige Roberts' help. I was on leave in Palo Alto and beginning to work on 'my' chapters when I sustained a diagonal break of my tibia, the same injury that had kept me in a wheelchair for many months as a nine-year-old. Craige happened to find out about this early on. She rescued me from my growing despair by suggesting that the two of us form a reading group and also discussing with me the chapter on presupposition I was drafting for the semantics text. And she's continued to support my work, including this book.

Not surprisingly, the chapter in the semantics text on lexical meaning was the most difficult for me to write (and the one about which Gennaro and I had the most intense arguments – I miss arguing with Gennaro, whom I see too seldom these days). For the second edition, published in 2000, I scrapped most of what I had said about lexical meaning in the first so that I could highlight the important work showing that even content words show considerable semantic systematicity, especially in abstract matters like causation. But I could not embrace the view that lexical meanings were *fully* analyzed by recurring components, even though I found many such analyses enlightening. In an earlier paper on adverbs, I had returned to matters of modification about which I had first written in my *good* paper. I proposed that, in a technical sense, adverbs actually shift the meanings of the verbs to which they attach. In an aside, I also suggested that adverbs like *botanically* or *technically* indicate alternative interpretations of some word and direct interpreters to interpretations serving particular purposes. Languages offer a range of resources for tinkering with what words mean, I somewhat tentatively suggested.

But this work had very little to do with social life or power. In the early 1970s, immediately after I got my PhD, I was hired for a visiting position at Cornell in what was then called Women's Studies (and at Cornell is now called FGSS, pronounced like 'figs' and standing for Feminist, Gender, and Sexuality Studies) and Philosophy. That first year I taught a seminar in the first semester that helped me develop an undergraduate course for the second semester called "Women and Language," which eventually became

"Language and Gender." The linguists then took me on to teach the undergraduate gender course (and other courses in the structure of English, semantics, and pragmatics). I was already influenced by feminist activism and popular literature like *The Feminine Mystique*, but teaching about the interaction of language with gender issues led me to explore not only the burgeoning literature in feminist scholarship (and later queer studies) but also some of the relevant theoretical literature in the social sciences. Jane-Carol Glendinning, a Penn PhD in linguistics who attended my first seminar, introduced me to empirically grounded studies of language use being done by William Labov and students. Our contact has been somewhat sporadic, but she remains a valued friend and supporter. With literary scholar Nelly Furman and anthropologist Ruth Borker (who, very sadly, died shortly after turning forty), I coedited and contributed to *Women and Language in Literature and Society* (with indexing help from Ruta Noreika, an undergraduate in that first language and gender course, who remains a close friend). My undergraduate education included no social science, and the only literature class I took was one in German. Nelly, Ruth, and anthropologist Kathryn March helped educate me. Kath had been a grad student in that initial seminar and later became a Cornell colleague with whom I taught several times and who remains a good friend. Other friends and colleagues in Women's Studies like social psychologist Sandra Bem (also dead far too early) and political scientist Mary F. Katzenstein (who read a draft of this book and offered useful suggestions) also helped expand my intellectual horizons to ideas about patriarchy, injustice, ideology, and more, as did Zillah Eisenstein, a major figure in socialist feminism at Ithaca College.

Initially I was uncomfortable thinking about issues of meaning and gender. After all, I had been reared with the myth that "*he* includes *she*" by virtue of some mysterious 'linguistic convention.' I even used male names in the invented examples of my dissertation. The study of meaning was abstract as I understood it, the sort of thing a former math major like me felt comfortable pursuing. Well, I could hardly ignore the social in thinking about gender, but I tried at first to contain it to matters I thought of as in the scope of sociolinguistics, safely not my field, or pragmatics. Maybe I could keep the social action to matters like variation in pronunciation (for others to study and me to teach), politeness, and whether women and men might perform different speech acts (or the same ones in different ways – or be understood differently). But students and colleagues fairly soon made my compartmentalization of the two strands of my research and teaching deeply problematic. From when I first saw Kath March slap stickers proclaiming "This is offensive to women" on posters and the like, the two strands got entangled. I began to suspect that saying generic masculines were "just conventional" was a cop-out. How might conventions like that arise? Empirical research already showed clearly that in actual linguistic practice *he* was not freely useable in all circumstances of reference to human beings. So I began to think, write, and give talks about pronouns in English and then about how it might be that expressions referring to women so often became infected with negativity. Soon there was no turning back.

I fully embraced research on the interaction of meaning with gender and sexuality in the early 1980s after I met and started talking with sociolinguist Penelope Eckert. Penny and I began actually collaborating at the beginning of the 1990s and published the first edition of our coauthored *Language and Gender* in 2003. Penny inspired me by just charging ahead and working on issues that concerned her without paying attention to the kinds of questions that always seemed to plague me. "Is this linguistics?" or "Is this semantics?" I used to ask myself, worried that the answer was "no." Of course, having tenure has made it much easier to ignore disciplinary boundaries, but Penny had ignored them before being so protected. She introduced me to Bourdieu and Goffman and many other important thinkers about language in our lives. And we talked and talked (and sometimes argued) when writing together, a highlight being a joint residency at the Rockefeller Institute in Bellagio in 1998. Penny's wonderful "Indexical Fields" paper was the basis of a talk she gave on the occasion of my retirement from teaching at Cornell. (My good friend and colleague Molly Diesing also gave a talk then that used syntactic and pragmatic theory to analyze spells in the Harry Potter books; she and I collaborated on developing the paper further, but, sadly, potential publishers wanted more revisions to it than we were willing to make.) Although I was glad in 2013 to see my first print copy of the second edition of *Language and Gender*, greatly changed from the first, I was sad that my work with Penny had ended. Our friendship, of course, continues.

I had begun thinking about writing this book (or something like it) after Betty Birner and Gregory Ward invited me in the early 2000s to submit a paper to the festschrift they were editing in honor of Larry Horn. (Gregory and I had become close colleagues and good friends through our work for the LSA and through co-teaching a course on language and sexuality at the LSA Linguistic Institute at Michigan State in the summer of 2003. I owe Gregory special thanks for useful comments on the draft of this book sent to Cambridge in August 2019.) That paper on defining *marriage* and the connected disputes over the institution of marriage was my first solo project fully embracing the "who cares if it's really linguistics?" orientation that Penny's example (and being tenured!) helped me finally adopt. And I thank Deborah Cameron for abridging it for inclusion in a collection she was coediting with Don Kulick on language and sexuality. (Debbie is another hero, who, long before being professionally secure, did not listen to "that's not linguistics." She just did and continues to do brilliant feminist work about language, now on her wonderful blog, *Language: A Feminist Guide*, at debuk.wordpress.com.) The *marriage* paper was followed by my LSA Presidential Address, "Words in the World." Encouraged by an editor no longer in the publishing business, I began then to think about writing a book that developed some of the ideas in that paper, a book pitched toward nonacademics.

And in 2015 I got several invitations pushing me forward. The first was from the Yale linguistics department inviting me to give a talk at a workshop celebrating Larry Horn on the occasion of his retirement. I used the occasion to explore linguistic issues of special significance to transgender people. (I should say here that without Larry's published work as well as his constant attentiveness to media sources attesting to changing linguistic practices I would have been hard put to write this book.) And then Brian King, to whom New Zealand linguist Janet Holmes, a wonderful feminist scholar and supporter, had introduced me years earlier, invited me to speak at IGALA (International Gender and Language Association) 9, the theme of which was *transition*. With valuable input from Andrea James, a transgender writer and activist I met online, I developed the paper from the "Hornucopia" event and, after giving that talk, met some inspiring transgender activists in Hong Kong in May 2016. (Chu-Ren Huang, my PhD student at Cornell, had invited me to spend a week at Hong Kong Polytechnic University in 2010; he and other linguists in Hong Kong, including his wife, Kathleen Ahrens, have been greatly supportive of my work.)

Perhaps most critically, in 2015 Sebastian Bücking invited me to participate in the two-week DGfS (Deutsche Gesellschaft für Semantik) summer school, "Mapping Meaning," that he was organizing at the University of Tübingen for late August 2016. "Meaning, Society, and Power" was the title of my eight-session course, which touched on many though not all the topics in this book. This book benefitted enormously from comments not only by the enrolled students but also from several faculty attending, Tübingen professors Erhard Hinrichs and Claudia Maienborn as well as visiting professor Nicholas Asher.

Coincidentally, my friends Fred Landman, a former colleague, and Susan Rothstein, also a distinguished syntactician and semanticist, were in the final weeks of eighteen-month research fellowships that had brought them to Tübingen from Tel Aviv. I was able to spend time with them, including a marvelous day at a nearby spa with Susan, where we soaked in mineral water and talked about my book project. Susan was enormously supportive of all my work and very insightful in her comments. Like many others, I was devastated by her unexpected and too early death in the summer of 2019.

I returned from Germany with the book still in its early stages. Donald Trump's defeat of Hillary Clinton a couple of months later helped move me to commit (finally) to writing this book. In the spring of 2017, I lunched with Andrew Winnard of Cambridge University Press. Andrew encouraged me to submit a proposal, which the syndics accepted that June. The worries of one of the Press's reviewers that I might focus too much on gender and sexuality spurred me to do even more reading and thinking than I already had about matters of race and ethnicity. And in late August 2017 I began teaching "Language in Society," a Cornell undergraduate course for which the text was Miriam Meyerhoff's *Introducing Sociolinguistics*. (Colleague Abigail Cohn had recommended to chair John Whitman that I step in while she was on leave; Abby also read and commented on part of this book.) I'd naively thought that I would combine drafts of my projected book with assignments from Miriam's text (one of her exercises originated in my language and gender course, which she'd attended while at Cornell on a postdoc) and thereby progress with my writing. Well, it worked less smoothly than I'd hoped. Drafts rolled out quickly at first but then slowed. And the organization I'd envisioned in my proposal did not work as I'd imagined. Nonetheless, the interaction with the undergraduates was stimulating and their enthusiasm helped me move along.

That same fall, Luvell Anderson invited me to give a talk, which I called "Truth, Trust, and Trumpery." A slightly different version of that paper had been published shortly before in a festschrift honoring Janet Holmes and edited by Meredith Marra and Paul Warren, to whom I owe thanks for getting permission for republication of that paper by the *Southern Journal of Philosophy* as part of the proceedings from the University of Memphis conference organized by Luvell. This book does not address directly the issues that paper raises, nor does it deal with a number of relevant matters covered in *Propaganda* by Jason Stanley, a former colleague. It was, however, Jason's invitation to speak at a Yale conference on language and authority in the spring of 2018 that helped me develop the chapter on semantic authority (Chapter 7). And David Beaver, coauthor with Jason of a published paper and of a book in progress on related matters, not only read the entire manuscript of this book in September 2019 but offered some very useful comments and suggestions.

Not long after the Yale conference, Heather Burnett invited me to spend a week in April 2019 with her and her colleagues and students in the stimulating linguistics group at Paris 7. I gave a talk based on the chapter on linguistic reform and resistance to it (Chapter 6) in their departmental colloquium and a new version of the semantic authority material in a workshop organized for the final weekend of my stay. Even more important, I got to talk with Heather, Andrea Beltrama (then a postdoc in Heather's group), and others in the department as well as the other workshop participants.

A host of others have given me useful references or read and commented on portions of the material in the book or read the manuscript and sent encouragement. In addition to people I have already mentioned, they include at least the following: Susan

Brison, Richard Brooks, Liz Camp, Susan Gelman, Karen Jones, Dan Jurafsky, Rae Langton, Barbara Deutsch Lynch, Sarah Murray, Donna Jo Napoli, Joan Ormondroyd, Mandy Simon, Will Starr, Zoltan Szabó, and Rob Voigt. Colleagues who gave me more substantial comments include not only David Beaver, Mary Katzenstein, and Gregory Ward, whose help I have already mentioned, but also Anne Adams (a Cornell colleague from Africana and a good friend), Mary Kate McGowan (a leading contributor to social philosophy of language whom I've met at a couple of conferences), Matt Shields (recent Georgetown PhD in philosophy who invited me to serve on his doctoral committee), and Mia Wiegand (Cornell grad student in semantics).

Other Cornell colleagues, especially but not only in linguistics and philosophy, have supported this work in various ways. I've mentioned Molly Diesing, Abby Cohn, and John Whitman already. The semantics reading group, begun by Sarah Murray and Will Starr, has been a wonderful resource and a lively audience for 'practice' talks I've given on material from the book.

It was Sarah who suggested Mia Wiegand (now Windhearn) serve as my research assistant in the final months of manuscript preparation. Mia has given me excellent substantive feedback and has also taken over technical details, including mastering Word's indexing capabilities. Funds for hiring Mia and for other expenses came from a PEARS (Podell Emeriti Award for Research and Scholarship) grant, ably administered by Cynthia Robinson in the office of CAPE (the Cornell Association of Professors Emeriti) and then by Gretchen Ryan, administrative manager of Cornell's Department of Linguistics. Albert P. Podell, Cornell Class of 1958, set up PEARS in 2005 to help "support research and scholarship related to making the world a better place for all peoples of the Earth." What impact a book like mine can have I'm unsure, but I hope very much that it does do at least some small good. I greatly appreciate Mr. Podell's support of mine and other projects undertaken by retired Cornellians.

I've already mentioned Andrew Winnard of Cambridge University Press, with whom I'd earlier worked on *Language and Gender*. Andrew was mainly involved in acquiring the book, but he also helped draft a licensing agreement for Figure 5.1 with Abby Muller of Algonquin Press. Isabel Collins, however, was my primary Cambridge editorial contact in late 2019. In December 2019, Grace Morris began managing production and by late January 2020 Stanly Emelson and Frances Tye were handling the (almost) final stages. Jayavel Radhakrishnan and team took over final typesetting corrections in April. In the pandemic shutdown of the Cornell campus, friend and neighbor Bonni Voiland scanned sheets for me to send Jay. CUP's Rachel Tonkin began the advertising push. Thanks to them all.

Many others, in Ithaca and afar, have also supported me – friends in Eastwood Commons, Drama Club, yoga class, Women Swimmin', theatre boards, and more. Diana Hotaling's political insights have been as invaluable as her cleaning skills. And I thank Judith Richwine and Alison Spransy, my sisters, along with nephews and nieces, cousins, as well as others who are 'family' by virtue of something other than a bit of shared genetic material. I do hope that at least some of you read this book.

Two people reading these acknowledgments may well be wondering why their names have not yet appeared. The first is Gillian Moore Jondorf, retired from Cambridge's Modern Languages Faculty and a Life Fellow of Girton College, Cambridge. Jill has been a close friend for six decades, beginning when I went to Cambridge on a Fulbright in philosophy. I sent Jill the manuscript in August 2019, hoping but not daring to expect that she would read and comment on it. Jill is a linguist in the sense of knowing very well languages other than her native English, but she is neither a philosopher of language nor a linguist as understood by most university departments and programs of linguistics. She is, however, a meticulous reader and proofreader, which I knew. I was delighted when she returned the manuscript a month or so later with copious and extremely helpful annotations. Typos, inconsistencies, unclarities: she is not to blame if some of these remain. I tried to respond to all her comments but I may have missed a few and may also have introduced new infelicities in making other revisions. I was especially touched and pleased that she said she found the process enjoyable. Thanks are inadequate.

The second is Carl Ginet, my husband. Carl has read and reread many versions of the material in the book, listened to me talk about it in public, discussed it with me over dinner and on many other occasions, and in countless ways propped up my sometimes flagging commitment to the project. Carl has been retired from Cornell's philosophy department for a couple of decades, but he still reads philosophy papers for pleasure. His own writing is beautifully clear. And he has always advised me as well as his students to use plenty of examples. Often as I was writing I heard that injunction. When I did hand over drafts, sometimes reluctantly, his careful criticism was leavened with what seemed like real enthusiasm (though I do have to remember that he's a very talented actor!). Without him I doubt if I could have finished.

Carl is also the love of my life, whom I met at age 20 just a few months before I met Jill. I dedicated my previous book to him. This one I want to dedicate to his and my now middle-aged children – Lisa, Alan, and Greg Ginet – and to Jill Dreeben, Greg's wife, and Bob Spatz, Lisa's husband. And I include our millennial grandchildren – Simon, Chris, Michael, and Vanessa Ginet. In different ways, they too have all cheered me on.

Ithaca, New York, USA
April 2020

Getting Started

Words (and meaningful silences) matter enormously in our lives. They enable us to cooperate, collaborate, and ally with one another – as well as to exclude, exploit, and subordinate one another. They script our performances as certain kinds of people in certain social locations. They are politically powerful, both as dominating weapons that help oppress and as effective tools that can resist oppression. But words in and of themselves are impotent. It is the socially structured practices and historically situated circumstances constituting our social lives that pour content into words, endow them with meaning and power.

This book explores how such meaning-making works. It does so by examining a number of concrete examples of linguistic practices, many of them very current. I am writing it not for specialists, although I hope some may find it useful, but for anyone willing to join me in examining critically their own ideas about language and its complicated connections to social conflict and change. As that invitation suggests, I am also writing it to help clarify my own understanding of these often complex and contentious issues. I do not expect that readers will always agree with my perspectives, either before or after reading the book. But I do hope they will, as I have tried to do, rethink familiar assumptions.

Do 'politically correct' efforts to change or regulate language sometimes go too far? Why do people keep changing the labels they use to identify themselves? Isn't speaking 'grammatically' important anymore? What does it mean to say that certain words or ways of speaking are 'sexist' or 'racist'? What might be meant by 'hate speech' or 'dangerous speech'? Are there words or ways of speaking that should be abandoned, maybe even

outlawed? Does 'free speech' license saying anything at all in any
context? What might be effective strategies for 'counter speech' to
help defuse words that increase social tensions? How are new
words, new meanings, or new ways of using familiar words
authorized, 'legitimated' as part of a shared language?

I explore these and similar issues with as little technical appa-
ratus, jargon, and ideological bias as possible and lay out my own
commitments as clearly as I can. I do include some notes at the
end of each chapter, but they mainly give information about
sources and occasional suggestions for further reading, so feel
free to ignore them. My emphasis is on everyday linguistic
encounters of many different kinds. I hope that readers who are
not already in the habit of noticing linguistic details of their own
experience will begin to do so more often, mining their own
observations for new insights into social life.

Although I occasionally range further afield, most (not all) of
my illustrative cases feature the US and practices involving the
English language. This geographic and linguistic parochialism
reflects my own limitations as well as biases in the research
literature. I hope that those with interests in other parts of the
world and other languages may nonetheless find this book
relevant.

I entered the field of linguistics via logic and the philosophy of
language. Abstracting away from the social identities of language
users and from their relations to one another, these fields were
able to enrich understanding of some important aspects of linguistic meaning, of how languages allow us humans to put complex and novel messages out in the public domain. The focus of
much of this work has been on understanding the direct, face-to-
face, linguistic transmission of information between interchangeable individuals presumed to be cooperating with one another.
But it was far from clear how to make sense of the role of linguistic
practices in social institutions and in social conflict and change.
And that's what we needed in order to understand why social
activists were so concerned about linguistic matters.

Beginning with black civil rights activists after World War II, identity-based groups began to 'politicize' everyday social relations, including linguistic practices. Many other identity-focused social movements soon followed: second-wave feminism, gay and lesbian rights activism expanding to other sexuality and gender-identity groups, panethnic movements like those initiated by Asian Americans or Latinos/Hispanics. Students in college classrooms were suggesting that what we older folks thought of as 'just semantic conventions' worked to the disadvantage of particular oppressed groups. The young women we were teaching, for example, did not always feel their experiences were being considered in courses with titles like "Man and His Place in Nature." "Black is beautiful," proclaimed some activists, and the label *Negro* began to fade away. "But don't they [!] want to be called African American now?" some white person would chime in. More recently, opponents to extending the right to marry to couples other than those consisting of one man and one woman relied on legally ratified 'definitions' of *marriage* to support their position. And so on. How to think about linguistic politics was not immediately obvious to those of us trained in formal semantics, pragmatics, or the philosophy of language. At least not to me.

Many researchers in linguistics and philosophy of language, however, have recently moved toward work that transforms the abstract isolated individual speaker into a socially situated being interacting with others. These new directions are exciting and inspiring not only to me but to young people entering our disciplines, whose work has been crucial in developing more socially realistic theories of language and linguistic communication. Increasingly, investigators are drawing on existing tools, and also developing new ones, to explore and to theorize social dimensions of meaning. This book draws heavily on such recent work, as is clear from both my acknowledgments and the references I cite.

A major impetus for these explorations has been political activism around everyday uses of language. Ideas of everyday people – people who are not linguists or language specialists – about the linguistic resources they encounter and about their own

linguistic actions and reactions have prompted those of us in our
ivory towers to rethink our sometimes simplistic accounts. There
has also been an increased willingness among linguists and philosophers to consider ideas about meaning from colleagues in
other academic disciplines: social theorists, anthropologists, social
and cognitive psychologists, literary scholars, and more. My discussion in this book of why and how words matter for our social
relationships draws not only from my own disciplines but, more
than is usual for a 'language' person, from studies in social theory,
psychology, history, and other areas. I do this in part to show how
deeply embedded language is in our lives.

Readers may sometimes not approve of the words I have put –
or failed to put – on these pages. In general, I try to walk a middle
line. For the most part I avoid recent coinages that will be unfamiliar to many readers – for example, I wait until the final chapter
to discuss *Latinx* as a possible non-gendered alternative to *Latina*
and *Latino*. But throughout the book, I choose *they* instead of *he*
or *she* to refer to someone whom I know does not want the
standard gendered pronouns used for them and also as a default
gender-neutral form of reference. (I confess that I still sometimes
find *they* in speaking of a specific individual far from easy. This
was recently confirmed when a university search committee asked
me to write a recommendation with no gendered references to the
candidate.) I discuss pronoun controversies in the sixth chapter,
returning to the issue in the final chapter.

Given that this is a book about language, sometimes I *mention*
words I myself might be reluctant to *use*. Let me illustrate this
distinction. Speaking of a fastidious old friend in my play-reading
group, I might say "She always said *damn* when there was a *fuck* in
the script, which made it hard in most contemporary plays for her
to read parts with any sense of authenticity." I have mentioned
damn and *fuck* but could go on to use them by saying something
like, "But she was a damn good reader even if she was a bit fucked
up." I italicized the mentions above. In speech and in much
writing, however, there is no distinction between a word and its
name, the word we use to mention it. So someone hearing or

seeing a metalinguistic mentioning of a word is not fully insulated from effects that might be produced by uses of the word.[1] I try to minimize mentions of words likely to wound or otherwise annoy some readers. I cannot avoid them altogether, however, and be clear. Of course, one of the issues the book addresses is debate over avoiding words because of possible offense to some.

This book is organized around three broad kinds of social and linguistic actions and practices. The first three chapters focus on what I sometimes call *identifying*, linguistic practices centering on labels for social identities. The next two emphasize what I call *placing*, using language to push one another around the social landscape. And then there are two chapters highlighting *change* and disputes about it. They deal more with language *about* language – *meta*linguistic actions and practices – and with how social arrangements, including power relations, affect success in metalinguistic projects. The *concluding* chapter of the book discusses more case studies in light of the perspectives emerging from the preceding discussion.

I have used *gerund* forms, a verb plus the suffix *-ing*, for chapter titles. I do this to emphasize that it is linguistic *practices* that are our focus, not static linguistic structures. Linguistic practices are socially recognized ways of *acting* or *doing* in which words figure centrally: wearing name tags at a social event, engaging in rap battles, standing and singing "God Save the Queen," quoting a dictionary definition or a passage from a grammar book to 'win' an argument, and so on. We do not all recognize or participate in the same linguistic practices: they are tied to particular communities. These communities can be small face-to-face ones like church choirs or book clubs, or they can be very large 'imagined' ones like nations.[2] I have organized this book around a range of illustrative examples, both very contemporary and from centuries past. My aim is to show some of the complexities of social meaning-making in action.

Identity politics is often mentioned with disdain, and it is also associated with bringing linguistic questions into focus, often in ways that outsiders mock. Although I early on recognized and endorsed what became known as *intersectionality*, the idea that, for example, racial and gender identities inflect one another, I knew far less than I wanted to about how this worked. (My often 'unmarked' whiteness made it all too easy to ignore my own racial identity.)

I realized that I had avoided discussing race, and more generally that I had done little to further understanding of talk about social identities as such. So that seemed the place to start this book.

Labeling, the first chapter, explores why and how sorting and tagging people with social-identity labels matters, given the historically contingent and changing nature of those identities. The second chapter, *Marking/Erasing*, looks at linguistic practices through which some identity groups dominate others and through which such dominance gets challenged. *Generalizing*, the third chapter, looks at the continuing significance of social identities and the need to speak about them even when they are socially constructed and not inherent in unalterable 'scientific' facts.

The next two chapters are less focused on identifying social groups and their members and more on individual social actors using words to position and reposition one another in a social landscape. The fourth chapter, *Addressing*, draws attention to everyday linguistic practices in which we participate with one another, the social significance of which we often overlook and which sometimes is only evident through statistical patterns. *Putting Down*, the fifth chapter, was another challenge to myself to think about hard and uncomfortable questions. What I found especially important here was realizing that the significance of, for example, explicit racial slurs goes far beyond their direct effects on targets they aim to subordinate. They often function in the absence of those targets to recruit potential allies for racist projects.

The topic of linguistic reform has already been foreshadowed by the earlier chapters, but the sixth and seventh chapters put these matters center stage. Linguists often say that languages change "in response to" social change, but of course such changes don't happen without human agency, which is sometimes but not always intentional and often encounters explicit opposition. *Reforming/Resisting*, the sixth chapter, looks at some specific reform proposals that show clearly the embedding of linguistic practices in social practices and arrangements more generally. The seventh chapter, *Authorizing*, tackles disputes over semantic authority, over controlling what words mean.

The arc of the book moves through shared social identities to interpersonal jockeying for position to explicit struggles over changing language. Because I am trying to show the complexity of linguistic politics I rarely issue definitive pronouncements or produce clear summaries of 'morals' to be drawn. In keeping with that stance, the eighth and final chapter, *Concluding*, does not emphasize drawing 'conclusions.' Rather, building on the ideas developed throughout the book, it opens discussion of some difficult ongoing questions through examining several more specific cases.

Words matter enormously, but often mainly because they bring into the light of day attitudes, assumptions, and actions that ground social relations and arrangements. They make public ideas, hopes and plans, commitments, values, and affiliations. Sometimes what's made public is only covert, thus at least in principle deniable. Still, linguistic awareness helps uncover what's happening. It helps challenge and disturb existing power relations. Linguistic and social change go hand in hand because linguistic practices are fundamental to social practices more generally. Words are woven into the social fabric.

Notes

1. "Talking about Slurs," an unpublished paper that philosopher Cassie Herbert kindly shared with me, offers a number of excellent reasons to avoid even mentioning very offensive language.
2. See Anderson 1983 for the notion of imagined communities.

1   Labeling: "What Are You, Anyway?"

Social identities are categories into which individual people are grouped by others and by themselves. Labels, or group names, are essential to social identities. Labels may shift over time as groups realign and develop different views of themselves and their relations to other groups. And new social identities come with new labels. Labeling people as certain 'kinds' of people can contribute to shaping the kinds of people they become.

Philosopher Ian Hacking wrote what I found a wonderful book a couple of decades ago called *The Social Construction of What?* By the mid-1990s it had become very fashionable among many in the social sciences and humanities to say that categories, 'kinds,' were 'socially constructed.' Yet just what was meant by that was far from clear. Did it mean 'anything goes'? Was social constructionism paving the way for the 'post-truth' era? Using a number of detailed case studies, Hacking tries to develop a clearer understanding of the insights of social constructionism while not denying the imperviousness of much of the world to what humans think or want. He distinguishes between 'interactive kinds' (which he had earlier called 'human kinds') and 'non-interactive kinds.'

As Hacking points out, social constructionists have generally been interested in what we might call 'social liberation.' They have wanted to challenge the idea that how things have been understood, categorized, and labeled is somehow inevitable. They are challenging existing power relations, "unmasking to liberate the oppressed, to show how categories of knowledge are used in power relationships."[1] But, Hacking argues, power is not only operated from above. The oppressed are not simply powerless victims, pawns in the hands of the oppressors. "It is an important feature of [interactive] kinds that they have effects on the people classified, but also [that] the classified people can take matters into

8

their own hands." This is what he elsewhere calls a 'looping effect.' Like Hacking, I want to emphasize the duality of power, its relational character, and the agency of those who suffer under current arrangements, while acknowledging their serious disadvantage.

Applying the label *pillow* to a rock doesn't protect you when you stumble over it. Rocks are not interactive kinds. Interactive kinds are not, however, only categories of people. They include kinds of human actions, relationships, and institutions – any categorization where people's attitudes and evaluations toward instances of the category matter. Applying the label *rape* to a husband's sexual assault on his wife rather than using the label *exercise of spousal privilege* or something similar matters a lot. And it was not those at the top of power pyramids who finally brought about that change, one I will talk about in Chapter 6. I start this chapter by looking at practices of labeling social identities.

Shifting Ethnic/Racial Labels for a Single Individual?

Many years ago, traveling in a VW camper around Europe with my husband and small children, I was often mistaken for someone from somewhere else in Europe rather than identified as American. (My language skills were far too poor for me to be thought a local!) At the time, the 'ugly American' stereotype was widespread in the areas where I was traveling, so I rather enjoyed being read as Italian in Spain or Greek in Italy. Readily labeled *white* or *Caucasian* back home and showing no trace of influences from any non-English language when I talk, my ethnoracial categorizing has never seemed to raise questions in the US.

People with darker skin or curlier hair or eyes shaped differently from mine do often get asked 'what' they are in the US and elsewhere. Individuals who are comfortably 'at home' in a range of languages and linguistic varieties also can puzzle would-be labelers. H. Samy Alim, Founding Director of UCLA's Center for

Race, Ethnicity, and Language, recounts an eighteen-hour period during which he was "raced and reraced at least eight times: *Indian, Algerian, Mexican, Turkish, American Latino, Colombian, Arab,* and *Black*."[2] Some of those identifications were triggered mainly by his appearance, others by the language he happened to be speaking at the time. In South Africa, he heard the label *Colored Muslim*. Elsewhere the labels applied to him included *Middle Eastern, half-White/half-Black, Black & Puerto Rican, Brazilian*, and, from a Spanish speaker, *Caribeño*. On being introduced to Alim, an elderly African-American man smiled and said "I hope you're not Cablanasian," lightly mocking the portmanteau identity label introduced by golfer Tiger Woods to convey his own complex ethnoracial heritage: Caucasian, Black American, American Indian, and Asian. Professor Alim describes himself as a multilingual light brown ("ambiguously brown," said one colleague) man with a beard, qualities that allow others to pop him into multiple categories. Still, they are often a bit puzzled. A new colleague of his summed it up nicely. "You're like the campus Rosario Dawson or Jessica Alba – no one knows what you are." At the same time many ask, "But what are you, really?" Although more and more people in the US get assigned by others and assign themselves to multiple ethnic and racial identities, labels like those attached to Professor Alim and others that also purport to track ancestral history on the basis of bodily features remain highly significant social identity categories into which people are regularly placed. Yet whether these categories actually mean anything like what most people think they do is highly dubious.

Escaping these category labels or shifting among them (*transracializing*, as Samy Alim puts it) is impossible for many. People whose appearance automatically gets them labeled as members of a subordinated and devalued social group seldom have the luxury of avoiding others' negative or misleading first impressions, even if such impressions are based on implicit attitudes and stereotypes that are not accessible to conscious awareness. Some time ago comedian Dick Gregory put clearly the challenge he faced as a black man trying to make a name for himself in comedy. "I've got to go up there as an individual first, a Negro second."[3]

What Do Ethnic and Racial Identity Labels Label?

For so-called 'natural kinds' like oak trees, dogs, dandelions, gold, and water, the world around us often seems to come carved at the joints, just waiting for us to label what we find in it. But, as philosopher Kwame Anthony Appiah so nicely puts it in his recent book on the topic, the social kinds to which we attach identity labels are sustained by "lies that bind."[4] Sorting people by color, country, creed, class, or culture, as he shows succinctly, is a human enterprise in which boundaries are contested and keep changing. Such sorting projects also do not yield groupings of individuals sharing essential properties. But even though the assumption that these identities are anchored by such essences has proven untrue, many of these identities are 'real' in important ways. They correspond to social, not biological, kinds. Nor does the existence of people like Samy Alim and others whose racial labelings may shift mean that race and racial labeling no longer matter, that we are in a 'post-racial' world. Increased sexual contact involving people from what have been seen as distinct racial groups and subsequent births of 'interracial' children have, however, changed the social dynamics.

For some time, biological scientists have known that human biological variation does not divide people into groups that could be labeled *races* in the traditional sense.[5] Since DNA sequencing on ancient human remains became feasible around 2010, genomics has made that even clearer. A spring 2018 *National Geographic* article explains: "There is no scientific basis for race. It is a made-up label. It's been used to define and separate people for millennia. But the concept of race is not grounded in genetics."[6] The idea that race has been used to separate people for millennia is perhaps a bit of an exaggeration. According to historian Nell Irvin Painter, differences in people's skin color were certainly known in antiquity, but "did not carry useful meaning." Where people were from was more significant, for example. She argues that European colonizing of parts of the world where people with darker skins already lived was what really launched race as a category used for establishing the superiority of European colonizers.[7]

In a book aimed at a nonspecialist public that appeared at around the same time as the *National Geographic* article, paleo-geneticist David Reich paints a fascinating picture of population movements and mixing, especially over the past 5000 years or so.[8] "Males from populations with more power tend to pair with females from populations with less," as Reich says. Racial 'purity' does not exist: we are all, as some say, 'mongrels.' The picture emerging from recent population genetics studies fits with that painted by archeological and linguistic studies. Most people with European ancestry are closely related to people of the near East and of Northern India, although for all of us our genealogy goes back to African beginnings. Humans have been amazingly peri-patetic, and they have regularly mixed their genes with those of the new groups they encountered on their travels (some such mixing has resulted from consensual sexual encounters but cer-tainly not all – the phenomenon of men raping women of other groups as part of their 'conquering' those groups has a long pedigree).

People around the world are very much like one another. There is less genetic difference among humans than among chimpan-zees, even though there are many more of us than of them. There are, obviously, some visible differences among people like the relative lightness or darkness of the skin. Darker skin is helpful near the equator, but the genes that are responsible for skin color do not seem to carry much other information, and there are several different genes that can be involved. As Elizabeth Kolbert, who wrote the *National Geographic* article mentioned above, explains, "the deepest splits in the human family aren't between what are usually thought of as different races – whites, say, or blacks or Asians or Native Americans. They're between

African populations such as the Khoe-San and the Pygmies, who spent tens of thousands of years separated from one another even before humans left Africa."

Human beings or *Homo sapiens* first appeared on the African continent between 200,000 and 300,000 years ago. Some 60,000 years ago, a relatively small group of them started moving. Some of them encountered and reproduced with other hominids, Neanderthals and Denisovans. They then fanned out around the world, reaching Australia about 50,000 years ago but probably not making it to South America, for example, until about 15,000 years ago. They did form isolated population groups, among which some genetic mutations took hold. To reiterate, however, the differences between certain African groups isolated from one another are far greater than those between many of the African groups that remained on that continent and the people who left them and then populated Europe and the rest of the world. As Reich's book makes clear, many population groups have roamed and mixed their genes. Some genetic 'markers' with implications for health are associated with particular racialized groups. But even there connections can be tenuous, and the racial labels we actually employ may be of far less use to medical professionals than is sometimes suggested.

The bottom line: people do not split into groups that "possess group-specific biologically-based inherent behavioral and psycho-logical tendencies and characteristics." Philosopher Lawrence Blum offers that succinct characterization of how the label *race* has been understood throughout most of American history, and probably continues to be understood by many Americans (and most English speakers elsewhere).[9] So what might we mean in speaking of racial identity labels? Blum proposes that instead of *races*, we speak of *racialized groups*. There are some phenotypic properties, like skin color, eye shape, and hair texture, that correlate to a considerable extent with these groups. Even these external properties are far from consistently distributed, but the critical point is that such features of external appearance predict essentially nothing else about people. There are no 'essences' that skin color (or any other feature of appearance linked to what we call 'race') indicates. Blum puts it this way. "Racialized groups are characterized by forms of experience they have undergone and a sociohistorical identity that they possess *because of* the false attributions to them ... of innate biobehavioral tendencies." To 'identify as,' say, black or white in the contemporary US, then, can be understood as identifying with shared experiences and "a sense of inheriting a certain history and a sense of peoplehood connected with that history."[10] Racializing comes from without and from within, Blum argues, and it can involve a host of factors, including linguistic practices.

Sociologists Michael Omi and Howard Winant may have been the first to talk about *racializing* in their richly informative *Racial Formation in the United States*, the first edition of which appeared in 1986. Drawing on their account in a paper first published in 2000, philosopher Sally Haslanger offered the following definition. "A group is racialized if and only if its members are socially positioned as subordinate or privileged along some dimension (economic, political, legal, social, etc.) and the group is 'marked' as a target for this treatment by observed or imagined bodily features presumed to be evidence of ancestral links to a certain geographical region."[11] Notice that, unlike Blum, Haslanger makes issues of differential power, of subordination and advantage, partly definitive of racialization. Retaining the word *race*, Omi and Winant put it this way in their third edition: "*Race is a concept that signifies and symbolizes social conflicts and interests by referring to different types of bodies*" (italic in original). Noting that the criteria used are "at best imprecise, and at worst completely arbitrary," they continue: "They may be arbitrary, but they are not meaningless. Race is strategic; race does ideological and political work. ... Corporeal distinctions ... become essentialized. [They] are understood as the manifestations of more profound differences that are situated *within* racially identified persons: differences in such qualities as intelligence, athletic ability, temperament, and sexuality."[12] Both these definitions are proposals to understand such distinctions in politically useful ways, what Haslanger calls 'ameliorative' projects.

Like Blum, both philosopher Haslanger and sociologists Omi and Winant are *stipulating* how we 'should' understand terms like *racialized group* or *race*. But, unlike them, Blum does not acknowledge directly that his definition is part of a strategy for most effectively engaging in discussions using words like *race* and *racial*. These discussions among academics over how best to understand such words preview the discussion in Chapter 6 of disputes among ordinary folks over how to apply words like *racism* and *racist*. Sometimes people are inclined to dismiss disagreements over defining particular words, how to apply terminology, as talking past one another, 'just semantics.' I agree, however, with those who argue that there is a kind of continuity of topic that is possible even when somewhat new and competing understandings, 'articulations,' are voiced. Substantive debates can underlie discussions that might seem 'merely' matters of language. I am not arguing that theoretical point here, but I hope by the time you have read this book, you will understand better how this might happen.[13]

Racial labels can be used to police racialized group boundaries. This can be done to mobilize a racialized group for collective action. It can be done to enforce group subordination. Laws were written in the post–Civil War southern US to specify limits of the label *white*, to try to make clear, for example, exactly who was excluded by 'whites only' signs in restaurants and on public transport. Well into the middle of the twentieth century, it was pretty clear that those with visible traces of anything other than European ancestry were excluded by such signs – for example, Indians from the Asian subcontinent as well as those so labeled who were native to the Americas. Indeed being of European ancestry was not always 'enough.' In the early part of the twentieth century, for example, Irish and Italian immigrants were not considered unproblematically white. And it was not only Hitler who thought that Jews and Romany people were inherently inferior to northern Europeans, the 'Aryans.' In the US, the honorific label *white* was pretty much limited to WASPs (White Anglo-Saxon Protestants) until well into the twentieth century.[14] And in

American English, "that's white of you" has been used to compliment the morality and integrity of the addressee.[15] Although
putting a 'whites only' sign in the window of a restaurant would
now be deemed illegally discriminatory speech in the US,[16] and
most state laws trying to specify boundaries for racial labels are
now off the books, people still pay considerable attention both to
drawing racialized boundaries and to just how groups so deli-
neated are to be labeled. But, as we will see in Chapter 3, they don't
like to talk about doing so. This avoidance of 'race talk' may be
explained in part by the fact that a once robustly anti-racist notion
of 'colorblindness' has been, in Omi and Winant's terms, 'rear-
ticulated' so that it can now support new more subterranean
forms of racism.

Racialized groups are historically contingent, and they keep
changing over time. At any given point, their boundaries are
fuzzy and contestable. And labels frequently shift in response to
various kinds of social factors. Social identity groups can be
racialized, on Blum's view, if biobehavioral essences are (falsely)
attributed to them. As Samy Alim's experience vividly illustrates,
the same individual may be sometimes in one and sometimes in
another of these groups, both as labeled by others and in terms of
self-identification. This does not mean, however, that such labels
are meaningless.

Deep Historical Antecedents to Recent Labeling Disputes: *Latino* vs *Hispanic*

There is long-standing tension between the panethnic label
Latino and its near twin label *Hispanic*.[17] *Latino* was mostly
self-generated and associated with individuals and groups
embracing more left-leaning political views. *Hispanic*, on the
other hand, was mostly preferred by those with relatively
conservative outlooks; it often was the choice of US bureaucrats and businesses not themselves embracing such an identity. There are now, however, Latinos for Trump, along with

plenty of people who label themselves Hispanic and also see themselves as progressive politically. The US Census and various other 'official' sites now treat these two panethnic labels as equivalent in scope. Some, however, draw a distinction. On this approach, *Latino* is used for those whose own origins or those of their forebears are anywhere in Latin America. In contrast, *Hispanic* applies to those who are connected to any country where the dominant language is Spanish, which would include Spain, across the Atlantic from the Americas. It would, however, exclude Latin American countries such as Brazil, where Portuguese dominates, and Haiti, where Haitian Creole and French are most widely spoken. There is also a long-standing tension between the panethnic *Latino/Hispanic* and more specific group labels like *Chicano* or *Tejan* or *Nuyorican* or *Cuban American*.

By just using *Latino*, I postpone discussion of the important gender issues connected to this terminology to the final chapter. *Latino* is gendered masculine in Spanish, though traditionally also considered gender-inclusive or generic, able to apply to all people. Women were labeled *Latina*, the feminine form. But many of them and, more recently, people outside traditional gender categories have interpreted *Latino* as only masculine and excluding them. In the final chapter I look at the use of *o/a*, *a/o*, and the 'at' (@) symbol instead of the traditional -*o* suffix to create alternative generic forms that include both women and men. I also discuss the more recent *Latinx*, which goes beyond familiar gender binaries to include those of any or no gender identity. (The same gender issues arise with *Chicano* and various other gendered terms from Spanish.) For now, however, I will speak as if *Latino* were unproblematically gender-neutral. Interestingly, labeling for these groups has been contentious even beyond these matters of gender.

Historian Ramón Gutiérrez has a useful discussion of some of the background in "What's in a Name," the first chapter in *The New Latino Studies Reader: A Twenty-First-Century Perspective*, which he and Tomás Almaguer edited in 2016. He

examine[s] three moments in the history of what became the
United States, looking at the contexts of power that produced
particular understandings of social boundaries and group
membership: the Spanish conquest of the indigenous people of
Mexico's north, which started in 1598; the United States military's
takeover of what became the American Southwest at the end of the
Mexican War in 1848; and the mass decolonization civil rights
movement undertaken by racialized minorities in the United
States during the late 1960s and the early 1970s.[18]

Gutiérrez explains that the soldiers invading Aztec cities
did not initially think of themselves as Spanish, but primarily
as Christian and from a particular region of what was becoming established as Spain. They came, however, to see their
origins in the Iberian Peninsula and their status as *españoles*
as part of what entitled them to take over the lands of the
indios, the term they took from Columbus and used as a tool
furthering their empire-building.

> [B]y calling the natives *indios*, the Spaniards erased and leveled the
> diverse and complex indigenous political and religious hierarchies
> they found. Where once there had been many ethnic groups
> stratified as native lords, warriors, craftsmen, hunters, farmers,
> and slaves, the power of imperial Spain was not only to vanquish
> but also to define, largely reducing peoples such as the mighty
> Aztecs into a defeated Indian class that soon bore the pain of
> subjugation as tribute-paying racialized subjects.[19]

Early during the colonial period there was established a *régimen
de castas*, which provided what Gutiérrez dubs a 'capacious lexicon' with which to categorize a wide range of 'racial types'
produced by sexual reproduction involving people of different
ancestral histories (Spanish, Indian, and African being the supposed 'pure' sources). The son of a Spaniard and an Indian was a
mestizo, for example, and if he had a child with a Spanish woman
their offspring was a *castizo*. These categories were spelled out for
six generations of possible combinations, but it became increasingly difficult to identify on the basis of bodily appearance, or

phenotype, where to categorize people. By 1760 the Spanish crown sold writs of whiteness, *gracias al sacar*, and the entire code was abolished when Mexico gained its independence in 1821. This does not mean that terms categorizing by color and presumptive ancestry vanished. Throughout Latin America, among the colonizers, the indigenous populations, and the Africans brought by the slave trade, there had already been and continued to be considerable 'interracial' sexual reproduction. Although there persisted a privileging of 'whiteness,' at this point there were far more varied bodies and more awareness of racial diversity.

By the nineteenth century, many of the people populating the north of Mexico identified themselves by the regions in which they lived: *Tejanos* in Texas, *Californios* in California, *Nuevos Mexicanos* in New Mexico. But after the US took over these regions in 1848, the *Anglo* and *Anglo-American* soldiers and settlers moving in followed the falsely universalizing strategy of the sixteenth-century Spanish colonizers: everyone living in these formerly Mexican lands was dubbed *Mexican* or the Spanish *Mexicano*, even though the newness of Mexico as a nation meant that they had never so called themselves. The Anglos, who were Protestants, saw Spanish-speaking Catholics and ignored the many social distinctions among the residents, some of whom had been living in these areas for generations. At this point there was some use among those residents of the term *nativo* to differentiate themselves from those they initially called the *extranjeros*, 'foreigners,' who were rapidly moving in and assuming dominance over these long-time residents. It would have been highly inaccurate to think of these long-time Spanish-speaking residents of the Southwest as immigrants, for many had been living in the same location since before the United States existed. "My family never crossed a border," proclaimed Mexican-American actor Eva Longoria at the 2016 Democratic National Convention. "The border crossed us."[20] This slogan is widely used in migrant rights' campaigns and reflects the reality of the US annexation of land that once was part of Mexico.

The Spanish-speaking local residents of territories acquired by the US in the middle of the nineteenth century found a range of less than flattering labels for the many English-speaking newcomers to their regions. Appearance frequently provided labels. Gutiérrez mentions *canosos* 'gray-haired,' *colora[d]o* 'red-faced,' *bollilo* 'doughy faced,' *cara de pan crudo* 'pan-of-dough face,' *ojos de gato* 'cat eyes,' and *patón* 'big foot.' *Gringo* apparently comes from "a linguistic corruption of a song that Mexican soldiers heard the Texas rebels singing at the Alamo ... 'Green Grows the Grass of Kentucky.'"[21] And there were more. Of course the Anglos also had disparaging terms for those they were encountering, like *greaser, taco-choker,* and, for a woman, *hot tamale.*

By 1850 the English label *Mexican* "signified a dominated population, stigmatized by defeat and subordination. 'Mexican' rapidly became the insulting expletive hurled to hurt its auditors as 'mex,' 'meskin,' 'skin,' and 'skindiver,' or modified with adjectives such as 'dirty,' 'stinking,' 'greasy,' 'lazy,' and 'ugly.'"[22] A century later linguist Arthur L. Campa asked long-term residents of New Mexico in Spanish how they identified themselves ethnically and most responded, "Soy mexicano 'I'm Mexican.'" Asked what they called someone from Mexico, they said "mexicano de México 'Mexican from Mexico.'" In English, however, they identified themselves as *Spanish American*. "I'd rather not be called Mexican because of the stereotype remarks that are associated with it. Such as lazy, dirty, greaser, etc."[23]

Not surprisingly, nineteenth-century self-labeling was often strategic. In California, long-time Spanish-speaking residents often called themselves *californios* to emphasize their differences from, for example, those lured up from Mexico by the Gold Rush. Panethnic labels emerged when some became affiliated with larger projects of imagining possibilities for alliances among the former Spanish, Portuguese, and French colonies in the Americas. These groups called themselves *latinoamericanos* or *hispanoamericanos*, shortened to *latinos* or *hispanos*, and appearing in English as *Latins, Latin American,* or *Spanish American*. Thinking of the hemisphere, a Los Angeles publication of 1858 wrote, "Two rival races are competing with each other … the Anglo-Saxon and the Latin one [*la raza latina*]."²⁴ That terminology was pretty much gone by 1920, not to be revived until the late 1960s.

One of the first citations the *Oxford English Dictionary* gives for *Latino* as an English word comes from a 1973 news story in *The Black Panther* newspaper about an "action group composed of Blacks, Latinos, and Whites." In that era those first dubbing themselves *Latino* were also rejecting whiteness and offering alternatives to the long-standing black–white dichotomy in the US view of racial identities. In cities people of different national origins united under the banner of *Latinidad* to press for better access to decent jobs, housing, voting rights, and bilingual education. Inspired by the Black Panther movement to resist their colonized status and to claim self-determination, many Mexican Americans in the late 1960s and early 1970s embraced the label *Chicano*, which was used by César Chavez and Delores Huerta in organizing farm workers and in other actions like school walkouts. Its origins are disputed, but there is general agreement that its use goes back to the 1920s, yet becomes widespread only after student activists use it in their 1969 "Plan Espiritual de Aztlán," which called for all racially oppressed groups to join together, for community control over institutions and culturally relevant schooling, for work "to defeat the gringo dollar system," and much more.²⁵ Many politically engaged Puerto Ricans began calling themselves *Boricua*, which is said to have been the (indigenous) Taino name for the island. Both these groups saw the utility of *Latino* in some contexts for collective organizing. Cuban Americans, in contrast, had mostly come from relatively well-to-do (and white-identified) backgrounds and were very focused on opposition to Castro, not generally invested in anti-racist activities. They were influential in persuading the US Census to adopt the label *Hispanic* for the 1980 census.

Sociologist Cristina Mora suggests in her 2014 book, *Making Hispanics: How Activists, Bureaucrats, and Media Constructed a New America*, that the government first went with *Hispanic* because it was seen as apolitical even though many pushing for this new census category were activists doing so precisely in order to further political agendas. At the same time, the emerging panethnic identity was being promoted by business interests. *Latinidad* could be highly marketable, especially by using Spanish-language media to promote 'lifestyles' and products. In a 2014 interview,[26] Mora notes that she grew up Mexican American, calling herself *Chicana* in the 1980s and 1990s. She became aware of how much diversity there was in Hispanic or Latino identity only after moving from the west to the east coast of the US and getting to know Puerto Ricans, Cubans, and South Americans. She mentions in that interview that recent polls suggest a nearly even split in "the community" between preference for the panethnic labels *Latino* and *Hispanic*, with the former embraced more in urban areas on the coasts, and the latter more in rural areas in places like Texas and New Mexico. Many organizations and many authors deploy both these panethnic labels. Philosopher Jorge Gracia, for example, titled his 2000 book *Hispanic/Latino Identity* and uses both labels often in his text, even though he argues in favor of *Hispanic* and its transatlantic possibilities. And, of course, the more specific ethnic labels are still very widely used.

So what should we make of this complex and ongoing history of naming practices? Clearly, such practices have helped form both specific identities like Mexican American or Chicano and an emerging panethnic social identity, Hispanic/Latino. It is clear that naming practices can create more inclusive groups from above in the interest of domination. Gutiérrez's discussion of the use of *indios* makes this point, which is developed further in the later section of this chapter on labels given to populations already living in the Americas when Europeans arrived. At the same time it is also clear that inclusive names can come from below in the interest of resistance (the *Latinos* who mobilized as part of anti-colonial efforts during the 1960s and 1970s).

Creating Labels to Mobilize Groups: The Case of *Asian American*

Ethnic groups involve (presumed) shared ancestry tied to a region, (presumed) shared culture related to that ancestral history, and a sense not only on the part of outsiders but also on that of group members of themselves as a distinct group on those grounds. My parenthetical 'presumed' indicates the often tangled links entwined in both genealogy and cultural products and practices. *Asian American* is a relatively recent panethnic group label linking people who, unlike most Latinos, have immigrated to the US from quite different and widely separated regions that are also culturally and linguistically very diverse.

Although there had been immigration to America from parts of what was then called 'the Orient' since the eighteenth century and white people did sometimes label these immigrants *Oriental*, the identity labeled *Asian American* did not emerge until the 1960s. *Asian American* lumps together, for example, Vietnamese with Japanese with Pakistani origins. In a *New York Times* opinion piece, novelist Lisa Ko put it this way: "Asian American … is a label that can be both empowering and exclusionary. Asian Americans aren't just East Asian, heterosexual and middle class. They're queer and working class and poor and undocumented: South Asian and Southeast Asian and Filipino and Central Asian."[27] The term arose in the 1960s as some of the people so labeling themselves struggled to circumvent the *black–white* dichotomy that had so long dominated American discourse about race.

Oriental was once a label applied to people from the countries now called Asian. But many people now agree with the judgment that "rugs are Oriental, not people," and chide older generations who have continued using it as an ethnic label. The basic reason for avoiding it seems to be its strong association with exoticizing and distancing stereotypes of earlier periods. Historian Erika Lee, author of *The Making of Asian America: A History*, says the term "has been used to reinforce the idea that Asians were/are forever foreign and could never become American. These ideas helped to justify immigration exclusion, racial discrimination and violence, political discrimination and segregation." San Francisco *Chronicle* columnist Jeff Yang finds the word "freighted with baggage ... you can't think of it without having that sort of the smell of incense and the sound of a gong go through your head." In 2016 President Barack Obama signed legislation forbidding use of the term in federal documents, a bill introduced by Representative Grace Meng from the state of New York, who described the label as both "outdated and insulting."

But not all to whom the label has been applied share Meng's strong aversion. Shortly after passage of Meng's bill, Dr. Jayne Tsuchiyama, who describes herself as a practitioner of "Oriental medicine," wrote an opinion piece in the *LA Times* entitled "The term *Oriental* is outdated, but is it racist?"[28] Although the quotes above endorsing the abandonment of *Oriental* as an identity label are from her piece, Tsuchiyama applies the term to herself and argues that it is not insulting or racist. She claims that, in contrast to the many slurring epithets that do exist for Asian Americans, *Oriental* lacks a history of being hurled at targets in order to wound them. "A funny thing I noticed," she says, "is that my Caucasian (dare I say Occidental?), not my Asian colleagues, are most eager to remove Oriental from public discourse." And she quotes Asian-American comedian Margaret Cho. "White people like to tell Asians how to feel about race because they're too scared to tell black people."

We'll return to the topic of slurs in Chapter 5 and to attempted linguistic reforms and some reactions to them in Chapter 6. In a very real sense, ethnoracial and other social identities *require* labels. Which labels are used can matter a lot, but that is secondary. Acts of labeling others and self and of being labeled by others and self are central to creating and sustaining social identity groups and their relations to one another. That does not mean that race or ethnicity is 'just' a matter of language, that such identities have only linguistic but not material reality.

"My Mom Says It's Not Polite to Call Someone *Black*"

In *Between the World and Me*, his searingly beautiful letter to his son, Ta-Nehisi Coates eloquently testifies to the great dangers a young man labeled *black* in America faces and also to the immense yet fearful love parents so labeled have for their children.[29] He uses that label, but there have been many shifts in past centuries to label Americans of African ancestry. (As we are all ultimately of African ancestry, this should be understood as encompassing ties back to Africa in the last millennium or so.) In what became the US, settlers from the British Isles and elsewhere in Europe killed off most of the indigenous populations of Native Americans through a combination of warfare and disease. At the same time, especially in the southern colonies, they used forcibly captured and enslaved Africans to do the most menial work. This history helps explain why differences in skin color were especially salient and provided material for racialized group names. The label *white* was distinguished from the label *negro* (which derives from *negro* 'black' in both Spanish and Portuguese, languages spoken by many in the slave trade). Indigenous peoples, whose labeling I'll discuss a bit more in a later section of this chapter, were called by the incoming English speakers not only *Indians* (because of Columbus's belief that he'd reached the Indian subcontinent) but also *redskins* (I'll discuss this more in Chapter 5). They in turn called the Europeans pouring into their land *white men*, both highlighting skin color.

Negro was applied to enslaved Africans and, along with what is now the deeply slurring and highly taboo epithet *nigger*, came to have strong associations with the master–slave relation and the white supremacist ideology supporting that relation. In a very informative article from over half a century ago, Lerone Bennett, Jr., a senior editor of *Ebony*, details the history up until the late 1960s of labels for the racialized group of those Americans "identifiable" as having African ancestry. (He points out that millions of those labeled by others and themselves as white also have some relatively recent African ancestry.) In the 1830s as the abolition movement strengthened, some began speaking of *colored people* or *people of color*. They were not extending the term as broadly as the current *people of color* or *POC* because they distinguished *colored Americans* from *red Americans* or *red Indians* as well as from *white Americans*. Early enslaved Africans did seem, so far as can be discerned from relatively limited records, to label themselves *black* or *African*, but the *African* label mostly disappeared when there were movements in the 1830s to try to return freed people forcibly to the African continent. Immediately following the Emancipation Proclamation, although a few embraced the term *negro* or *black* for self-labeling, the overwhelming preference was *colored*, which predominated through the end of the nineteenth century. Bennett suggests its popularity peaked in the early twentieth century with the founding in 1909 of the National Association for the Advancement of Colored People (NAACP). *Colored* continued, however, to be widely used across the Jim Crow–era South. It was used to label water fountains and bathrooms in NC during my childhood there in the 1940s and early 1950s, a practice which continued well into the 1960s. The move to reclaim *negro*, especially in capitalized form, had already had considerable success by the late nineteenth and early twentieth centuries and the term was used frequently by leaders as different as Booker T. Washington and Frederick Douglass. It was also urged in opposition to *African* by W. E. B. Du Bois and Marcus Garvey. On March 7, 1930, the *New York Times* included the following announcement on its editorial page. "In our 'style book' 'Negro' is now added to the list of words to be capitalized. It is not merely a typographical change; it is an act of recognition of racial self-respect for those who have been for generations in 'the lower case.'" The word *black* continued for self-labeling, especially among more politically active advocates for ending Jim Crow and racial segregation. Du Bois used it often as well as *Negro*, and such initiatives as Black Power and Black is Beautiful movements in the middle of the twentieth century gave it an initial capital letter.

What prompted Bennett's article was the late 1960s push among some activists to replace *Negro* with *Black or African American* (or some variant thereof). *Negro* was rapidly fading as a relic of the Jim Crow years. The more radical anti-racist movements proclaimed *Black Power* and groups like the Black Panthers initially saw black civil rights movements in America making common cause with oppressed people of color around the globe. Martin Luther King, Jr., was not speaking to the labeling question, but on April 4, 1967, exactly one year before his assassination in Memphis, he made his famous speech against the Vietnam War (perhaps sealing his death warrant). "These are revolutionary times. All over the globe [people] are revolting against old systems of exploitation and oppression. The shirtless and barefoot people of the land are rising up. ... We in the West must support them."[30] The *black/Black* terminology did not figure in King's address and was still being seen by most ordinary blacks as too 'confrontational,' but by the early 1970s it was dominant both in media and among most of those so labeled. But the more revolutionary and sometimes separatist anti-racist groups were being contained during the 1970s, and by the 1980s they had lost most of their power.

Relatively 'moderate' leaders like Jesse Jackson urged the descendants of enslaved Africans to see themselves as like other ethnic groups who ultimately melted into the 'mainstream.' In a 1988 speech to black leaders from around the country, Jackson issued the following statement.

> To be called African-Americans has cultural integrity. It puts us in our proper historical context. Every ethnic group has a reference to some land base, some historical cultural base. African-Americans have hit that level of cultural maturity. There are Armenian-Americans and Jewish-Americans and Arab-Americans and Italian-Americans; and with a degree of accepted and reasonable pride, they connect their heritage to their mother country and where they are now.[31]

By the mid-to-late 1980s, *African American* had begun to be the preferred term in most mainstream publications. *Black*, both

lower- and uppercase, has continued to be widely used, especially
for self-labeling, but *Negro*, the term that was considered 'polite'
among people of both white and black racialized groups in the
American South into the early 1960s, has pretty much disappeared. (Its contemporary use, as I illustrate in the final chapter,
can be very shocking.)

Matters have become more complicated in recent decades, in
part because of substantial waves of people with at least some
recent African ancestry arriving in the US from the Caribbean and
Central and South America as well as from the continent of Africa.
Historian Howard Dodson, then chief of the Schomburg Center
for Research in Black Culture of the New York Public Library,
argued in a 2007 keynote conference address that these recent
arrivals pose "major questions about the definition of African
Americans. ... How do [they] fit within the construct and definition of African American? Do the differences in language, culture,
ethnicity and nationality that they bring with them limit their
ability to be admitted to the African American group?"[32] Dodson
notes that virtually everyone in the US with visibly apparent
recent African ancestry identifies or is identified as black. He
also observes that both those with American enslaved black
ancestry and those whose families arrived more recently sometimes label themselves and are labeled by others as *African
American*. That designation and *black*, Dodson notes, are often
used strategically – for example, in mobilizing protests of police
brutality against darker-skinned people.

Official US government forms often collapse *African American*
and *Black*. The 2020 census is using the same social identity
categories that were on the 2010 forms: *White, Black/African
American, American Indian/Alaska Native, Native Hawaiian or
Other Pacific Islander, Asian,* and *Other*. These are followed by the
question "Do you consider yourself of Hispanic, Latino, or
Spanish origin?" with *yes* and *no* the options for answering. At
the same time, when you or your parents arrived in the US, and
from where, matters for some categorizing purposes. Linguist
Renée Blake notes that once other linguists learned that her

parents were Trinidadian and Venezuelan immigrants, they no longer considered her a truly 'native' speaker of African-American English. She was, however, a black American who had grown up speaking English in the US. Blake opens her thoughtful discussion of the sociolinguistic dimensions of categorizing black people in twentieth-century locales in the US by introducing us to Dana, a young black woman born in the US to a Jamaican mother and a Jamaican father. "I consider myself a Jamerican," Dana says.

> Because if I tell the American kids that both of my parents are Jamaican, they tell me I'm Jamaican. And if I tell the Jamaican kids that both of my parents are Jamaican, some of them will tell me I'm Jamaican, but for the most part, all you hear is you're a Yankee, and that means that you're American. [LAUGHS] But, yeah. So I just say I'm a Jamerican.[33]

In the mid-1990s anthropologist Mica Pollock taught for a year at "Columbus High School," the invented name she uses for the California public school in which she worked. Pollock stayed on for several more years of ethnographic study of how students and teachers and other staff at the school talked – and avoided talk – about race.[34] The school district's listing of racial categories for students at Columbus had the labels *Filipinos* (28 percent and actually from linguistically diverse areas), *Latinos/Hispanics* (29 percent, sometimes all called *Mexicans* by the students though their parents came from a variety of Caribbean and south American locations as well as from Mexico), *Black/African-Americans* (22 percent), *Chinese* (8 percent), a bureaucratic *Other Non-White* (which included the racialized group linked to Pacific Islands that teachers and students labeled *Samoan* at about 8 percent), and *Other Whites* (5 percent). These were the major racial category labels used by students and teachers alike.

Michael, a Columbus High School student whom Pollock met early on, resisted all the labels, at least sometimes. In a class discussion led by Pollock early in 1994, Michael refused to identify himself racially and later, speaking privately to Pollock, he said that though he 'appeared' white (and was categorized as 'other

white' on school forms), "there are hecka races in me." He sometimes called himself a "white black kid." Months later in a class
discussion debating whether white people were an ethnic group,
Michael offered a trenchant analysis of racial/ethnic labeling.
"They say all people from Europe are supposed to be white,
right? And all the people from Africa are supposed to be black,
right? And all the people – Indians are supposed to be red, right?
And all the Asian people are supposed to be yellow, right? Those
are the colors people are givin' 'em. So it seems just like sports –
they put 'em all in teams, like categories." When asked "why?" he
responded: "To make 'em compete!"

Michael is, I think, essentially right. Ethnoracial identities still
figure in ongoing histories of exploitation and oppression and in
current institutions and practices. Recognizing their 'social construction' and the 'lies' sustaining them does not eliminate their
real effects. We do not live in a 'post-racial' world, at least not in
the USA.

Tracking People: Sex/Gender Labels

Unlike distinctions signaled by skin color, distinctions based on a
binary sort at birth into female and male bodies are universal in
human societies. Human babies' bodies are immediately *sexed* at
birth, usually on the basis of visual inspection of external genitalia.
In English, the words *female* and *male* label both the human
bodily distinction and somewhat analogous distinctions in
(potential) reproductive role in many other animals and indeed
plants as well. What varies enormously is exactly what significance
different social groups attach to those distinctions of sex, and what
expectations and experiences flow from that initial sex sort (and
also what happens when binary expectations are occasionally
upset in some way).

Feminist scholars in the 1970s and 1980s tried to reserve the
word *sex* for the (almost) binary bodily split (and being labeled
female or *male*) and to use *gender* for the sociocultural significance

of sexing (including being labeled *girl* or *boy* and subsequently being labeled *woman* or *man*). But these distinctions fell apart for a host of reasons.

On the one hand, the use of *gender* for the basic bodily divide has spread among those who continue to buy into somewhat traditional views of the sexes and their relations to one another. This shift was probably helped along by avoidance of the word *sex*, given its strong association with sexuality and sexual activity. Now that sonograms can 'sex' a growing fetus, many expectant parents in the US host 'gender reveal' parties or send out 'gender reveal' announcements to friends and family. Indeed, there seems to be a healthy industry offering advice and stuff on how to manage this announcement most imaginatively. Most approaches rely on the blue for boy, pink for girl code that is widespread in the US now (but was more or less the other way around a little over a century ago and is by no means familiar across the globe). For example, a plane overhead can drop pink or blue balloons, a neon sign with the letters "Baby" can be switched on in either blue or pink, the soon-to-be mother can wear white over the swollen abdomen and have someone create pink or blue handprints, and on and on. Intriguingly colors give way to words sometimes, according to a recent *New York Times* account. "[T]he old pink-or-blue short-hand has given way to amped-up gender signifiers and strangely lurid themes [verbally indicated as well as in other ways], like 'Rifles or Ruffles?' and 'Guns or Glitter?'"[35]

It is clear that many people care a lot about sex-sorting and that they assume babies come in just two sexes/genders: *girl* or *boy*, *she* or *he*. (I'll discuss pronouns further in Chapter 6.) The information about apparent bodily characteristics that is "revealed" is made available to soon-to-be parents by modern medical technology. But many people do not embrace this exuberant contemporary 'anatomy is destiny' outlook. Some, indeed, resist actively.

From several different directions, people traditionally over-looked have begun to speak out. They include (1) *intersex* people not readily assigned either *female* or *male* on the basis of their bodies, (2) *transgender* people who find their initial assignment discordant with their own sense of gender identity, and (3) those who reject standard binary gender identities altogether (among some relatively recent labels associated with different stances: *nonbinary, genderqueer, genderfluid, postgender*). The term *trans** (with or without an asterisk) sometimes functions as a cover term for all three groups, though they are quite different (and within each group there are important differences). Such gender activists have played a large role in challenging and changing sex/gender identity talk, including reliance on binary labeling. But it is not only these social activists who have changed the discourse: researchers in anthropology, biology, and medicine as well as humanistic disciplines have added their voices, as we will see.

These days it is common among gender activists to distinguish gender *identity* from gender *expression* (or sometimes, *performance*). Gender identity is said to be the label one pastes on oneself: *girl/woman* or *boy/man* or neither or both or shifting. (In Chapter 7 we'll discuss the contested semantic authority over labels like *woman* and *man*, including objections some raise to allowing individuals ultimate say over how they are labeled.) Gender expression or performance (a term some criticize as suggesting unconstrained choice) has to do with how one presents oneself *as* gendered: clothing, hairstyle, ways of moving and holding one's body, bodily maintenance practices, leisure activities, and the like.

Sometimes *feminine* and *masculine* are used in speaking of what are seen as matters of gender. What is often left out is that sex categorizing (which gets conflated with gender categorizing) matters so much because sex/gender is not simply a matter of individual identity or expression. Virtually every society has what sociologist Raewyn Connell called a *gender order*, social institutions and arrangements in which sex/gender categorization is a fundamental organizing principle. And sex/gender labels are a major tool used by the state and other institutions to track individual people, a point to which I will return.

Chromosomal makeup (XX vs XY), external genitalia (labia and clitoris vs penis), reproductive anatomy (ovaries and fallopian tubes vs testes and vas deferens), hormonal environment (estrogen dominant vs androgen dominant): these are major bodily features that sort somewhere between 98 to 99 percent of human babies definitively into the female or the male class. But not all, which is why categorization into exactly two sexes is not biologically determinate.

Although precise figures are unavailable, between 1 and 2 percent of infants fall outside the binary split. This is not always obvious at birth (and indeed 'sexing' happens at different points in the life cycle). In the February 18, 2015, issue of *Nature*, science writer Claire Ainsworth laid out clearly some of the kinds of complications that defeat the simple binary, summarized in the table in Figure 1.1. A beautiful interactive graphic developed by Amanda Montañez for the August 2017 issue of *Scientific American*, which cannot be reproduced here, gives an even fuller picture of what is going on. In Queensland, Australia, a push began in early 2018 to allow for an alternative to the standard sex categories on birth certificates. Yet opponent Deb Frecklington's claim that a baby can "only be born male or female" would still strike many, probably most, English speakers as common sense.[36] So-called common sense can, however, mislead.

Figure 1.1 The Sex Spectrum

A typical male has XY chromosomes, and a typical female has XX. But owing to genetic variation or chance events in development, some people do not fit neatly into either category. Some are classed as having differences or disorders of sex development (DSDs), in which their sex chromosomes do not match their sexual anatomy.

	Chromosomes	Gonads	Genitals	Other characteristics/examples
Typical male	XY	Testes	Male internal and external genitals	Male secondary sexual characteristics
Subtle variations	XY	Testes	Male internal and external genitals	Subtle differences such as low sperm production. Some caused by variation in sex-development genes

Figure 1.1 The Sex Spectrum (cont.)

	Chromosomes	Gonads	Genitals	Other characteristics/examples
Moderate variations	XY	Testes	Male external genitals with anatomical variations such as urethral opening on underside of penis	Affects 1 in 250–400 births
46,XY DSD	XY	Testes	Often ambiguous	The hormonal disorder persistent Müllerian duct syndrome results in male external genitals and testes, but also a womb and fallopian tubes
Ovotesticular DSD	XX, XY, or mix of both	Both ovarian and testicular tissue	Ambiguous	Rare reports of predominantly XY people conceiving and bearing a healthy child
46,XX testicular DSD	XX	Small testes	Male external genitals	Usually caused by presence of male sex-determining gene *SRY*
Moderate variations	XX	Ovaries	Female internal and external genitals	Variations in sex development such as premature shutdown of ovaries Some caused by variation in sex-development genes
Subtle variations	XX	Ovaries	Female internal and external genitals	Subtle differences such as excess male sex hormones or polycystic ovaries
Typical female	XX	Ovaries	Female internal and external genitals	Female secondary sexual characteristics

From *Nature*, 518, 288–291 (February 19, 2015) doi:10.1038/518288a
Accessed at www.nature.com/news/sex-redefined-1.16943#/spectrum

Intersex births are seldom reported as such and both doctors and parents are often eager to be able to answer the ubiquitous query "Is it a boy or a girl?" as soon as possible. Increasingly, however, doctors and parents have become more hesitant to perform unnecessary surgery on infants. The medical terminology now is not *intersex* or *hermaphrodite* but *DSD*, read by most doctors as *Disorders in Sex Development* and by most intersex activists as *Differences in Sex Development*. Some jurisdictions now allow for birth certificates to carry something other than the standard two sex categories – for example, Germany has a possible X for babies not assigned male or female. Adult intersex people may identify as one of the two polar sexes but nonetheless want their complicated bodily histories to be recognized by changing the sex designation on their birth certificate to 'intersex' or something similar. In December 2016, NYC became the first US jurisdiction to issue a birth certificate specifying *intersex*: this was done at the request of fifty-five-year-old Sara Kelly Keenan. Keenan was reared as a girl and lives not unhappily as a woman, but wanted her complex history recognized (chromosomally male, she endured surgeries as well as massive hormonal therapy to force her down a female pathway). Similarly, some transgender people whose gender identity carries a binary label but not the sex/gender assigned to them at birth want their birth certificate changed to recognize the identity they affirm.

Of course, a major reason that a binary sex/gender label has long been entered on birth certificates is the assumption that the label can be used permanently to help identify that individual. As officials in NYC said to transgender activists who were pushing in the first decade of this century for getting these labels changed on birth certificates, "How will we know who you are?" A transgender woman who has succeeded in getting the label F on her passport will encounter huge problems if she has a penis detected by an airport scanner. Several US states along with NYC now have the option for birth certificates to indicate X or some other alternative to the usual binary choices. So far in the US these choices are only available as a change requested by an individual, not as something entered immediately after birth, though sometimes the sex/gender box has been left blank. Of course, so long as the federal government or a state motor vehicle office requires a binary choice, someone wishing to avoid binaries still faces potential difficulties in navigating their life. And changing documents from one binary label to the other remains challenging.

Some non-Western societies have long had more than two 'sex' categories into which to place people. These 'extra' categories, however, are not all the same. Some who fit the criteria for binary sexing at birth (and even perhaps thereafter) might get assigned to a 'supernumerary' class on grounds that most current Western analysts would treat as gender-nonconformity or non-heterosexuality. Others whom Western medical practitioners would categorize as DSD could end up in one of the 'standard' binary categories rather than in an 'extra' one.[37] Biologist Anne Fausto-Sterling has been pursuing these matters for decades. Her 2000 book, *Sexing the Body*, makes clear what a lot of sociocultural work goes into sorting people by sex. And in a short 2017 paper, she argues cogently for a dynamic interactive approach to understanding sex, gender, and sexuality, essentially offering the same kind of approach in this area as we saw proposed for racialized groups.

Recently, a small number of parents of children whose bodies are readily assignable to the female or the male pole at birth are trying to rear their children without having them steered toward traditionally feminine or masculine gender expression, leaving the child free to decide their own gender (one of the two binaries or neither). In doing so, of course, they need somehow to shield the child from the genderizing efforts of others and to do so they do not 'reveal' any information about the child's bodily configuration. They refer to their child using the pronoun *they* and ask others to do so as well, forgoing the more familiar binary *she* and *he*. (Just as *you* can be used in speaking to and of a single addressee, so *they* can be used in speaking about, referring to, a single person. Some changes in practices of English pronoun choice will be discussed in Chapter 4. In Chapter 6, there is an account of recent trends in specifying pronouns people want others to use for them and related issues.)

Some in the media now use the term *theyby* (pl. *theybies*) to label children being so reared. The parents expecting and trying to rear theybies and those throwing ever more elaborate gender reveal parties nicely show the huge social fissure on both gender conformity and gender binarism. Although it is only recently that deciding one's own gender assignment has been widely recognized, parents influenced by the second wave of feminism often tried to allow their children to follow their own inclinations in their performing gender. The story of "Baby X" in the early 1970s proposed an approach similar to that which parents raising theybies typically follow: keep others in the dark as long as possible as to the genitalia and other sex-relevant features of one's child's body so as to minimize the child's exposure to gender assumptions. Social psychologist Sandra Bem proposed that one raise gender-aschematic, potentially gender non-conforming, children by teaching them that their genitalia were all that was relevant to whether one was a girl or a boy. (Current ideas about gender identities outside the binary were not then very widely discussed.) Her goal was to assure them that whether one had a vulva or a penis did not constrain one to choose certain kinds of toys, play certain sorts of games, wear certain kinds of clothes. You could have a penis and wear barrettes in your long hair – you were still a boy. And if you had a vulva, playing with toy trucks was irrelevant to your being a girl. It is possible that a society without what writer Cordelia Fine calls "delusions of gender" might be one where gender identity simply became a non-issue. It's clear, however, that such a society is nowhere on the horizon.

It is still the case that the vast majority of people in the US and most other Western countries simply assume that they and others are easily sorted into two sex/gender categories on the basis of bodily characteristics ascertainable at birth. And they also assume that the sort is not only in fact important but necessarily so, far beyond any implications it might carry for baby-making. Thus it is hardly surprising that gender-labeling still plays an enormous bureaucratic role in so many social locations. Philosopher Robin Dembroff has argued that the state really has no business using sex/gender labels to track people, even if those labels can be shifted and include nonbinary options.[38] This proposal is relevant to the discussion in Chapter 3 about needing labels to generalize.

"One Name to Rule Them All": Strategic Labeling Dances

In *The Inconvenient Indian*, his often entertaining but profoundly unsettling history of the indigenous peoples of North America, Thomas King turns to *Lord of the Rings* to characterize how European settlers in North America tried to cope with the disturbing (to them) realization in the nineteenth century that in spite of great population shrinkages among native tribes due to disease and armed conflict "too many" of those native peoples were still around. "[T]oo many tribes, too many languages … a great sprawling mess. … So, out of ignorance, disregard, frustration, and expediency, North America set about creating a single entity, an entity that would stand for the whole. The Indian."[39] (As mentioned earlier, Spanish-speaking colonizers in parts of the Americas further south created the term *indios* to lump many different groups together.)

With his nod to J. R. R. Tolkien, King continues.

> No one really believed that there was only one Indian. But as North America began to experiment with its "Indian programs," it did so with a "one size fits all" mindset. Rather than see tribes as an arrangement of separate nation states in the style of the Old World, North America imagined that Indians were basically all the same. Sure, Mohawk were not Apache, Cherokee were not Cheyenne, but the differences among Native peoples were really just a matter of degree. … What could North America expect of this Indian? What might be this Indian's place, if any, in the new order? With the proper guidance, what might this Indian become?

In his introduction to the book, King had already addressed the issue of terminology.

When I was a kid [over half a century ago], Indians were just
Indians. Sometimes Indians were Mohawks or Cherokees or Crees
or Blackfoot or Tlingits or Seminoles. But mostly they were
Indians. Columbus gets blamed for the term but he wasn't being
malicious. He was looking for India and thought he had found it.
He was mistaken ... and various folks and institutions tried to
make the matter right. Indians became Amerindians and
Aboriginal Indians and Indigenous People and American Indians.
Lately, Indians have become First Nations in Canada and Native
Americans in the United States, but the fact of the matter is that
there has never been a good collective noun because there was
never a collective to begin with.[40]

That, of course, is the point of his appropriation of Tolkien's "to
rule them all" – creating (and naming – sometimes renaming) the
collective was essential to the US and Canadian governments'
projects of 'dealing with' the various groups of people whom
Europeans pushed aside as they poured into North America.
King goes on to say that any of these terms is fine but that he
will use *Indian*, as that seems to him the North American default.
(He confesses that he did consider titling his book *The Pesky
Redskin*, a name he and friends gave some years ago to their
band – I'll discuss *redskin* and similar terms in Chapter 5.) In a
wide range of contexts, however, he and many others identifying
as descendants of those living in North America when Europeans
first arrived prefer to use *nation* or the name of a specific band or
tribe or group of nations.

But in many cases, the versions familiar to English speakers of
those names no more represent self-chosen labels than terms like
American Indian or *Native American*. Legal scholar Peter d'Errico
outlines the situation.

Some of the traditional or "real" names are not actually derived
from the people themselves, but from their neighbors or even
enemies. "Mohawk" is a Narraganset name, meaning "flesh
eaters." "Sioux" is a French corruption of an Anishinabe word for
"enemy." Similarly, "Apache" is a Spanish corruption of a Zuni
word for "enemy," while "Navajo" is from the Spanish version of a

Tewa word. If we want to be fully authentic in every instance, we will have to inquire into the language of each People to find the name they call themselves. It may not be surprising to find that the deepest real names are often a word for "people" or for the homeland or for some differentiating characteristic of the people as seen through their own eyes.[41]

In late January of 2020, I visited Kitt Peak National Observatory in Arizona, which is located on land belonging to the people of the Tohono O'Odham nation and is a sacred spot for them. On that visit I was reminded that the Tohono O'Odham, literally 'people of the desert,' were once known as the Papago. That name derived from the Spanish rendition of *Ba:bawĭko'a*, literally meaning 'eating tepary beans,' a label bestowed by the other Piman groups who were in competition with them.[42] Ofelia Zepeda, a distinguished linguist and poet honored with a MacArthur 'genius' award and herself a member of the Tohono O'Odham nation, used the name *Papago* for her people and their language in her early publications. For some time now, like most others in the group, she has used *Tohono O'Odham*.

Cornell University, my home institution, stands on land that was once home to the Cayuga, whose name is an Anglicization of the name they used for themselves (transliterated *Guyohkohnyoh*). On August 25, 2017, Martha E. Pollack made sure that her inauguration as Cornell's thirteenth president began with a traditional prayer of Thanksgiving in the Cayuga language, delivered by a member of the Cayuga nation. The Iroquois Confederacy, to which the Cayuga belong, is now reclaiming the name *Haudenosaunee*, as explained in the statement in Figure 1.2. Reclamation of earlier names has been spreading.

There continues, however, to be widespread agreement among indigenous North American populations with the tolerant and eclectic outlook on naming expressed by Thomas King at the beginning of this section. Yes, all of the distinction-erasing names are problematic. Even *indigenous* can be problematized as it is used only for populations that have been 'conquered' by foreign invaders of their homelands. At the same time, names first

Haudenosaunee is the general term we use to refer to ourselves, instead of "Iroquois." The word "Iroquois" is not a Haudenosaunee word. It is derived from a French version of a Huron Indian name that was applied to our ancestors and it was considered derogatory, meaning "Black Snakes." Haudenosaunee means "People building an extended house" or more commonly referred to as "People of the Long House." The longhouse was a metaphor introduced by the Peace Maker at the time of the formation of the Confederacy meaning that the people are meant to live together as families in the same house. Today this means that those who support the traditions, beliefs, values, and authority of the Confederacy are to be known as Haudenosaunee.

The founding constitution of the Confederacy brought the Seneca, Cayuga, Onondaga, Oneida, and Mohawk nations under one law. Together they were called the Five Nations by the English, and Iroquois by the French. The Tuscarora joined around 1720, and collectively they are now called the Six Nations.

We also refer to ourselves as "Ongwehonweh," meaning that we are the "Original People" or "First People" of this land. The Haudenosaunee is actually six separate nations of people who have agreed to live under the traditional law of governance that we call the Great Law of Peace. Each of these nations have their own identity. In one sense, these are our "nationalities." Many of the names that we have come to know the tribes by are not even Indian words, such as Tuscarora or Iroquois. The original member nations are:

Seneca, "Onondowahgah," meaning The People of the Great Hill, also referred to as the Large Dark Door.
Cayuga, "Guyohkohnyoh," meaning The People of the Great Swamp.
Onondaga, "Onundagaono," meaning The People of the Hills.
Oneida, "Onayotekaono," meaning The People of the Upright Stone.
Mohawk, "Kanienkahagen," meaning The People of the Flint.
Tuscarora, known as "Ska-Ruh-Reh" meaning The Shirt Wearing People.

Figure 1.2 Who are the Haudenosaunee?

imposed from above can be useful sometimes for furthering self-determination, reclaiming of "the power of naming." Peter d'Errico makes this point:[43]

It may be that the shortest way to penetrate the situation of Indigenous Peoples is to critically use the generic name imposed on them. "Native American Indian Studies," then, is a way to describe an important part of the history of "America," of the colonization of the "Americas." It is a part of world history, world politics, world culture. It is a component of "Indigenous Peoples Studies." By using this terminology, we aim for a critical awareness of nationhood and homelands, of Indigenous self-determination.

The differences among those misleading names assigned from above often cancel out. As Susan Shown Harjo said in a 1992 appearance on Oprah Winfrey's talk show, "Call us whatever you want; just don't call us names [like *injun* or *squaw*]."[44]

Labeling vs Describing

Although terminology is by no means standardized, linguists have long noted important differences between *labeling* someone using nouns or noun phrases, the focus of this chapter, and *describing* them, using adjectives or verbal expressions. In what I am calling labeling, a noun or multi-word nominal is typically used to categorize a person, to identify them as a certain *kind* of person. In describing, an adjective or verb phrase ascribes some property to the person. What I'm calling 'describing' is also sometimes called 'labeling' by social scientists, but I adopt this way of talking about the different grammatical structures and their meaning as a handy shorthand.

Linguist Anna Wierzbicka described the distinction this way more than three decades ago:

> [I]f one categorizes a person as a cripple, a leper, a virgin, or a teenager, one is not mentioning one characteristic among many; rather, one is putting that person into a certain category, seen at the moment as "unique." One is putting a label on that person, as one might put a label on a jar of preserves. One might say that a noun is comparable to an identifying construction; "that's the kind of person that this person is."[45]

Writing just a few years earlier, linguist Dwight Bolinger made a very similar observation:

> [T]he noun objectifies in a way the adjective cannot. A quality may come and go. If we are disappointed at Jane's lack of appreciation we can call her *ungrateful*, or solidify it a step further and call her *an ungrateful person*. But if we call her an *ingrate* we put the brand on her: the name implies that the world puts people like this in a class by themselves.[46]

Bolinger suggests that saying "Maria is Mexican" brings with it fewer stereotypes and assumptions than saying "Maria is a Mexican" and also points out that racial and ethnic slurs, which we'll discuss in Chapter 5, are nouns rather than adjectives. Nominal labels and categorization tend to suggest clusters of properties that make the category cohere, whereas a description simply ascribes a single property and does not necessarily suggest that any particular other properties might also hold of the individual so described.

Formal models of natural language meaning that draw on the resources of logic and other formal languages have generally treated *Dana is female*, a description, and *Dana is a female*, a labeling, as equivalent. They have tended to ignore the distinctions noted by linguists like Bolinger, Wierzbicka, and others before them. Philosopher of language Kate Ritchie, however, has recently proposed incorporating into formal semantic theories the distinction between the meaning of nouns and noun phrases (*a female* or *females*) and of adjectives (*female* without an article preceding it or a plural ending following it) and other verbal expressions used in predicates.[47] In showing why it is important to do so, she offers considerable evidence from social science research showing the systematicity of the different interpretations. For example, research by psychologist Susan Gelman and associates found that children told a story about a girl labeled "a carrot-eater" were far more likely to 'essentialize' her carrot-eating than those told she "eats carrots whenever she can." Those who heard the nominal label were significantly more likely than those who got the description to infer that she would continue eating carrots in adulthood, that she had eaten carrots as a much younger child, and that she would eat lots of carrots even if she lived in a family whose other members did not eat carrots.[48] And the Gelman research is just the tip of the very large iceberg that Kate Ritchie has exposed for theorists to consider.

In fact, multitudes of ordinary speakers of English exploit the contrast between labeling and describing (between nouns, on the one hand, and adjectives and verbal expressions, on the other) regularly. They did not wait for people who study language to give them license to do so. "I've smoked cigarettes occasionally, but I am not a smoker." "Yes, I drink the occasional beer, but I am not a drinker/an alcoholic." "Chris is intellectual but not an intellectual – Chris is someone you'd really like to hang out with, enjoy yourself with."

Of course it matters what is involved. Anyone who agrees to "Lee murdered someone" is hard put to deny "Lee is a murderer." On the other hand, if Lee's commission of murder is far in the past with considerable atonement for that crime in the meantime, some might want to say that Lee should no longer be 'defined' by that long-ago misdeed, that continuing to refer to Lee using *murderer* is no longer appropriate. Indeed precisely that claim was made by a letter-writer responding to "When a Murderer Wants to Practice Medicine," an article that appeared in the *NY Times*, January 29, 2008. On February 5, 2008, the paper published this response from reader Elise Wang:

> Dr. Lawrence K. Altman refers to Karl Helge Hampus Svenson repeatedly as "killer" or "murderer." I have worked in prison-to-work rehabilitation and I know that the insidious practice of referring to people – no matter how long ago their crimes occurred – as "killers" or "illegal aliens" steps beyond semantics [!] and reduces these human beings to the law they have broken. These terms prejudice the discussion from the start.

Linguist Larry Horn, who brought this and other examples to my attention, calls the letter-writer's objection the result of *noun aversion*. Noun aversion generally leads to what we might call *noun avoidance*.

Sometimes noun avoidance succeeds, sometimes it does not. "I have lied but I am not a liar," said Michael Cohen, Donald Trump's former lawyer and go-to "fixer" in testimony to the US Congress on March, 6, 2019. "I have done bad things, but I am not a bad man." But "If you've lied, you are a liar," retorted Rep. Jody Hice of Georgia. And, not surprisingly, President Trump weighed in via Twitter, pasting the *liar* label on Cohen. Cohen's strategy was to try to separate his essence, the *kind* of person he was (and is), from the obviously blameworthy things he has done over a period of many years. He blamed his earlier wrongdoing on Trump and his own misguided loyalty to Trump, being willing to see that as evidence for his being *a fool* – but not for being *a liar* or *a bad man.*

Noun aversion is responsible for what has sometimes been called the people-first strategy for renaming certain marginalized groups. In the 1990s, many organizations began issuing guidelines for "bias-free" language and endorsed, for example, choosing *a person with schizophrenia* rather than *a schizophrenic*, or *people with learning disabilities* rather than *the learning-disabled*. And others responded positively to these proposals. Again, Larry Horn's files, which he has generously shared with me, offer nice examples. "Kay Jorgensen does not minister to 'the homeless.' She ministers to people who happen to live on the streets. Please update your language guidelines: Families live on the streets, mothers, fathers, young people, elders, people with and without disabilities ... " So read a letter in January 2002 from Harold A. Maio to the editor of the *Unitarian Universalist World*. And the *NY Times* published a letter from Susan Lesburg on December 26, 2006, also criticizing labeling practices. "Thank you for your article. But you do a disservice to all those with diabetes by referring to them as 'diabetics.' We are not our diseases; we are individuals with lives and families. Such a reference is demeaning and promotes just the discrimination you were reporting."

But the strategy of preferring adjectival or verbal descriptions to nominal labels for those who might face physical or other challenges is not always fully embraced by those being spoken of.

I am an addict – or, as my father prefers to say it – I *have an addiction*. There's no need, he insists, to so thoroughly pigeon-hole myself. I think I know what he means. If I have an addiction, then maybe one day I can throw it away, or misplace it, or refuse to be seen with it. But if I am an addict ... well, that feels more permanent, more all-defining.

These words by Benoit Denizet-Lewis appear near the beginning of his 2009 book, *America Anonymous: Eight Addicts in Search of a Life*.[49] And there are others who find the formulaic 'people-first' expressions quite overblown sometimes and would prefer just being labeled. The author of a *NY Times* piece on autism reports that Michelle Dawson, a woman from Montreal to whom he spoke, cautioned him against such ways of speaking, at least of her. "I would appreciate it," she said, "if I end up in your article, if you describe me [or, in my terminology 'refer to me' or 'speak of me'] as 'an autistic' or 'an autistic person,' versus the 'person with.' Just like you would feel odd if people said you were a person with 'femaleness.'"

There is no word magic on which we can draw to eliminate oppressive categorizing. It is useful, however, to be aware of the many functions labeling can serve. Even if social identity categories often rest on problematic assumptions, social identity labels and labeling can be important components of social practice.

Notes

1. Hacking 1999, pp. 58–59.
2. See Alim 2016. This quote is from p. 42.
3. This quote appears in an obituary in the *Southern Illinois University Alumni News* (August 19, 2017). It is followed by "I have to be a colored funny man, not a funny colored man." *Southern Illinoisian* online at https://thesouthern.com/news/local/comedian-civil-rights-activist-dick-gregory-dies/article_9ef72d39-f3fe-5a11-9417-f0d412f4312c.html.
4. See Appiah 2018.
5. See Lewontin 1972, Gould 1981.

6. Elizabeth Kolbert, "There's No Scientific Basis for Race – It's a Made-Up Label," *National Geographic*, 2018, www.nationalgeographic.com/magazine/2018/04/race-genetics-science-africa/.
7. Painter 2010, p. 1.
8. Reich 2018.
9. See Blum 2010. This quote is from p. 300.
10. Blum 2010. The first quote is from p. 300, the second from 302.
11. Haslanger 2012 [2000], p. 236.
12. Omi and Winant 2015. The first, italicized, quote is from p. 110; the longer quote is from p. 111.
13. Haslanger 2012 [2000], already cited, addresses these issues as does Haslanger 2012 [2010]. In his 2019 Georgetown PhD dissertation "The Pragmatics and Epistemology of Conceptual Disagreement" philosopher Matthew Shields argues that *stipulation* is a distinctive kind of speech act, something we can do with words in order to 'improve' our collective exploration of our shared ideas.
14. Again, Painter 2010 is an excellent resource.
15. See "Ask Language Log: 'White of You,'" *Language Log*, June 4, 2011, http://languagelog.ldc.upenn.edu/nll/?p=3179.
16. Philosopher Mary Kate McGowan notes that such signs did indeed legally count as 'speech.' Like crying 'fire' in a crowded theatre, such speech was not protected by the 'freedom of speech' doctrine enunciated in the First Amendment to the US Constitution, courts determined. See McGowan 2012 and also the discussion in Langton, Haslanger, and Anderson 2012.
17. The term *panethnic* is used in the literature to characterize groups that include multiple ethnicities, not, as the etymology of *pan-* might suggest, *all* ethnicities.
18. Gutiérrez 2016, p. 20.
19. Gutiérrez 2016, p. 23.
20. www.youtube.com/watch?v=K_pc7g9GOJ8.
21. Gutiérrez 2016, p. 30.
22. Gutiérrez 2016, p. 32.
23. Gutiérrez 2016, p. 32.
24. Gutiérrez 2016, p. 34.
25. See Roque Planas, "Chicano: What Does the Word Mean and Where Does It Come From?" *HuffPost*, October 21, 2012, www.huffpost.com/entry/chicano_n_1990226, with references to scholarly work and see Gutiérrez 2016, esp. pp. 40–43.
26. Yasmin Anwar, "I Say Hispanic. You Say Latino. How Did the Whole Thing Start?" University of California website, April 29, 2014, www.universityof

california.edu/news/i-say-hispanic-you-say-latino-how-did-whole-thing-start.

27. Lisa Ko, "Harvard and the Myth of the Interchangeable Asian," *The New York Times*, October 13, 2018, www.nytimes.com/2018/10/13/opinion/sunday/harvard-and-the-myth-of-the-interchangeable-asian.html.

28. Jayne Tsuchiyama, "The Term 'Oriental' Is Outdated, But Is It Racist?" *Los Angeles Times*, June 1, 2016, www.latimes.com/opinion/op-ed/la-oe-tsuchiyama-oriental-insult-20160601-snap-story.html.

29. Coates 2015.

30. Martin Luther King, Jr., "Beyond Vietnam," https://kinginstitute.stanford.edu/king-papers/documents/beyond-vietnam.

31. "Leaders Say Blacks Want to Be Called African Americans," *AP News*, December 20, 1988, https://apnews.com/089fc3ab25b86e14deeefae3adb7a5ad. Cited in Martin 1991, a highly relevant article I only encountered as this book was in press.

32. Dodson 2007, p. 1.

33. Blake 2016; the quote from Dana is from pp. 158–159.

34. Pollock 2004. Figures on "official" racial labeling of students are from pp. 7–8. The first quotations from Michael are from p. 25 and the longer closing quotation is from pp. 39–40.

35. Carina Chocano, "When Gender Reveal Videos Go Spectacularly, Cathartically Wrong," *The New York Times Magazine*, August 1, 2019, www.nytimes.com/2019/08/01/magazine/gender-reveal-fail-videos.html.

36. Jordan Hirst, "Queensland Opposition Leader Slams Non-Binary Birth Certificate Proposal," *Q News*, n.d., https://qnews.com.au/queensland-opposition-leader-slams-non-binary-birth-certificate-proposal/.

37. Amanda Montañez, "Visualizing Sex as a Spectrum," *Scientific American*, August 29, 2017, https://blogs.scientificamerican.com/sa-visual/visualizing-sex-as-a-spectrum/. See also www.nature.com/news/sex-redefined-1.16943#/spectrum, an article by science writer Claire Ainsworth, "Sex Redefined," *Nature*, February 18, 2015. See also Fausto-Sterling 2000, 2017.

38. Dembroff 2018.

39. King 2013, 82. The next quote is from p. 83.

40. From King 2017, xiii–xiv.

41. I encountered d'Errico's words in Dunbar-Ortiz and Gilio-Whitaker 2016. What I reproduce is from p. 147. A fuller version of D'Errico's interesting material on names can be found at http://people.umass.edu/derrico/name.html.

42. See Indigenous Peoples. (n.d.). Tohano O'Odham (Papago) Literature. www.indigenouspeople.net/papago.htm.

43. In the full article at http://people.umass.edu/derrico/name.html.

44. Quoted in Dunbar-Ortiz and Gilio-Whitaker 2016, p. 145.
45. Wierzbicka 1988 [1986], p. 468.
46. Bolinger 1980, p. 79.
47. Ritchie 2019.
48. Gelman 2003 reports on this and much other relevant research.
49. Denizet-Lewis 2009; again, I owe Larry Horn thanks for this reference.

2 Marking/Erasing: "Instead of Saying 'Normal Americans,' You Can Just Say 'Americans'"

Labeling is part of categorizing our world, organizing its contents to help make sense of them.[1] Part of that organization is relating categories to one another, and one linguistic strategy for relating categories is explicitly marking one and not the other. African Americans are Americans: the first identity label *marks* a subcategory included under the second overarching category. African Americans are labeled as a 'special,' a 'distinctive,' kind of American.

Sometimes those in the marked subcategories can be erased, forgotten, in talk of the overarching category. Joy Cho, American-born daughter of immigrants to the US from Thailand, talks about the "What are you?" questions she faced as a child. "I wanted to be American SO bad. I knew I was American in theory but I wanted to be American American."[2]

Marking and Erasing: First Pass

Often what gets marked is what is not expected, what is not 'normal' in that statistical sense: the *male nurse* or the *female jockey*. *Female nurse* or *male jockey* would in most contexts be surprising labels simply because in most contexts it can and does 'go without saying' that nurses are female and jockeys are male. But statistical normality certainly does not always settle matters for what gets marked. The label *lion*, for example, can designate any of the species, but *lioness* only applies to females, who certainly statistically just as normal. In some species the male is marked with its own distinctive label: *bull* applies only to male bovines but *cow* can cover creatures of either sex. In human populations, females and males are more or less equal in number,

50

with females usually slightly in the majority (and, as we noted earlier, there are a few people who for various reasons are outside that binary sex/gender split). Nonetheless, there used to be many contexts and there still are a few in which the labels *man* and *men* can be understood as applying to people in general, unmarked for sex/gender, whereas *woman* and *women* are always marked.

Marking a social identity can also be a matter of highlighting it, drawing attention to it, when speaking of some person or group of people. Doing so of course suggests its relevance to the particular exchange, and when and how particular identities are relevant can often be a socially loaded question. Over forty years ago, as the second wave of feminism was just beginning to move into academic pursuits but when the gender binary was still generally assumed, philosopher Elizabeth Beardsley argued that linguistic practices promoted the view that a woman's sex was always relevant. A woman was a 'poetess,' a 'draftswoman,' a 'female philosopher' – whereas her male peer could far more readily be represented without his sex being noted.[3] That highlighting of marked female identities in some contexts often accompanied what looked like their erasure in others – talk of 'poets', of 'draftsmen', and of 'philosophers' had all too often simply ignored those who were women. When we speak of *heroines*, have we excluded women from our discussions of *heroes*? Beardsley was drawing attention to the fact that marking gender identities was often done in contexts where it should have been irrelevant, and to the related tendency to forget about, to erase, women when their presence was not explicitly marked. I discuss below evidence that even without 'sexist' markers of gender, women are not always included in supposedly 'inclusive' language. Nonetheless, that marking clearly sometimes promotes erasure in contexts where the marking is absent.

The point I want to make here is that assumptions about what is and is not relevant in particular contexts are crucial in detecting erasure of marked subcategories. In the autumn of 2018, a friend sent me the headline, "Americans are Divided over Kavanaugh," with the comment "not African Americans." In fact, as a group, African Americans were not divided but

overwhelmingly *against* approving Brett Kavanaugh for a place
on the Supreme Court, a place he eventually did get. Were they
being erased in this headline? As linguist Mia Wiegand has
reminded me, *divided* is a complicated predicate. And, as we
will discuss in more detail in the next chapter, the semantics of
generic claims about groups, especially but not only social identity groups, is very complicated and contestable. We certainly
don't require a claim that a group is 'divided' to apply to all
subgroups. Sometimes a focus on particular subgroups, including marked ones, might be what is relevant for establishing the
claimed division. The headline writer might conceivably have
continued (but did not), "Most white Americans support him
but African Americans are nearly unanimous in their opposition." In that case the division of the overall group would be
grounded in the opposition between the two subgroups, so
neither would be erased. My friend read the headline as erasing,
and I concurred because we judged the near unity of African
Americans in their opposition to be highly relevant in the context, something that should have been made explicit. Differences
between what people think needs mentioning and what goes
without saying often arise from social divisions.

The term *erasing*, which I use in this chapter, suggests intentional removal. Sometimes, in fact, what is going on is more
a matter of *ignoring* or *overlooking*, simply failing to consider.
Once you start looking you will find many cases where marked
groups are erased or ignored, 'squeezed out,' in talk of the larger
groups to which they belong. Literally 'inclusive' language does
not always include everyone and sometimes defaults to
a dominant subgroup. Contexts may change, however, in terms
of which group is the default, even where there are larger patterns
of social power. It always matters who is speaking of what to
whom – and what projects their linguistic practices serve.

And there is also a different kind of erasure. Social dominance
of one group vis à vis another is sometimes manifest in the
absence of marking of the dominant group, whose members can
present themselves as just 'normal,' as the default in the larger

social scene, with just individual characteristics and nothing 'special.' In this case, power and privilege are erased because we *fail* to mark 'default' identities; we *erase* them as identities that distinguish those bearing them from those that do not. Resistance to the dominance of those default identities can take the form of calling attention to them by labeling them – launching and promoting the form *cisgender*, a term which I discuss below, illustrates this kind of move.

I need to acknowledge that my uses of *American* and *America* at most points in this book are instances of conventionalized erasure. *American* is widely used in English to designate only those in the United States of America. It has erased the many others living in and identified with the Americas, eliminating Canadians and all those in Latin America. Similarly, the political dominance of the US has led to *America* being used in a way that erases the other countries in the Americas – North, Central, and South. The slogan "Make America Great Again" is not about improving life in Honduras, Ecuador, Peru, Mexico, or even Canada, also once a British colony. America Ferrara makes this point quite eloquently in the preface to her recent *American Like Me*. In a very moving passage she speaks of how often people she has met in the USA assume that she has been named by immigrant parents eager to honor the United States of America, their new home.[4] But, she explains, she is named for her mother. Her mother was born in Honduras on a holiday called Día de Las Américas, a holiday that "celebrates *all* the Americas, South, Central, and North, not just the United States of . . . my name has nothing to do with amber waves of grain, purple mountains, the US flag, or your very narrow definition of the word." Ferrara's learned grandfather, a librarian, had used his daughter's day of birth to name her. His granddaughter, now an extremely successful actor, director, producer, and public figure in the USA, is proud that her name connects her to her mother and to her family's central American roots. America Ferrara enjoins us to "refrain from limiting the meaning of my name, erasing my family's history."

Us vs Them Marking

Languages often use a single word to designate both humans in general and also 'us', that is, the group of humans who speak that language. The general form then is modified or 'marked,' in one sense of that linguistic notion, in talk about people from other communities, about 'them.' Linguist Joseph Greenberg reported that in the Maidu language the word *majdy* would typically designate Maidu speakers but also, if modified, could denote people more generally. So, for example, Greenberg translates *kombom majdy* as 'Yana person' whereas he translates *wolem majdy* as 'white person.' The modifier *kombom* distinguished Yana from the Maidu, and the modifier *wolem* distinguished the lighter-skinned incoming people of European descent from the Maidu. It is highly plausible that for the Maidu speakers, unmodified *majdy* could convey not just the 'us' who speak this language but also something like just 'person' or 'human,' perhaps understood as 'normal' or 'typical' or even only 'familiar' humans after non-Maidu people were encountered. After all, fellow Maidu speakers were the only people Maidu speakers first knew. They were the kind contrasting with the wildcats, dogs, and other animals they encountered in their home in the Sierra Nevada mountains of what is now northern California. Wildcats roar or yowl, dogs bark, and the Maidu people speak the Maidu language. Only in encountering other groups was there any need for Maidu people to think of themselves or their fellow Maidu speakers as having some special, distinctive social identity beyond their common humanity. Labeling a Yana person *kombo majdy* acknowledged the shared humanity of the Yana people (they were clearly much more like the 'us' of the Maidu than like wildcats or dogs or other animals) but assigned to them a marked social identity.[5]

The distinction between *ingroup*, those who share some identity the speaker claims, vs *outgroup*, those who do not share that identity, is often important for how we speak both about and to people. This is true even when there are no significant power differences between the groups, but differential resources and status of the groups can magnify these effects, as we will see.

How Did English *Man* Lose Its Generic Inclusiveness?

Interestingly, *Wikipedia* glosses Maidu *majdy* as 'man,' and Greenberg follows his discussion of Maidu by contrasting English *man*, unmarked, with *woman*, marked. The English word *man* is now seen as semantically ambiguous. It can indeed still designate humans generally, the 'unmarked' or generic sense. More often it designates a distinct group of adult human beings, the masculine sense or 'marked' sense that applies to people who are not women. (This becomes slightly more complicated when we recognize people outside gender binaries, but the points to be made here are unaffected by that complication so I ignore it in this discussion.) In many contexts, only the masculine interpretation of *man* is now available. On the door of public toilet facilities, the plural *Men* unambiguously excludes a particular kind of people, those directed to the door labeled *Women*. If someone says "I saw a man sitting out under the tree," the claim is that it was an adult who is not a woman out under the tree. "There are three men sitting at that table" is not judged true if there are three people but one is categorized as a woman.

Generic uses of *man* (and *men*) have declined somewhat since feminist critics noted that the masculine sense often infects the generic. They do, however, continue in contexts such as "Man's relation to other primates" or, in the suffix pronounced differently from the independent word, "A chairman for the university's concert committee will be appointed by the dean of the faculty." (Changing the spelling of the singular suffix *man* to *mun* and of the plural *men* to *min* might have been a helpful reform as, arguably, the suffixed forms were far less heavily gendered than the independent form. It is probably too late for that now.) Still, *man* is far less common in gender-inclusive contexts than it once was. (As I'll discuss in more detail in Chapter 6, there has also been a decrease in the use of the pronoun *he* in contexts where both sex/gender groups are potentially spoken of and where the sex/gender binary is at issue.)

What's especially relevant for this discussion is that around the time of the Norman invasion of England, 1066, Old English *man* had only the generic sense. To indicate that one was speaking specifically of female humans, the modifier *wif* (from which the modern *wife* descends) was prefixed, *wifman*. To indicate that one was speaking of male humans, the prefix *wer* (related to Latin *vir* and modern English words like *virile*) was added. Within a few centuries, however, the masculinizing prefix had been abandoned even when it was clear that the 'man' spoken of was male. There must have been a considerable period during which analysts might have hesitated to say that *man* had a conventionalized meaning 'male human being,' in which it could be understood as not extending to female human beings. At the same time, linguistic practices that increasingly used the modified form *wifman*, explicitly marked feminine, whenever speaking of women but also increasingly dropped the masculine prefix when speaking of male human beings eventually forced recognition that *man* could be taken 'literally' to mean 'male human being.' We don't have and cannot obtain anything like a detailed record of these changing linguistic practices. It is highly likely, however, that in this arena men's greater social power played a significant role in conventionalizing the use of unmodified, unmarked, *man* to designate male-sexed humans in particular as well as human beings in general, once its sole conventional meaning.

The ubiquity of the masculine interpretation of *man* and also of the pronoun *he* led US feminists in the 1970s and 1980s to protest so-called 'he/man' or 'sexist' language and to push for terminology that is unambiguously sex-neutral: *firefighter* rather than *fireman*, for example. That movement had some success as we'll see in Chapter 6, but matters remain complicated.

Squeezing Marked Subcategory Members Out: Where Are the Women?

It continues to be the case that widespread ways of speaking, commonly encountered linguistic practices, suggest that there are human beings and then there are people in this specially 'marked' category designated by the term *woman*. We also find other forms like *wife* where there is another presumptively gender-neutral term that might have designated the person. History texts in my school days would speak of "the settler and his wife" or "the pioneer and his wife," erasing women as settlers or pioneers.

There is a continuing "illusion of inclusion," as linguist Deborah Cameron points out in an August 2018 posting on her blog *Language: A Feminist Guide*. Words that are conventionally 'inclusive' or gender-neutral (as *man* once was but no longer is, at least in its most common meaning) continue to be used in contexts that covertly render them masculine. She cites a recent news report: "The lack of vitality is aggravated by the fact that there are so few young able-bodied adults around. They have all gone off to work or look for work, leaving behind the old, the disabled, the women, and the children." The old, disabled, and children clearly don't fit the description "young able-bodied adults," but surely at least some of "the women" do. It is not semantically odd to say "She is an able-bodied young adult," whereas in modern English replacing *adult* by *man* in that sentence would seem semantically weird. Semantically *man* is masculine whereas *adult* is not. Semantically, *adult*, even if modified by *able-bodied*, clearly includes both men and women, but pragmatically it can be used in contexts that exclude women.

And Cameron offers a host of other examples where what is semantically gender-inclusive language is used in ways that exclude women. Consider "We cannot tolerate attacks on the wife of an American citizen," in a context that has made clear that the woman attacked is herself an American citizen, or "A forty-five-year-old man has been charged with assaulting his neighbor's wife," where the person assaulted also lives next door and could be referred to using "his neighbor." These seem bizarre unless we suppose that the woman's status as wife is deemed of greater relevance than her status as citizen or neighbor. Back in the late 1980s, linguists Francine Frank and Paula Treichler dubbed such examples 'false generics.' An example modeled on actual sentences in well-known anthropology texts went something like this: "We awoke in the morning to find that the villagers had all stolen away in canoes under cover of night, leaving us behind with the women and children." The women (and also the children) have been erased from "the villagers," squeezed out as not counting.

That such covert masculinizing of formally gender-neutral terms persists well into the twenty-first century shows that abandoning *he/man* language, though it can be helpful, by no means guarantees the linguistic inclusion of women as fully equal human beings. Are men ever excluded by uses of semantically gender-neutral words? Yes, but such exclusions are far less common than the exclusion of women. Here is one of the few cases I've encountered.[6] Flight attendants in the early days of the airline industry were young women and called *stewardesses*. The feminizing *-ess* suffix marked their sex/gender status. (Feminizing affixes occur in many languages; masculinizing affixes are very rare although the *-er* in *widower* is one example.) A woman who was among the first to work as a stewardess was reminiscing in an NPR interview about those days of yore and remarked that "people quit working back then when they got married." It is clear that she has used *people* here in a way that excludes men, who she certainly was not suggesting quit working when they married.

Exclusion or erasure of marked members of a category often arises from highlighting the unmarked members, focusing on those taken as central, as default category members. Such a focus makes it easy to overlook those outside that central unmarked group. Light sometimes shines only on the unmarked group: those marked are in deep shadow, easy to ignore. At the same time, marking can highlight. We seem to have a paradox, and indeed marking and erasing are in considerable tension with one another.

Who Is an 'Unmarked' - 'Normal' - American?

In late summer of 2018 the US film *Crazy Rich Asians* opened to considerable critical acclaim and huge box office success. It was the first major film produced by a Western studio with a cast where all leads were "Asian" – that is, of recent Asian ancestry – since *The Joy Luck Club*, based on Amy Tan's novel of the same name, twenty-five years earlier. *The Joy Luck Club* was well received, though, inevitably, it was criticized for offering only a limited perspective on Asian Americans' lives. On August 18, 2018, Jennifer Ludden of NPR's *Morning Edition* program interviewed Janet Yang, executive producer of the earlier film. Oliver Stone's company, for which Yang had worked in the early 1990s, had finally agreed to take on the film after a number of other studios had turned it down. Yang answered Yellen's query about what concerns executives at all those nay-saying studios had expressed. "You know," Yang said, "in some cases, it was very blunt. I know Chris Lee, who was working at TriStar at the time, remembers, specifically, when he was trying to push for the movie, they said, oh, but there are no Americans in the movie. And he said, oh, they are Americans. They just don't look like you. And then that executive said, oh, you know what I mean."[7]

Indeed, most readers, whatever their own nationalities and ethnic origins, will immediately know what the executive meant but did not say: "There are no white Americans in the movie." Asian Americans and all the others who look different from 'white' Americans do not fully count as American. What is going on here? How is it that the label *American* can convey what is literally expressed by *white American* or *European American* or something similar? Although there are some important differences between sex/gender distinctions and other identity differences, what lets ethnically and racially marked groups of

Americans get excluded from the range of *American* or of *normal American* is very like the process that lets semantically gender-inclusive terms like *neighbor* or *villager* or the like be used so that women and girls are not included.

Some analysts promote a view of many categories as internally graded or ranked, with some members more central, 'prototypical', than others.[8] So does *American* convey whiteness because Americans not classified as white are seen as less typical than their compatriots of mostly European ancestry who are so classified? Although typicality may play a role, I think there is more going on.

A favorite example among those advancing prototype theories of category meanings is that of *bird*. Penguins are not typical birds; they do not, for example, fly, and yet their not flying seems compatible with the truth of a generalization like "Birds fly" (I'll have more to say about generalizing about social kinds in the next chapter). In other words, unless penguins or other examples of flightless birds have been made especially salient, their being unable to fly does not seem to threaten the truth of "Birds fly." Most kinds of penguins are not only flightless but are also much larger than typical birds. There have been many critiques of the quasi-documentary film *March of the Penguins*, but if someone asked whether there were birds in the film, viewers would certainly have said yes. In other words, the atypicality of penguins does not seem to get them ejected from the bird category.

Judgments of atypicality do not as such push or attempt to push atypical category members out of the category altogether. Yet in the case of social groups, there is often talk suggesting that 'peripheral' or 'marked' members do not count as group members, either qualitatively or quantitatively. It is not that they are not 'normal' members of the group in the sense of statistically typical. It is that they are not 'normal' members of the group because they are different in a value-laden way from what is expected for the group. (Actually, the pervasive marking of women in contrast to men, who set the norm in so many contexts, shows that norms involved in such markings need not be a matter of statistical frequency. There are, after all, slightly more women in most populations than there are men. I will return to the tension between statistical norms and value-setting norms in the next chapter.)

It is certainly the case that Americans with recent Asian or African (or, somewhat ironically, even Native American or American Indian) ancestry are seen as less 'typical' Americans than those classed as white. This is especially likely if their skin color or eye shape or hair texture is not that associated with recent predominantly European ancestry. But there is more than 'typicality' going on when *American* is understood as excluding Americans of color. Such exclusions in many contexts constitute negative judgments of acceptability and worthiness.

Beginning with philosopher Paul Grice, students of language have offered explanations of how and why conveyed meanings depart so often from literal meanings.[9] As linguist Larry Horn has put it, there is an ongoing struggle between two competing communicative principles. The speaker should "say enough" (he calls this Q for quantity) but "not too much," leaving the hearer to fill in what "goes without saying" (he calls this R for relevance).[10] The studio executive complaining that the cast includes "no Americans" probably had not even noticed that the addressee would need to fill in "white." It "goes without saying" (and probably even "without thinking" for many white people) that white American lives and experience are of general interest to Americans, any of whom can identify with characters played by white actors. In contrast, the 'special' – that is, 'marked' – lives and experiences of Asian Americans or other 'ethnic' or 'racialized' groups are often assumed to be of interest only to those in that 'special' group. (Sometimes this assumption is indeed spelled out. In the case of *Crazy Rich Asians*, at least one studio offered to produce the film if the female romantic lead, Rachel, were changed to be a young white woman.)

Withholding the label *American* from native-born citizens who don't 'look' American downgrades those Americans. Studio executives who turned down *Joy Luck Club* (and also *Crazy Rich Asians*) may well not personally have harbored overt negative attitudes toward Asian Americans. But in not 'counting' the

Asian-American actors as Americans they participated in linguistic practices that help sustain a social system that not only systematically overlooks and renders invisible, but also devalues and disadvantages Americans who don't look like 'normal' Americans – those who count as 'white.'

America Ferrara, whose reflections on her own first name appeared earlier in this chapter, offers other childhood memories relevant here. At the age of nine, the boy she has loved since age six tells her "I like Jenna more than you ... Because she has blue eyes and lighter skin than you." Shortly afterwards California passes Proposition 187 to deny undocumented immigrants and their kids access to public schools. Many immigrant parents worry and her mother says to her, "You are American. You were born in this country. If anyone asks you questions, you don't need to feel ashamed or embarrassed. You've done nothing wrong." The nine-year-old doesn't understand what this is all about but starts discussing her mother's words with friends, to whom the idea of being questioned about being American is completely novel and makes no sense. An older kid interrupts, "They don't care about *us*. It's just Americans like you." Ferrara's nine-year old self narrates.

> My mind short-circuits. Americans like me? What does that mean? I wasn't aware there were different kinds of Americans . . . . Is it about my name? . . . Maybe this has something to do with my skin and my non-blue eyes again . . . Are there different words for different kinds of Americans. Am I half American? Kind of American? Other American? I am nine years old, and suddenly I am wondering what do I call an American like me?[11]

Modifiers and Marking

As I have already pointed out, it is not a matter of what is *literally* meant by *American* that some Americans don't always 'count' as such. Their somewhat peripheral status as Americans is, however, indicated by the widespread linguistic practice of using modifiers, with or without a hyphen, to speak about them: *Vietnamese American, Chinese American, Korean American, Pakistani American, Sudanese American,* or *Mexican American.* This linguistic practice contrasts with the relatively rare use in recent decades of modifiers when speaking of white Americans generally.

Modifiers do occasionally occur for some white Americans when shared heritage is being either celebrated or denigrated. In some areas of the US, people still designate themselves and others by such labels as *Greek American, Scandinavian American,* or *Irish American.* But these same people in other contexts just get the label *American.* In contrast, an individual can immigrate on their own from, for example, Nigeria, and no matter how little they associate with others originally from that country they are likely to be dubbed or even call themselves *Nigerian American* or *African American* or *black American.* In contrast, consider someone whose ancestors for over a millennium have lived in or near Cambridge in England. Such a person can immigrate to the US and become a US citizen, but is highly unlikely to be called or to call themselves *British American* or *English American* (even if their accent might clearly indicate their origins on the other side of the Atlantic from the US).

The terminology *hyphenated Americans* seems to have originated early in the twentieth century. The new term spiked in popularity after Teddy Roosevelt used it repeatedly in a speech he gave on October 12, 1915, to the Knights of Columbus, a fraternal Catholic organization that had been founded in the late nineteenth century to help immigrant and working-class Catholics in the US.[12]

> When I refer to hyphenated Americans, I do not refer to naturalized Americans. Some of the very best Americans I have ever known were naturalized Americans, Americans born abroad. But a hyphenated American is not an American at all. This is just as true of the man who puts "native" before the hyphen[13] as of the man who puts German or Irish or English or French before the hyphen.

> Americanism is a matter of the spirit and of the soul . . . The one
> absolutely certain way of bringing this nation to ruin, of preventing
> all possibility of its continuing to be a nation at all, would be to
> permit it to become a tangle of squabbling nationalities, an intricate
> knot of German-Americans, Irish-Americans, English-Americans,
> French-Americans, Scandinavian-Americans or Italian-Americans,
> each preserving its separate nationality, each at heart feeling more
> sympathy with Europeans of that nationality, than with the other
> citizens of the American Republic. The men [note!] who do not
> become Americans and nothing else are hyphenated Americans;
> and there ought to be no room for them in this country.

Because immigration from other parts of the world is so
severely limited that he can ignore it, it is European allegiances
worrying Roosevelt. TR is resoundingly endorsing the assimila-
tionist model of immigration and trumpeting a strongly nationalist orientation. Theodore Roosevelt is, of course, a complex
figure. Even though conservative anti-immigration commentators often quote this speech approvingly, those supporting immigrant rights can also find passages that resonate with their views.
For example, Roosevelt says at another point in the speech, "We
cannot afford to continue to use hundreds of thousands of immigrants merely as industrial assets while they remain social out-
casts." But, unsurprisingly, his views on immigrants and on racial
diversity often reflected the openly racist assumptions common to
his era. He did recognize the possibility of, for example, outstand-
ing talents among black Americans. He also believed that the
government should protect ordinary people from exploitation
by business interests. What I am interested in here, however, is
the way his anti-hyphen rhetoric has struck a responsive chord
with those currently seeking to "make America great again." That
mythic "greatness" did not value diversity in the population but
assimilation.

The words of Donald Trump addressing the UN General
Assembly on September 25, 2018, echo Roosevelt's nationalism:
"America is governed by Americans. We reject the ideology of
globalism, and we embrace the doctrine of patriotism." Both

Roosevelt and Trump are endorsing views of America as the great 'melting pot,' where all speak the same language (English, of course), eat hamburgers and apple pie, look pretty 'colorless' (various pinky-orange shades, which in my childhood were dubbed 'fleshtone'), pledge allegiance to the American flag, and are suspicious of other countries and other ways of living. They do not question that European settlers had the right to seize the land on which indigenous populations had been living for years and, aided by germs as well as guns, to borrow Jared Diamond's vivid phrasing, to kill off most of the people they found on arrival. Nor are they counting, at least not fully, descendants of the enslaved Africans. Neither slaves nor black freedmen were considered a part of the 'founding' American polity. And of course women were not fully American either. (Teddy Roosevelt's use of *men* in the extract quoted above pretty clearly does not include them.)

We can travel back even further in American history. Here is how J. Hector St. John de Crèvecoeur, who crossed to America from France, described the situation in his 1782 *Letters from an American Farmer*.

> What then is the American, this new man? He is either an European, or the descendant of an European, hence that strange mixture of blood, which you will find in no other country. I could point out to you a family whose grandfather was an Englishman, whose wife was Dutch, whose son married a French woman, and whose present four sons have now four wives of different nations. He is an American, who leaving behind him all his ancient prejudices and manners, receives new ones from the new mode of life he has embraced, the new government he obeys, and the new rank he holds. ... Here individuals of all nations are melted into a new race of men, whose labours and posterity will one day cause great changes in the world. ... The Americans were once scattered all over Europe; here they are incorporated into one of the finest systems of population which has ever appeared, and which will hereafter become distinct by the power of the different climates they inhabit. ... Wives and children, who before in vain demanded of him a morsel of bread,

now, fat and frolicsome, gladly help their father to clear those fields
whence exuberant crops are to arise to feed and to clothe them all;
without any part being claimed, either by a despotic prince, a rich
abbot, or a mighty lord.[14]

De Crèvecoeur's views of the "American, this new man" were
more complex than this extract suggests. They clearly suggest,
however, that the unmarked, canonical American was born from
a melting pot, but one that melted down only those supposed to
have exclusively European ancestry in the past few millennia.

If not explicitly spoken of, then, hyphenated Americans often
get eliminated from talk of Americans. When they are spoken of,
the modifiers so often used to designate them, whether with
a hyphen or not, mark them as special, as not canonical, not
'normal' Americans. The hyphens (or other modified forms)
currently relevant mostly label Americans who are visibly or
audibly distinguishable from those with European roots.

Professor Anne V. Adams, a friend and Cornell colleague, read
an earlier draft of this discussion. She was reminded of
W. E. B. Du Bois's discussion of related issues far before formerly
enslaved black people in the US and their descendants got the
two-pronged (sometimes) hyphenated label that at least in principle marks them as American. In "Of Our Spiritual Strivings," the
first essay in Du Bois's *The Souls of Black Folk*, Du Bois eloquently
speaks of the duality of identity, the "double-consciousness," that
African Americans experienced long before that label with
African modifying *American* was used.

> One ever feels his twoness, – an American, a Negro; two souls, two
> thoughts, two unreconciled strivings. . . . The history of the
> American Negro is the history of this strife. . . . He simply wishes
> to make it possible for a man to be both a Negro and an American,
> without being cursed and spit upon by his fellows, without having
> the doors of Opportunity closed roughly in his face.[15]

Du Bois's notion of "double-consciousness" is much richer than
the simple idea of markedness. It brings out clearly how those who
take themselves to be 'unmarked' Americans can distort the notion

of self readily accessible to 'marked' Americans. As Du Bois puts it, they deny the 'Negro' access to the 'opportunity' of the American dream and to the simple civility offered other citizens. I am grateful indeed to Anne Adams for sending me to Du Bois's words.

Reading Du Bois reminded of something else I had recently read. On August 18, 2019, the *New York Times Magazine* announced the 1619 Project. The 1619 Project marks 400 years since the landing at Point Comfort in Virginia, some time late in August 1619, of a ship containing twenty to thirty enslaved Africans, who were sold to British colonists. Its purpose is to reframe American history in ways that put that institution of chattel slavery at its center, rather than treating it as just an aberration. The issue begins with an essay by Nikole Hannah-Jones that opens, "Our founding ideals of liberty and equality were false when they were written. Black Americans fought to make them true. Without this struggle, America would have no democracy at all." And she closes, "We were told once, by virtue of our bondage, that we could never be America. But it was by virtue of our bondage that we became the most American of all."[16] Derrick R. Spires, drawing on recently discovered documents from as early as 1808, shows that black Americans were already constituting themselves as citizens long before the Emancipation proclamation. Working to promote the abolition of the slave trade, they addressed one another as "fellow citizens" and practiced citizenship through networks of letters and meetings that Spires likens to modern social media.[17]

"Jocks, You're Not Aware of It": Becoming 'Normal' People

In many American schools, somewhere around grades 7 or 8 as students enter their teens (or even earlier), there emerge distinct and opposing social groups with very different orientations toward the school and its institutions and what has been dubbed its 'corporate culture.'[18] That culture includes not only special interest clubs but, importantly, student 'government' and performing groups, not only dramatic and musical but, most centrally, sports teams that represent the school in competition with other schools. In her groundbreaking *Jocks and Burnouts*, an ethnographic study of a Detroit-area high school, linguist Penny Eckert shows how students use a range of symbolic resources, including but by no means limited to language, to construct social groups within the school. Patterned pronunciations of certain vowels, for example, were as meaningful as, or more meaningful than, the kind of jeans one wore in affirming one's social identity, in positioning oneself in the social structure of Belten High, the (fictional) name Penny bestowed on the (real) high school. *Jocks and Burnouts* reported on the ethnography and Penny's social analysis of the school. Just over a decade later, *Linguistic Variation as Social Practice* reported her sociolinguistic findings from Belten High – not only vowel pronunciation but such other matters as the use of double negatives ("I didn't start no fight").

Between those two publications Penny and I began working together on how gender identity interacts with language.[19] (I use Penny's first name throughout this section as that is the way we've referred to one another in all our joint work.) Drawing on her work at Belten High and on other studies, we argued that large-scale demographic categories like sex/gender, social class, or race were not in themselves triggers for talking in certain ways. Rather the kids at Belten High (and people more generally) develop styles and social personae, ways of acting and presenting themselves, as they engage with one another in the context of relatively small-scaled groups centered on some mutual endeavors. And they create localized social identities that actually play a role in channeling them into adult social trajectories.

Early on the kids at Belten focused on two distinct and opposed identities, which they labeled *jocks* and *burnouts* (or sometimes, *jells*). The label *jocks* drew on the central role of sports in school life. It was, however, by no means confined to athletes and was also used to designate a group oriented toward success in school-supported institutions. *Burnouts/jells* were labels that drew on stereotypes of the effects of drug consumption, behavior associated with a group more oriented toward activities and older friends in the nearby urban center. Those in this group were disdainful of what they saw as infantilizing of students by school authorities. Teachers and administrators set the rules whether inside classrooms or not, and burnouts saw the jocks as toadies presenting a 'goody-goody' face to the adults running the school. Burnouts resisted adult control over their lives. In junior high the two groups seemed to be maneuvering for ascendancy within the school, but by the last couple of years of high school the burnouts had mostly disengaged from that struggle. They recognized that they would not prevail in an institution like Belten High. Jocks, on the other hand, no longer even had to try to dominate the burn-outs – that was now taken for granted, and the jocks tended to deny that there had ever even been a struggle. They focused their after-class time on the school's extracurricular activities, they were securely on the school-endorsed track to college and eventual middle-class corporate lifestyles, and they could view the burnouts as losers, not among the 'normal' Belten High students.

Linguistic practices of labeling (or not) showed this shift of burnouts from being essentially on a par with jocks, one of two competing groups, to being marked as a subordinated group, out of touch with the dominant student ethos. The jocks, in contrast, got erased as a group trying to dominate. By high school, they could present themselves as just individual students, obscuring their school-based privileged status and the advantages it gave them. Extracted transcripts from Penny's 300 or so hours of recorded interviews, which she let me read, show the process very clearly.

Here is a burnout girl describing the original junior high split as stemming from competing interests and values.

> Yeah, OK, there was, you know, kids that got high and smoked and thought they were really cool like us (laughter) and then the other ones that didn't party or anything, were always getting into sports and being goody-goodies and, you know, all that stuff so we just started putting down those people, calling them *jocks* and

everything, and they call us *burns*, and that was just going on for
a while, while we were all at [name of junior high school].

Notice that she mentions name-calling, deploying group labels, as
a way each group put down the other. And, according to one jock,
there was at least talk about physical altercations between the two
groups during that period (Penny's questions appear in caps).

There was like, at least once a week it was, "Jocks are going to fight
jells after school, you know." DID THEY REALLY? DID YOU
GET IN FIGHTS OR WAS IT JUST A LOT OF TALK? Never.
Talk.

These groups did not really exhaustively account for the junior
high's population, but they were very visible and influential polar
opposing social identity groups, toward one of which more or less
all the students oriented, even those describing themselves as 'in-
between.' Here's how one girl who calls herself an 'in-between'
describes the regulative power of these polarized labeling practices. She speaks poignantly of the conflicts she experienced from
those practices and the social divisions they supported.

[O]nce I hit junior high, you know, that's all you heard was, "She's
a jock," "She's a jell," you know. And that's all it was. You were
either one. You weren't an in-between, which I was. I was an
in-between because here I was. I played volleyball, now what,
three years. Baseball, I'll be going on my eighth year. OK? So, I get
along really good with, quote, jocks. OK, and I get along really
good with jellies, because I'm right – I'm stuck right in the middle.
And in my ninth-grade and tenth-grade year, that kind of tore me
apart a little bit too. Because I didn't – my parents wanted me to
make a decision. "Now which way are you going to go?"

By high school, however, the jocks have convinced themselves
that they are not really a group opposing burnouts. They see their
own orientation toward school-endorsed values and activities as
more or less inevitable, what happens in the absence of some
marked social pathology. Interestingly, even those marked as
burnouts have accepted that they are not 'standard-issue' Belten

High students. Early on, a burnout boy asked Penny whether she
had yet talked to any 'normal' people. And here a jock girl
responds when Penny asks her whether she thinks that jocks
and burnouts are separate groups in the high school.

> The burns, yes. Well, not so much in high school. Like jocks,
> you're not really aware of it.

Many US high schools in the late twentieth century had
similar divisions. Groups opposing the institutionalized social
norms of the school were more or less always named – *stoners,
greasers, hoods*, and many more terms, varying regionally and
over time. Many times, however, the group oriented toward
corporate culture went unnamed or, as at Belten, the name of
the school-oriented group lessened in social significance. Those
in the dominant group at Belten resisted being labeled, moving
ultimately toward enjoying unmarked default or 'normal' status
within their school. Simply labeling a subgroup within some
larger group marks off that subgroup as distinctively different
from those who are not labeled within the larger group. The
'leftovers,' those not in the marked subgroup, simply lack spe-
cialness. Unless someone is said to be in the marked subgroup,
the default is that they are not. But the default subgroup is
typically not marked at all, not treated as an identity (even
when in fact defaults actually leave out some of those who are
not in the marked subgroup, 'loners' or 'misfits' or others not
identifying with or accepted by the dominant group).

Trying to Mark Dominant Groups: The Politics of *Cisgender* and Its Kin

Back when I was in high school, there were plenty of words around
to designate individuals whose sexual preferences were for those
who shared their gender/sexual identity. Most of these words
I heard my peers using were slurs, but they were used to label
others in our age group (and sometimes older people as well). I do

not recall ever hearing a peer labeled as a guy who preferred girls (or women – still in our mid-teens, we called ourselves and were called *girls* then) or a girl interested in guys. There was certainly talk of such people's sex/romantic lives – or, more often, the lack thereof. When someone bearing one of the two sex/gender labels pasted on us all seemed to direct their erotic interests only toward those bearing the other of the binary sex/gender labels, which was most often the case, we never noted that 'other-sex' orientation as a phenomenon at all. Girls hot for boys, boys lusting after girls – that was expected, non-noteworthy. It just went without saying and didn't make them special 'kinds' of people. And back in the 1950s, challenges to assumptions of the gender binary – that people sort into exactly two non-overlapping sex/gender classes, female/women and male/men – were seldom heard at all. (In the labeling chapter, I discussed some of the objections to this binary assumption.) It's not that no one expressed such challenges then, but those expressions were few and muted. They were certainly not part of most young people's talk with one another.

For sexual orientation, there was the word *heterosexual*, but it was very uncommon (I don't recall hearing it, though of course I may well have) and certainly used far less frequently than *homosexual*. Both carried (and carry) a medical flavor (many now consider them derogatory). The word *straight* that has now become widely used, even for self-labeling, has a checkered history. It begins with talk from those with same-sex desire of '*going straight*.' Initially (and perhaps still to some extent), *straight* evoked a contrast with *crooked* or *deviant*. Eventually, however, *straight* became fairly widely used to label those with what had been just the default 'normative' orientation and in many contexts it has lost its somewhat self-satisfied lexical associations. Terms like *het*, *hetero*, and *breeder* (used somewhat derisively by some in gay communities) have also been deployed for what was previously the 'default' sexual orientation, what once might have been said to "go without saying."

In recent years, however, there has been a lot more 'saying' around sexual identities and even more around gender identities, especially among the young. Many websites or other guides to these matters explain the distinction between sexual and gender identities in terms like this: "your sexual identity is who you want to go to bed *with*, your gender identity is who you want to go to bed *as*." (I will discuss controversies over an individual's being the authority for labeling their own gender identity in Chapter 7.) Organizations that are involved in advocating for those identifying with the LGBTQ community often rightly judge that the increased 'saying' leaves many feeling perplexed, left behind not only by social but also by linguistic change. The Human Rights Campaign, one such organization, introduces their glossary of thirty-one expressions (most but not all identity labels) with this attempt to reassure the uninitiated:[20]

> Many Americans refrain from talking about sexual orientation and gender expression identity because it feels taboo, or because they're afraid of saying the wrong thing. This glossary was written to help give people the words and meanings to help make conversations easier and more comfortable.

The familiar label *lesbian* conveys both sexual orientation/ identity and gender identity, and the increasingly familiar *LGBTQ* or longer variants like LGBTQ(IA+) also include both terms marking sexual identity (*lesbian, gay,* and *bisexual*) and those marking gender identity (*trans* or *transgender* or *trans**). *Queer* (sometimes the Q indicates *questioning*) is a complicated word, which is sometimes used to cover sexual orientations other than the normative hetero – and sometimes to include playing around with, perhaps challenging, the gender binary (*genderqueer* makes explicit what is being 'queered'). It is no accident that gender and sexual identity get conflated. After all, cultural gender norms – what to wear, bodily practices, interests, and activities – arguably exist in the interest of policing sexuality, especially though not only women's reproductive sexuality. Yet it is important to be aware that whether someone rejects the gender identity associated with the sex/gender label assigned them at birth is quite independent of their sexual/romantic preferences (if any). To identify as transgender is not to embrace any particular sexual orientation.

In the summer of 2014, the *Telegraph* reported that Facebook in the UK had added twenty-one new gender-identity labels to their earlier list of fifty from which to choose.[21] And in February 2015 a free-form field was added for those who "do not identify with the pre-populated list of gender identities," as announced on FB's diversity page. FB is just one example of expanding possibilities for gender identification, albeit a very prominent one. In 2020 there are well over a hundred different English gender-identity labels circulating. FB also offers users the option of specifying their 'preferred gender pronoun' or 'PGP,' that is, the pronoun they would like others to use when speaking of them. I will discuss PGPs and some of the issues they raise in Chapter 6 on reforming language.

So where does the label *cisgender* (and its kin, *cishet*) fit? Caesar's *Gallic Wars* uses *cis* 'on the same side as' in contrast to *trans*. *Gallia cisalpina* designated the part of Gaul on the same side of the Alps as Caesar's home base, Rome, whereas *Gallia transalpina* labeled the part of Gaul lying on the other side of the Alps. There was also *Gallia cispadana* and *Gallia transpadana* used to differentiate between Gaul on 'this side' and Gaul on 'that side' respectively of the Po River from the perspective of home base, Rome. These contrasting Latin affixes *trans* and *cis* continue to be used in technical terminology in chemistry. It is not surprising then that when transgender theorists wanted terminology to designate people who are *not* transgender, people whose current gender identity matches that standardly associated with the identity assigned them at birth, they used the affix *cis*. Of special importance in popularizing *cis-* was Julia Serano's *Whipping Girl*, which used *cis-* liberally, not only in *cisgender* but also in such coinages as *cissexism* for biases against transgender women. [22] In 2015, the word *cisgender* was entered in the *Oxford English Dictionary*, defined as meaning "not transgender; someone whose gender identity is unchanged from that assigned at birth." Some online commentators were outraged that the *OED* seemed to be 'authorizing' this new coinage, because they did not recognize any need at all to 'mark' what they saw as simply the 'normal' condition of life. (In Chapter 7, I'll discuss dictionaries and their 'authorizing' function in more detail.)

The prevalence of that rage is shown by the fact that the top 'definition' for *cisgender* in the online *Urban Dictionary* is "a derogatory word used by members of the trans community to refer to all the disgusting people in the world who don't hate their genitalia." In many, many contexts, it still "goes without saying" that people are cisgender – that is, resoundingly the unmarked case – and, though to a somewhat lesser extent, that they are heterosexual. People benefitting from cis status often want simply to ignore other possibilities, to view them/ourselves as just 'normal' humans, the folks we are talking about when we speak simply of people. They often profoundly dislike proliferating terminology, resent being forced to think about matters that they are accustomed to ignoring.

Social change and conflict highlight the tension I mentioned earlier between saying enough, giving necessary information, and not saying too much, that is, leaving out what seems to "go without saying." What some see as necessary specification, others claim need not be said. To say that I am cisgender, which I am, is to acknowledge explicitly that my comfort with my birth-assigned gender does not (at least not always) go without saying. And doing so also affirms that I do not pathologize transgender people, that I recognize them as legitimate inhabitants of the (historically shifting) landscape of human possibility. Applying the *cis* label to myself announces me as an 'ally' of trans people. To apply the *cishet* label would be to acknowledge also that I am identified with the dominant sexual orientation, to accept that I benefit from being seen as a woman whose romantic life has involved only men (in fact, having been happily married for many decades to one particular man). Sometimes I use these terms to describe myself, but I do indeed often let them "go without saying."

The current multiplication of gender identities seems to puzzle many who themselves do not conform to normative gender expectations, including norms of heterosexual orientation. This is part of why some resist a *cis* label. Even if they are not hostile to transgender people, they may themselves endorse alternative strategies for resisting gendered expectations and gender-based oppressive practices. For the bulk of English speakers over age forty, labels like *cisgender* are barely on their radar. On most forms they encounter the choice is still binary, and the labels provided are F(emale)/W(oman) or M(ale)/M(an). To mark the default group as *cisgender* is to protest erasure of the advantages its members enjoy because of that default status.

Marking any group tends to erase differences among its members, at least from the perspective of those not in the group. Those who *can* resist being marked often do so. They decry labels as 'divisive' and affirm people's individual distinctiveness. Treat us as individuals, they say. Don't lump us all together. Don't generalize.

Notes

1. The title of this chapter is a quote from columnist Kurt Schlichter; see "Conservative, Inc., Is Being Replaced by Us Militant Normals," *Townhall*, September 25, 2017, https://townhall.com/columnists/kurtschlichter/2017/09/25/conservative-inc-is-being-replaced-by-us-militant-normals-n2385943.
2. In Ferrara 2018, p. 99.
3. Beardsley 1973. The particular examples are mine.
4. See Ferrara 2018, vii–viii.
5. Greenberg 2005 [1956] discusses this cases and markedness generally in chapter 1 of the reprinted edition.
6. See Eckert and McConnell-Ginet 2013 for this case.
7. Jennifer Ludden, "The Connection Between 'The Joy Luck Club' and 'Crazy Rich Asians', NPR, August 18, 2018, www.npr.org/2018/08/18/639822957/the-connection-of-the-joy-luck-club-and-crazy-rich-asians.
8. The work of psychologist Eleanor Rosch is foundational here; see especially Rosch 1973, 1975 and the discussion in chapters 3 and 4 of Taylor 2003.
9. The secondary literature on Grice's ideas is enormous, but most of his papers about how meaning is conveyed linguistically can be found in Grice 1989.

10. Horn 1984 is the classic source for the 'neo-Gricean' Q and R simplification of what Grice called conversational maxims.

11. Ferrara 2018, p. xvii.

12. This extract (and more) of his speech can be found on the pro-Trump website unhyphenatedamerica.org at https://unhyphenatedamerica.org /2015/11/16/the-frog-the-scorpion-and-the-lessons-of-paris/. The entire speech is available at https://en.wikisource.org/wiki/ Address_to_the_Knights_of_Columbus.

13. There are at least two reasons that it is unlikely that Roosevelt meant what is now meant by *native American* when he speaks of those who put "native" before the hyphen. First, at the time of his speech the indigenous people of North Americas were not American citizens. Second, TR frequently overtly expressed very racist views of those descended from the earliest inhabitants of the continent, whom he considered "savages."

14. http://web.utk.edu/~mfitzge1/docs/374/creve.pdf, p. 3 of Extract from Letter III, "What It Is to Be an American." But see also Alan Taylor, "The American Beginning: The Dark Side of Crèvecoeur's *Letters from an American Farmer*" at https://newrepublic.com/article/113571/crevecoeurs-letters-american-farmer-dark-side.

15. The quotations are from paragraphs 3 and 4 of the first chapter, at www .gutenberg.org/files/408/408-h/408-h.htm#chap01. See Du Bois 1999 [1903] for a much fuller discussion.

16. The first quotation is on p. 14; the second is on p. 26.

17. See Spires 2020.

18. This section draws extensively on Eckert and McConnell-Ginet 1995, reprinted in McConnell-Ginet 2011.

19. Eckert and McConnell-Ginet 1992 was where we introduced the idea of using Jean Lave and Etienne Wenger's notion of 'community of practice' to help develop a richer understanding of the interaction of language and gender.

20. www.hrc.org/resources/glossary-of-terms.

21. Rhiannon Williams, "Facebook's 71 Gender Options Come to UK Users," *The Telegraph*, June 27, 2014, www.telegraph.co.uk/technology/ facebook/10930654/Facebooks-71-gender-options-come-to-UK-users.html.

22. See Serano 2007. Serano continues to write engagingly and insightfully on gender and linguistic politics; see juliaserano.com.

3   Generalizing: "All the Women Are White, All the Blacks Are Men, but Some of Us Are Brave"

As we saw in the last chapter, subordinated 'marked' subgroups are often erased in talk about a larger group in which they are included.[1] Marked subgroups can be squeezed out of the discussion because they are overlooked, hardly noticed as comembers by the dominant.

Black women were the first to recognize that sexism and racism interact, both systemically and at the level of individuals' experience. Gender identity is inflected by racial identity and vice versa; gender and racial oppression and resistance also intertwine. In 1989, legal scholar Kimberlé Crenshaw coined the term *intersectionality* for such phenomena.[2] That name was new, but the insights involved can be found much earlier in black women's thinking. The complex history of black women's engagement in social life in the US, including their anti-racist activities, is one in which their identities as women and as black Americans are inextricably interwoven.

The Combahee River Collective, a black feminist lesbian group active from 1974 to 1980, is the source of the epigram in the title of this chapter. Black women recognized their double erasure in talk of 'Women' and in talk of 'Blacks' by most of those ostensibly pushing for the rights of those two groups to which they belonged. Their distinctive interests and perspectives within each group were often ignored, 'squeezed out' as marginal. (In Chapter 6, I discuss how this erasure led to rejection by some black women of the term *feminism*.) There were some exceptions among the 'second-wave feminists,' but generalizations about women's oppression in the 1960s and 1970s seldom recognized either racial or class diversity among women. And of course the women's suffrage movement of the late nineteenth and early twentieth centuries was rife with racism. Similarly, generalizations about the severe problems blacks faced and strategies for responding to them advanced by civil rights movement leaders and those who followed them typically ignored the very different ways in which racism affects women and men. Neither the perspectives of white women nor those of black men can be identified with those of black women.

Whenever there are generalizations offered about some large group, the question arises of whether they have given adequate attention to potentially marginalized subgroups within the larger group. And there are other issues about their relevance to individual group members.

There is nothing wrong with generalizing. Far from it. One cannot think or act without linking together distinct things as similar, arranging the "buzzing blooming confusion" that might otherwise reign in our heads into manageable patterns. But we need to attend to how we generalize, the uses to which we put generalizations, the kind of support we have for generalizing, and the language we use to express generalizations. First, however, I want to look at generalizations that are often not only unexpressed by those whom they influence but also hidden from them, at least *as* influences on themselves.

Implicit Stereotypes and Prejudices

In the past few decades, *social cognition* has been extensively studied by psychologists, neurologists, and philosophers. The word *cognition* here covers not only rational thinking, pondering, inquiring, and deliberation. It also includes evaluating, fearing, hoping, and much more. The term *social* focuses on people's relations to one another, their beliefs about and expectations of one another, the influences of others and their presumed values and norms on an individual's actions. The study of social cognition combines a long tradition of social psychology with the more recent research techniques and theories of *cognitive science*, using a wide array of approaches to figure out what moves people to speak and act as they do and how their brains and related systems (e.g., vision and hearing) enable them to navigate their social world. The term *implicit social cognition* covers social knowledge, attitudes, and the like that are not made explicit to others and sometimes not even to oneself. For the studio executives who did not categorize Asian Americans as (fully) American, their bias was very likely hidden even from themselves until they were forced to confront it. Their words revealed it when others were unwilling to go along with the erasure.

Since the late twentieth century, the study of what is standardly called *implicit bias* has burgeoned. One strand of research in implicit social cognition focuses on the kind of language people use in speaking of one another, the study of *Linguistic Intergroup Bias*.[3] (Thanks to linguist David Beaver for suggesting the relevance here of this work.) What seems to be emerging from such investigations are a number of tendencies. For example, there is an apparent tendency to speak in relatively more abstract, more general, terms when an outgroup member confirms a negative stereotype and relatively more concrete, more specific, terms when they disconfirm that stereotype, whereas there are the opposite patterns in speaking of ingroup members. So a white man might say of a black woman, "Ayesha is a mathematical moron" when Ayesha does poorly on some math test but when she does well he might say, "Ayesha got 98 percent on that math test yesterday." In contrast if he's talking about Jeffrey, a white man, a poor performance might prompt, "Jeffrey got 41 percent on that math test yesterday" whereas a good one might well be reported, "Jeffrey is a mathematical whiz."

Perhaps the best known research tools from the study of implicit social cognition are the *implicit association tests* (IATs). These find, for example, that even white people who sincerely affirm support for racial justice will be quicker to associate words like *crime* or *danger* with the picture of a black than with a white face. Many readers may already have taken such a test themselves and been dismayed by the results.[4] Philosophers, including philosophers of language, have appealed to the notion of such biases in exploring the social significance of our talk about one another. There has been, however, considerable debate about the strength of the research. Some in the popular press, which initially hyped the IAT, have now proclaimed that the whole body of research on implicit bias has been discredited. The topic is complex, but I am persuaded by my reading of some of the recent discussion that there is indeed strong empirical evidence that our minds do make associations that may clash with views we (sincerely) avow and that these associations can have a variety of problematic effects. Shortly before this book went to press, I reread the excellent entry on implicit bias by Michael Brownstein in the online *Stanford Encyclopedia of Philosophy*, which had just been updated from the version I had initially read, in part to take account of recent critiques. And I learned there of a book which will appear at about the same time as this one and which is aimed at nonspecialist readers. *An Introduction to Implicit Bias: Knowledge, Justice, and the Social Mind* is edited by philosophers Erin Beeghly and Alex Madva. The authors are all philosophers with significant grounding in relevant social science research. Readers of this book should gain a more sophisticated and nuanced appreciation of the issues involved than the popular press and blogosphere offer. They will also find far more accessible accounts of the empirical work than are available from the highly technical discussion found in psychology journals.[5] One criticism sometimes offered of implicit bias research is that it is too focused on individual psychology and not social structural factors, but Beeghly and Madva argue in their introduction that structural racism and individual biases, both implicit and explicit, interact in many ways.

Another excellent recent resource is *Biased: Uncovering the Hidden Prejudice that Shapes What We See, Think, and Do*, a very readable and informative book by social psychologist Jennifer L. Eberhardt.[6] We typically have more biases about groups to which we do not belong, and the less familiar we are with people in those groups the more biases about them are likely to lie in us. We can, however, as Eberhardt shows with a number of poignant anecdotes about her own sons and about black police officers, have biases about a group with which we identify ourselves. For example, her five-year-old son, noting a man who "looks like Daddy" (except that the only resemblance was that he was also a black man) was on their plane, expressed the hope that "he doesn't rob the plane." When his mother said "You know Daddy wouldn't rob a plane," he acknowledged that. Then she asked why he'd said what he had, and he responded "I don't know why I said that. I don't know why I was *thinking* that." She sums up the story this way. "Even with no malice – even with no hatred – the black-crime association made its way into the mind of my five-year-old son, into all of our children, into all of us."

Implicit biases like these do not in and of themselves make people racists or bigots. There does seem to be evidence, however, that they can prompt engagement in racist practices like unfair schoolroom discipline, profiling in policing, and disparate sentencing in court-rooms. And such practices only strengthen the biased linking of crime and black Americans. Bigotry and racism bring biases out into the open in some people's minds: that is, biases that were once implicit can become explicit in triggering social circumstances. People often, however, try to hide them. So, for example, the words *crime* and *criminal* can become 'dogwhistles,' coded ways to talk about black citizens and their communities that can succeed with audiences for whom the biases are very easily accessible.[7]

Implicit biases are not linguistic as such. They do, however, get attached to words and affect what we say. They are part of what I call *lexical baggage*.[8] This extra material associated with a word can produce effects though it need not. I say to you "My surgeon wants me at the hospital tomorrow by 6 a.m." and you respond "Couldn't he schedule the surgery at a more reasonable hour?" You've assumed, taken for granted, that my surgeon is a man even though being male is not part of the semantic content of *surgeon* (it is perfectly fine to say "She is a surgeon") nor need it be part of what I meant to convey. Your assumption will probably persist unless my surgeon happens to be a woman and I correct you, perhaps by saying "She says she's in top form in the early hours before fatigue sets in," maybe putting a little extra stress on the initial *she*. Of course, even if my surgeon were not a woman, I could notice your assumption and criticize it – "As it happens, my surgeon *is* a man, but don't forget that women can be and are top-notch surgeons." But that's not a very likely move on my part in many communicative contexts. You might well experience such a rejoinder as my adopting a sanctimonious attitude, taking it on myself to instruct others in order to promote gender equality in the field of surgery. "After all, Sally, surgery still *is* predominantly a male stronghold – stop being so politically correct!" With no challenge from me, which is the likely scenario if the surgeon I've mentioned is indeed a man, there's no weakening and perhaps a little strengthening of your view (and perhaps mine as well) of surgeons as presumptively male.

I like to think of acquiring a word like *surgeon* as opening a mental file folder into which a lot of material gets deposited. There will be information on pronouncing the word (or on signing it in a manual-visual language), its phonological and phonetic properties. (People who are literate will have information on spelling.) There will be what linguists call morphosyntactic information, which comes into play when fitting words into larger structures, no matter whether the folder belongs to an English teacher, a child of three, or an illiterate adult. (You may not know grammatical terminology but you actually know a lot about such matters, not necessarily about what schoolteachers or editors prescribe but about the distinctions needed to talk with friends and family.) And of course there will be some representation of semantic content (or at least of which experts you might consult to find out to what the word applies). This sort of stuff seems properly called linguistic knowledge. But there is much more in that folder. Some is perhaps tied to experience with what the word denotes. For example, *surgeon* may conjure up that cold fish of an arrogant man who removed your burst appendix when you were a kid. And so on.

Such lexical baggage, which certainly differs significantly across speakers, can produce all kinds of effects, both directly on those addressed but also indirectly on others. And people cannot access all of the baggage that is there in their word folders. There may be biased kinds of associations of which we are not aware. The folder metaphor cannot do justice to all that accretes to words, some of which is highly affective, like a quickened heartbeat when certain insults are heard or the visceral thrill of naughtiness that may accompany utterance of certain tabooed words. Ultimately, some of this lexical baggage moves people to action. They may become angered, saddened, emboldened, sympathetic, or antagonistic. And the biased baggage can affect their generalizing about what the lexical item denotes.

Remember that social identity groups are what Hacking called interactive kinds. Negative aspects of stereotypes associated with a social identity one is assigned and claims, hidden biases, can have a wide range of bad effects. There is now a substantial literature on what social psychologist Claude Steele has dubbed 'stereotype threat.' Steele's 2011 *Whistling Vivaldi: How Stereotypes Affect Us and What We Can Do* offers an accessible account of much of that research, investigation which continues and has broadened in scope. What Steele and his colleagues have found is that awareness of negative stereotypes about a group produces all kinds of problematic impact on those identified with the group. For example, African Americans aware that stereotypes paint them as less intelligent than whites can fear that they will somehow confirm those stereotypes even though they know themselves to be intellectually capable. This can lead to lowered performance on tasks presented as measuring intelligence – framing the task differently (as, for example, an exploration of different problem-solving strategies or as a recreational puzzle) can boost performance substantially. Similarly, suppose women are asked to check a gender-identity box just before taking an exam on which they believe women tend to do less well than men. Checking that box heightens the salience of that feature of their identities for them and tends to introduce performance anxiety, lowering performance on difficult tasks. If, however, they are told that women do just as well as men on the test, the stereotype threat lowers and they perform well. But performance on things like tests is a very small part of the picture. Stereotypes can lead people to avoid certain domains or to emphasize certain interests at the expense of others. Negative stereotype awareness can have a range of effects, including affecting whether (and, importantly, also how) one interacts with members of other groups. White Americans often worry that they will be seen as racist in interactions with people of color, which can lead them either to avoid such interactions altogether or to do things like stand or sit further away than they do with other white people.

Sometimes actions people take in attempts to counter negative stereotypes can be highly effective. Steele's title points to one illustration. Brent Staples, an author and *New York Times* editorial writer who won the 2019 Pulitzer Prize for editorial writing, lived in the Hyde Park neighborhood of Chicago in the 1970s. He was then studying and doing research at the University of Chicago. Like many others, he had to contend with the stereotype of black men as violent and dangerous, hulking monsters from whom white people, especially but not only women, needed to protect themselves. White people tend to see black men as larger than they are and black boys as older than they are, their own fearfulness affecting their perceptions. Tired of seeing people cross the street, clutch their purses tighter, or quicken their pace when he approached, Staples took to 'whistling Vivaldi.' Sure enough, the strains of classical music emerging from his lips tended to calm those stereotype-induced fears of him. The stereotype of classical music lovers as peaceful and restrained (white) people managed to drive out (or at least reduce) fears of the whistler as a black man. But such options are not available in all situations or to all people affected by hidden (as well as openly displayed) biases.

Colorblind?

Many well-meaning white Americans profess to be 'colorblind.' Categorizing people by the color of their skin is often thought to be buying into ideas of racial 'essences,' the scientifically discredited essentialist kind of view that underlies and helps perpetuate racism. "I don't see black or yellow or white – I only see people who all bleed red." An earnest middle-aged white woman, who described herself as the mother of a biracial child, passionately uttered these words at an anti-racist rally I attended in Ithaca, NY, in August 2017. The rally was one of many in the US affirming interracial solidarity in the face of a man's deliberately driving a car on August 12 into a crowd peacefully protesting the white supremacist gathering he was supporting in Charlottesville, Va. The driver hit and killed Heather Heyer, a young white woman committed to supporting racial equality. (That the driver sympathetic to white supremacist ideology murdered a white woman undoubtedly increased the publicly displayed outrage at his action and at the blatant racism the Charlottesville event highlighted.) A young African-American woman with fairly dark skin who was in the Ithaca rally crowd responded to the speaker claiming colorblindness. "I'm very glad you see me as human like you," she said. "Thank you. But let me remind you that people with skin colored like mine rather than yours have had more opportunities for people to see the color of our blood. Some places are dangerous for people who look like me. I often call on a white friend to go with me when I want to go somewhere that could endanger me, but most black people don't have such white protectors available."

Generalizations about color-based (and other) social identity categories have often been deeply problematic, disparaging people of color as such and using these 'generalizations' to justify race-based subordination. As we saw in Chapter 1, the boundaries of race-based and other identity categories are fuzzy and labels can shift in many ways. And recent scientific work has demolished earlier views that such characteristics as skin color and hair texture are causally connected to anything like behavioral tendencies, intelligence, or similar attributes. Labeling people as members of a common racial or ethnic category, however, tends already to suggest to labelers and to those labeled that there are significant likenesses beyond skin color and other superficial phenotypic properties among the labeled that distinguish them from people put in other categories, likenesses that 'tie' them together. There has long been and continues to be a strong tendency to see these ties as shared 'essential' important properties, important 'intrinsic' ones that the people sharing a particular racial or ethnic label inherit. Such (mistaken) essentialism holds skin color to be a reliable guide to an intrinsic essential 'nature' that determines dispositions and talents, and even possible life trajectories.

"We all bleed red" is intended to be a rejection of racist essentializing, of those discredited intrinsic generalizations, of the 'lies.' And I am sure that the woman I heard say that was committed to anti-racist activities. But of course it requires one to be color-conscious to recognize that people who are grouped together by others and themselves on the basis of color share important 'extrinsic' properties, histories of others' treatment of them because of those labels and of their own collective projects and shared cultural practices. The young black woman's response vividly illustrates why colorblindness is not now an option and certainly will not be so in the foreseeable future. There are 'extrinsic' generalizations requiring color-consciousness that need to be made about the destructive effects of racialization on the family histories of people of color as well as the ongoing threats it poses to their potential life trajectories. There are also more positive but equally important 'extrinsic' generalizations to be made about courage, resilience, and creativity in the face of such challenges.

Many white people, whether or not they claim to be colorblind, are frequently color-mute (that useful term was coined by anthropologist Mica Pollock, whose work was mentioned in

Chapter 1). That is, they refrain from talk about racialized groups in contexts where such talk might in fact be useful. Why? Not only do they want to deny that they do in fact 'see' color, as they must in order to engage in talk about race. Presumably they/we also fear where such talk might lead. (I have put the 'we' here in order to indicate that I do not consider myself exempt from such fears or, more generally, 'pure' in these matters. I have certainly benefited from white privilege and also from being both well educated and financially secure. I will mostly continue with 'they' both because it reads more smoothly and because 'we' would often be misleading, not only about my own stances but also about expectations of potential readers.)

Skin color is in fact something that humans, even quite young humans, readily notice. It's a useful sorting tool. What we make of it, however, is culturally quite variable. Some people have skin that is neither very dark nor very light, 'ambiguous.' In the US context, whether those people get labeled *black* or *white* has all sorts of implications for how others respond to them. Yet many white children get the message that it is 'rude' to mention or even notice people's skin color, and they (along with many white teachers) often try not to do so. (Not *actually* noticing it is not really an option for them if the person observed has dark skin.) Ironically, however, attempted colorblindness and associated color-muteness can make it more difficult for people actually to notice racial discrimination, which is essential for doing anything about it.[9]

In part because they have so often encountered and accepted comforting but profoundly distorted accounts of US history and 'the American dream,' white Americans may find it difficult to recognize how very much that 'dream' has depended on social arrangements and actions that many of them would now be loath to endorse. "All men are created equal" proudly proclaimed the US Declaration of Independence back in 1776. But of course the "men," all of whom were said to be equal, did not include any women. Nor did they include the enslaved Africans on whose coerced and cheap labor the young republic's economy depended.

The indigenous people whose lands were seized to make room for the invading Europeans were also left out of that ringing endorsement of equality. Philosopher Charles Mills puts it clearly. "The opposition between white and nonwhite has been foundational to the workings of American social and political institutions. (The United States Congress made whiteness a prerequisite for naturalization in 1790, and social and juridical whiteness has been crucial to moral, civic, and political status.)"[10] In this connection, Mills reports research showing that laws in the American colonies frequently included the word *white*, always to grant rights and never to limit them. Mills also draws attention to the so-called "discovery doctrine," which the Supreme Court of the US enunciated in its 1823 decision *Johnson v. M'Intosh*. This doctrine magically transferred lands from native American use into the hands of the descendants of the European 'discoverers' who had begun arriving on the already populated American continent at the end of the fifteenth century. These incursions from Europe had continued for almost 300 years before British colonists in what is now the eastern United States decided to launch their own nation.[11]

There is, of course, an excellent reason to hope for a world in which all are colorblind on certain matters. As Dr. Martin Luther King Jr. famously put it, "I have a dream that my four little children will one day live in a nation where they will not be judged by the color of their skin, but by the content of their character."[12] What King meant, which I strongly endorse, was that superficial physical characteristics like skin color should not lead us to draw conclusions about a person's intelligence, talents, tastes, or general worthiness. He did not mean that skin color or other such superficial differences needed to disappear.

King's solution was not to stop talking about race but to point to the many arenas of life in which skin color did in fact determine the distribution of rights and goods, did in fact limit opportunities and life trajectories. The civil rights movement he was central in founding accomplished many things, but it did not erase racism at either personal or institutional levels. However, there has been a change in how that racism works. We have what sociologist Eduardo Bonilla-Silva dubbed *color blind racism* in the 2018 fifth edition of his *Racism without Racists*. Sociologists Michael Omi and Howard Winant, whose work on racial formation I mentioned in Chapter 1, suggest that this shift is at least partly due to what they call *rearticulation* of some key notions, including *colorblind* and also *racism* and *racist*. I will talk more about shifts in *racism* and *racist* in Chapter 6. My main aim in this section has been to highlight the shift from King's aspirational colorblindness to the often racist colorblindness so prevalent in current American discourse, a shift in which accusations of "reverse racism" and "playing the race card" have a central role.

In an inspiring 2014 TED talk, Mellody Hobson, a black woman who heads a very successful investment firm, urged a different approach. She issued a challenge to other business executives, to teachers, to parents – to all who claim to want racial justice. "It's time," she said, "for us to be comfortable with the uncomfortable conversation about race. If we truly believe in equal rights and equal opportunity in America, we need to have real conversations about this issue. We can't be color blind, we have to be color brave." Color bravery is difficult for people of any skin color or racial categorization, but it is squarely in the tradition of the fight for racial equality that Martin Luther King, Jr. helped move along many decades ago. Colorblindness as currently understood by many white Americans is not.[13]

Black Lives Matter ... Or Should!

On February 26, 2012, seventeen-year-old Trayvon Martin was walking back into the housing complex in Sanford, FL where he and his father were visiting friends. The young African-American boy was wearing a gray hoodie and talking on a cell phone to his girlfriend, Rachel Jeantel, when he was challenged by George Zimmerman, the volunteer neighborhood 'watchman.' Zimmerman called the police to report seeing someone who "looks suspicious" and was told police investigators would come but that he should not accost the stranger. Zimmerman ignored that advice and within a few minutes he had pulled out his gun and killed young Trayvon. Initially there was widespread sympathy for the loss experienced by Trayvon's family and friends. The public tide soon turned, however, especially after then President Barack Obama expressed his own compassion for Trayvon Martin's parents. "This is a tragedy. I can only imagine what these parents are going through. And when I think about this boy, I think about my own kids. ... You know, if I had a son, he'd look like Trayvon." Obama's careful statement, which included words about the necessity of investigation, nonetheless triggered an onslaught of support for George Zimmerman, especially but not only from white supremacist groups. The trial a year later ended in July 2013 with Zimmerman's being found 'not guilty.' (Linguist John Rickford and colleagues have argued that the jury completely ignored the testimony from Rachel Jeantel that Martin was accosted by Zimmerman and felt himself very much threatened; Rickford makes a strong case that the testimony from Jeantel was ignored largely because she used a variety of African American Vernacular English that the jurors – and even the court transcriber – did not understand and which they took as indicating her general lack of credibility.[14])

The hashtag #BlackLivesMatter took off in response to Zimmerman's acquittal. Alicia Garza, Patrisse Cullors, and Opal Tometi launched a social media protest over what was widely seen as the trivializing of Trayvon Martin's death. They later called for demonstrations in the face of the all-too-many cases of black men dying at the hands of police or in police custody. Michael Brown in Ferguson, MO and Eric Garner in New York City were two of the many cases that prompted #BlackLivesMatter. Sybrina Fulton and Tracy Martin, Trayvon's parents, started a foundation in his name and have pushed against gun violence and the "stand your ground" laws that helped 'legitimize' Zimmerman's actions. A 2018 miniseries for TV links Trayvon's death and the rise of the (non-centralized) Black Lives Matter (BLM) movement.[15]

What was meant by the phrase "Black Lives Matter" was crystal clear at its inception – namely, that black lives matter *also*, that the continuing treatment of black people as of lesser value than whites, their lives expendable, needs to be acknowledged and ended. The counter "All Lives Matter" pretends that #BlackLivesMatter means that *only* black lives matter, a willful distortion in the context of the origin of BLM. As Trayvon Martin's mother, Sybrina Fulton, put it: "It's not taking away from anyone else's life. It's just putting emphasis on black lives because black lives seem . . . so disposable."[16]

"All lives matter" advanced in response to "Black lives matter" is suspect. "All lives matter" in response to "Black lives matter" gives little reason to believe that those so responding actually do endorse the full humanity and value of people of color. Just as all the women were white and all the blacks were men, so all the lives that matter are all too often overwhelmingly white lives.

Quantificational Generalizing: Who Counts?

One way to generalize is to say "how many" or "what proportion" of the category members have the property being discussed – how many lives matter, for example. English and other languages use explicit quantificational expressions, 'quantifiers,' to express such generalizations. Quantifying expressions in English include *all, every, some, most, many, a few, seven, half, sixty-nine percent, no*, and so on. Armed with quantifiers, we express generalizations like "No Americans had major roles in *Joy Luck Club*"; or "Most ten-year-olds have their own smartphones"; or "Everyone toasted Democrats' regaining control of the House of Representatives"; or "Seven kids in my class went to the University of Colorado"; or "89 percent of the 2019 recipients of DDS (Doctor of Dental Science) degrees graduated with at least $200,000 of debt in student loans." (English also has adverbial quantifying expressions like *generally*, *occasionally*, and the like – for our present purposes they don't bring anything new.)

But to understand fully what is said requires something further, what semanticists call the *domain of quantification*. Which Americans, ten-year-olds, or people are to be counted here? The domain of quantification depends on what the generalizer is trying to do. Sometimes what is happening is restricting the boundaries of the label to which the quantifier is attached, treating only some of those so labeled as the ones that 'fully' belong to the category. As we saw in the preceding chapter, that is probably what explains the interpretation of 'Americans' to exclude Asian Americans in the case of the *Joy Luck Club*. Asian Americans acting in the movie, if they are excluded from the domain of Americans, become irrelevant to assessing whether it is true that the actors included no Americans. Often, however, the generalizer is not so much excluding but just ignoring certain individuals who fit into the labeled category. It is probably a safe assumption that not only the generalizer but also those interpreting the generalization will only be interested in the restricted group. Someone in the US saying "Most ten-year-olds have their own smartphone" is unlikely to have given any thought at all to children in Nepal or even to children in their own country living in extreme poverty. Those Nepalese ten-year-olds or those US ten-year-olds from lower economic strata are not necessarily being dismissed *as* ten-year-olds, but they are being ignored, treated as of no interest for the generalizer's present purposes. Ignoring may reflect treating people as of lesser status, less valuable, but it certainly need not. It may sometimes just reflect people's necessarily limited interests and experience.

Sometimes the discourse situation, the context in which an utterance is produced, provides the domain straightforwardly: "Can everyone hear me?" is not used to inquire about those outside range of the speaker's voice but only about those taken to be potential hearers. (Interestingly, "Everyone was looking at me" and many similar examples including "Can everyone hear me?"

leave the speaker out of the domain.) Or maybe I have just been telling you about the election night gathering I attended when I say "Everyone toasted . . . " – here it seems clear that the domain I assume is those attending the party.

Yet even where the discourse setting is central to delineating the domain, exclusion from the domain can be part of social subordination. If the election night party was catered, those catering are probably not included among those said to have toasted. "We had the restaurant to ourselves – no one else was there" would typically not claim absence of those who keep the restaurant running – the cooks, dishwashers, those who wait on tables, those who clear away dirty dishes, those who seat customers and take their coats, and so on. People in service positions are often tacitly excluded as discourse participants. Those being served simply speak as if the servers were not there, certainly not part of the present 'we.' This need not be done and probably usually is not done with any deliberate intention to slight those serving. Establishing a domain, however, reflects and sustains hierarchical social relationships in many subtle ways. And it is almost always implicit, not out on the table to be debated.

With *everyone, someone,* and *no one,* setting up domains for generalizing becomes a not-so-subtle tool for setting up social structures and hierarchies. The kid who says to a parent "But everyone is going to that party" is not including their parent (or younger sibs or teachers or . . .). They are just not part of the social landscape at issue here. More significantly, familiar but devalued peers may also be excluded. "No one goes there anymore because everyone's going there these days" switches domains from those considered 'of consequence,' those whom the speaker values who no longer go 'there,' to those the speaker treats as inconsequential, lacking in status, those who've now started going 'there' and whose distasteful presence keeps away the valued group. *Everyone* and *no one* are frequently used to affiliate or disaffiliate with others. And "She really thinks she's *someone,* doesn't she?" can comment on another's perceived sense of entitlement, her assumption of superiority, here implicitly criticized, perhaps challenged.

Domains of quantification can give considerable insight into who or what is taken to matter, to 'count.' Quantifying expressions often range over the speaker's ingroup, their *we*, the boundaries of which are seldom specifiable, certainly virtually never specified. I wore a button in the autumn of 1991 during the Clarence Thomas hearings to determine his fitness to be appointed to the Supreme Court. My button proclaimed "We believe her," where "her" was Anita Hill, the specific woman alleging sexual harassment. The implicit message was that I (and unspecified others allied with me in some unspecified respects) would tend to believe the female complainant in such cases rather than her male supervisor. *We* always implies *they*, an outgroup not aligned with the speaker (at least not for the purposes of the particular speech act). Because of the generality of the message on my button, I could recycle it twenty-seven years later when Christine Blasey Ford was testifying that Brett Kavanaugh, also a nominee for the Supreme Court, had sexually assaulted her when both were teens.

Determining domains can reveal and sometimes worsen divisions and exclusions in social life. These matters become even more challenging when we turn to generalizations that do not really say anything about the quantity or proportion of individuals in a group. When people say "don't generalize" it is generalizations like these that come immediately to mind.

Generic Generalizations: When Do They Essentialize?

Not all generalizations are quantificational. "Americans Are Divided About Kavanaugh," a headline in the fall of 2018, did not say that some/none/most/half of Americans were "divided about Kavanaugh." In fact, being "divided about Kavanaugh" does not really designate a property of any individual American. Of an individual unsure about Kavanaugh we'd be more inclined to describe them as 'conflicted' than 'divided' on the judge's suitability for appointment to the US Supreme Court.

And the article was certainly not about dithering, in-the-middle individuals. It was about the larger population as a group. Being divided about Kavanaugh says Americans can be split into two distinct subgroups, more or less equal in size, on the basis of their support of Kavanaugh (with perhaps many in-betweens). (And by not mentioning any subgroups it seems to imply that the roughly equal division would apply even if we singled out African Americans or women or other potentially significant subgroups of which the claim might be problematic.) Properties of the members of the group being spoken of are certainly relevant, and it certainly matters which members are being considered, but there is not a straightforward connection since the property in question does not apply to individual group members as such.

My focus in this section, however, is on *generic generalizations* that are not so clearly about kinds. "Americans oppose fetal heartbeat bills," which I read in my morning paper in June 2019, is an example. (For those unfamiliar with recent debates about abortion in the US, a fetal heartbeat bill is legislation outlawing abortion at any time after a heartbeat can be detected in the developing fetus, which can now be as early as six weeks after gestation and often before a woman knows she is pregnant.) Here indeed there is what might seem to be a claim directly about individual members of the kind designated by *Americans*, but the generalization is not expressed using overt quantifiers. Generic generalizations like this associate an *individual-level property*, the kind of property that an individual might have, with a *kind*. The 'kinds' that are of interest for this discussion are mostly social identity kinds. In the context of the newspaper article below the headline about opposition to fetal heartbeat bills, the generic generalization appears to be summarizing a study that shows that *a significant majority* of Americans oppose such legislation but clearly far from all. (The study report, based on a survey of a small number of Americans, used quantificational language.) But suppose someone asks "How many/what proportion of Americans oppose fetal heartbeat bills?" An appropriate reply to such a question needs an explicit quantifying expression – *65 percent, over 200 million, most, a lot, nearly all, only a few,* or some such. The quantifier may be extremely imprecise – for example, *a lot* – but there must be a quantifying expression present. Even if *Americans* is stressed, the sentence just does not answer the question. I emphasize this point because people sometimes think of generic generalizations as having an implicit, unpronounced, quantifier, maybe equivalent to *almost all* or *most* or even just *many*. But we need to remember that these generalizations tell us nothing about frequency of the property across group members.

Generic generalizations say something about a category or kind, associate a property with the kind. Exactly what they are saying is not readily specifiable, however. What is *not* being said is anything about the distribution of the property across the individual members. *Americans* or *ten-year-olds* are called 'bare plurals' because they don't have expressions of quantity like *all* before them. Bare-plural subjects are a common way to express generic generalizations in English. Not coincidentally, stereotypes are often expressed as generic generalizations: "Asian Americans excel at math," "White men can't jump," "Black Americans are musical," "Mothers bond immediately with their new-born babies," and so on. English generics can also have a non-bare singular subject – "An American has access to cutting-edge medical technology" or "The experienced cook who lacks an ingredient specified in the recipe can come up with a substitute." I will, however, focus on examples with bare-plural subjects because they are most common. There has been lots of analytic work from linguists and philosophers of language on how best to think about the abstract meaning of such sentences and other generics.[17] In what follows, however, I emphasize investigation that sheds light directly on everyday linguistic practices of generalizing and their impact on social stereotyping.

Susan A. Gelman, a leading figure in the field of cognitive science and developmental psychology, has spearheaded an extensive exploration over several decades of how we human beings generalize, how we categorize the world and make sense of the world we live in. She has been especially interested in how children develop concepts and other generalizing capacities, including those they rely on in "navigating the social world."[18] There is a huge amount of research now showing that we are born with cognitive *biases*, though not necessarily of the sort that appear in social stereotyping. These apparently 'inborn' biases do lead us astray sometimes, but they can also be very useful.[19]

Children do not need to be taught to lump things together into certain kinds of categories. Early on they distinguish other species of animals from humans, and they distinguish artifacts from both. They also seem already prepared to distinguish dogs from cats and to distinguish both dogs and cats from goldfish. But they 'essentialize' animal kinds whereas they do not 'essentialize' artifact kinds. What does 'essentializing' amount to? Even young children know that painting a racoon can't make it a skunk. Nor do they think that a bear raised by a tiger could become a tiger. They see bear-ness and tiger-ness as deriving from 'essential' internal properties that are not really malleable, and they see the members of each species as linked by their sharing of those properties, that species-defining essence. On the other hand, they see that one could disassemble a chair and use its materials to make a table.

With respect to human beings and social kinds, however, the child's biases are more variable. Children do early on recognize visible indicators, like skin color, that are used in delineating racialized groups. If those in their immediate social world (visibly) mostly belong to the same racial category, they become more adept at distinguishing those within that category and less adept at distinguishing those in different categories. But if their immediate environment is racially diverse, even if that diversity arises mainly from their own visible differences from caretakers (say, a black child with white adoptive parents), they retain the capacity to distinguish among individuals from different groups. Whether a child essentializes particular social kinds and how they do so, that is, which properties they take to define the 'essence' of the kind, both depend on social practices within the child's community. Linguistic practices such as generic generalizations might well play a role, Gelman reasoned, in which groups kids would come to essentialize. She had already found that learning about new animal kinds via generics hastened essentializing, but she knew that animal kinds would ultimately get essentialized by the child in any case. So a big question has been whether generic generalizations might lead children to essentialize one group but not another. She and others, including her former student Marjorie Rhodes and philosopher and cognitive scientist Sarah-Jane Leslie, have been exploring for some time now how both children and adults respond to generic generalizations, quantified generalizations, and specific talk about individual humans.[20]

One interesting series of studies used picture books about Zarpies, the name the research team gave to a new social group they created, one that showed racial and gender diversity. Both four-year-olds and their parents were asked to read the books, which showed Zarpies doing unusual things, and they did so several times. The same picture of a Zarpie eating flowers some-times bore one caption, sometimes another. Some readers might encounter "Zarpies eat flowers" or another generic form "A Zarpie eats flowers." Other readers were given specific statements: "This Zarpie eats flowers" or "This one eats flowers," with no identity label at all. To test for essentialization of Zarpies, partici-pants were asked, for example, about a baby Zarpie adopted at birth by a non-Zarpie mother, who did not eat flowers but ate crackers instead. Both child and adult participants who had cap-tions with generics were significantly more likely to think that the baby would grow up to eat flowers rather than crackers than readers who had gotten specific captions. (In their study, whether the specific caption included the identifying label *Zarpie* was not significant.)

Although that first Zarpie study showed the contribution of generic generalizations to essentializing, it did not address the question of whether adults who essentialize a group would pro-duce more generic generalizations in talking about that group than those who do not. So the team explored that issue with a new set of four-year-old and adult study participants. This time the study participants were divided into two groups. One set of parents got a little introductory paragraph to read that emphasized that Zarpies were very different from other social groups, though it said nothing about similarity of Zarpies to one another. The other set got introductory material that emphasized that Zarpies were highly similar to other social groups. (Independent testing had shown that such prompts did indeed lead to much greater essentializing of Zarpies by those told that the group was exceptional.) The Zarpie book was exactly the same except that this time it had only pictures and the adults were asked to talk about it with their kids. And indeed the group prompted to essentialize Zarpies used far more generics to talk about them than the group prompted to think of Zarpies as like groups with which they were familiar. So one plausible hypothesis is that hearing adults in your family or your playschool or your church regularly produce generic generalizations about some social group may be an important way kids come to essentialize that group.

That kids do not inevitably develop exclusionary views of the world was part of the (overt) message of Rodgers and Hammerstein's *South Pacific*, which premiered in 1949 and was made into a wildly successful film in 1958. In Act 2, Lieutenant Joe Cable sings a song that movingly tells listeners "you've got to be carefully taught" intolerance and fear of those who look different from yourself. "You've got to be taught before it's too late . . . to hate all the people your relatives hate," he proclaims, apparently now trying to overcome his own racism. Although that song in particular struck raw nerves in many explicit US racists of the time, Andrea Most has argued compellingly that *South Pacific* actually helped reinforce exoticization of Asians and other problematic racist ideologies widespread in American culture.[21] Nonetheless, the lyrics of Cable's song, widely available online, beautifully reject the view that it's human 'nature' to be fearful of other racial groups, to distrust and hate difference. Rather, children are taught racial biases, though of course much of the teaching is covert. One component of that teaching may indeed be hearing overt generic generalizations about other groups, but this will certainly be far from the full story. There are many, many covert sources in most American kids' environments that produce hidden biases. But it is useful to explore explicit linguistic promoters of bias.

Are generics the only overt source of problematic essentializing? A question that arises immediately is whether quantified generalizations with quantifiers like *most, many, nearly all*, and the like might have the same effect, and there is a recent study suggesting that perhaps they do.[22] The picture is further complicated by research that suggests people who have heard an explicitly quantified statement often report having heard a generic generalization. And, as my headline about opposition to fetal heartbeat bills illustrates, research that is about statistical frequency is often reported using bare-plural subjects, not only by headline writers but also by those who did the research. Although we know that children do not necessarily essentialize (and demonize) social groups to which they do not belong, both children and adults may be biased toward generic generalizations, not just about people but about all sorts of categories. When we are talking about people, there are many pitfalls.

In other work, Sarah-Jane Leslie has pointed out that people use sentences like "Sharks attack swimmers" or "Ticks carry Lyme disease" even though they are perfectly well aware that only a few sharks mount attacks and only very few ticks are transmitters of Lyme disease.[23] What Leslie proposes is that such (over)generalizations spring from a quite primitive cognitive strategy: avoid putting oneself in situations of grave danger even if one does so by also avoiding many perfectly safe situations. Generic generalizations, she proposes, often suggest that there is something in the essence of the kind that 'disposes' all its members to instantiate the property – although most sharks stay far away from swimmers, being a shark 'disposes' such a fish to attack. (This generalization is undoubtedly unfair to sharks, which seldom attack unless provoked.) She doesn't put it quite this way, but we might think of some generic generalizations as proposing that we act 'as if' any member of the group in question might pose a danger to us. This is especially true for what she calls *striking-property* generics like those about deer ticks and sharks. Better by far to avoid them all than risk debilitating Lyme disease or death in the waves. We certainly essentialize deer ticks and sharks as animal species. So do people cling to this default generalizing strategy when faced with instances of striking (and potentially very dangerous) properties in some of their fellow humans? Perhaps; but shunning all members of some social group on the basis of dangers posed by a very few of them has quite different kinds of consequences than shunning all deer ticks or sharks.

What Leslie has suggested in several papers is that post-9/11 proclamations by some (non-Muslim) Americans of the form "Muslims are terrorists" may stem from this quite primitive built-in strategy for avoiding frightening situations. At least some of those making such claims are perfectly well aware that the overwhelming majority of Muslims are not indeed terrorists. What is happening here is constituting a social kind (people who follow Islam) as having distinctive essences that contribute significantly to certain highly negative (dispositional) properties. Members of the group are taken as being 'fundamentally different' from those generalizing about them while at the same time being 'fundamentally all alike' in their being somehow 'disposed' to display these negative properties, in this case, to engage in terrorist activities. That they are taken as 'fundamentally different' is a mark of their being taken as lesser, readily and properly 'shunnable.' In some respects, such striking-property (over)generalizations seem to treat human beings who follow Islam more like deer ticks and sharks than like the generalizer's next-door neighbors.

I speak of next-door neighbors because, strikingly, negative actions engaged in by someone in a group to which the generalizer belongs or with which they affiliate themselves do not tend to lead to such generic generalizations. Timothy McVeigh, the Oklahoma City bomber, was not taken as emblematic of young white American men or Gulf War veterans. Rather his actions were explained in terms of his own very specific personality and particular life history rather than his social group membership. More recently, some Americans have indeed said things like "White supremacists now engage in public hate speech of a kind that promotes acts of domestic terrorism." It is important to note that those who say things like this characterize the group of which they are speaking so that it is clear they would not themselves identify as members of that group. Expressions like "White supremacists" or "Anti-Semites" label groups based on the beliefs of their members relevant to vicious acts targeting other groups in which group members might engage. "Muslims" includes many whose beliefs strongly oppose the actions being attributed to the group. "Western-hating Muslims" or "Anti-American Muslims" would be more directly comparable groups to "White supremacists."

Generic attributions of very negative properties to social kinds *tend* to be resisted by those who have close and warm relations with members of the kind. I emphasize 'tend' because familiarity with members of a group, even intimacy and even membership in the group, does not preclude all generic claims or negative stereotypes about them. Gender generalizations are pervasive about members of the other gender category (with those left out by the binary split generally forgotten). There are also internalized generalizations about the category to which one has been assigned oneself. In the case of gender generalizations, there are often strong beliefs in biological essentialism playing a role. These generalizations also play a role in sustaining the heavily elaborated social norms (for appearance, activities, tastes, etc.) that support gender above and beyond the differences in reproductive biology.

Norms

The English word *norm* is used in just a frequential or statistical sense to mean what is average, typical, or usual. It is also used to designate what is socially or morally approved, what is accepted or valued. It is hardly surprising then that generalizing about identity

groups and policing the behavior of those assigned and/or claiming those identities go hand in hand. "Women don't do well in
law," said my high school counselor. Lacking the courage of Ruth
Bader Ginsburg, a half-decade or so older than I am, and being far
more a conformist, I took that generalization as not just
a prediction that, since I would become a woman, I would not
do well in law but as advice not to try to pursue a legal career.
"Careers matter more to men than to women," said my mother,
instructing me to make family my primary interest. That's all long
ago, of course, but generalizing and guidance are still closely
connected. "Girls aren't interested in being scientists," pronounce
pundits. And indeed other research by Marjorie Rhodes and
Sarah-Jane Leslie and their colleagues has shown that girls are
significantly more likely to respond positively to an invitation to
"do science" than to one asking them to "be scientists." Many of
them see *scientist* as labeling an identity inconsistent with the
gender identity they are cultivating for themselves. Of course
kids can get the generalizations very wrong. Reportedly a young
boy growing up in Thatcherite England was asked whether he
wanted to be prime minister someday. "Of course not," he replied.
Prime ministers are women." The normative function of generalizing sentences is often illustrated by instructions to children to
change their behavior so as to make it consistent with some
generic generalization about gender. "Boys don't cry" is usually
aimed at a sobbing young lad, trying to pressure him into ceasing
his sobs. One child might say to another "Girls don't play with
trucks" while wresting the truck away from the child they identify
as a girl (whether that child so identifies is not relevant – the
truck-snatcher is assuming 'she' does and is trying to get 'her' to
conform to the presented gender norm).

It is not just with respect to social identities that what we might
think of as 'objective' ('statistical') norms intertwine with 'value-
laden' norms. When we are gathering evidence to assess the
'factuality' of generalizations, including the stereotypes fueled by
hidden biases, we observe individuals and their actions and other
properties. But we do so biased by what we already assume or

hope to be the case. We give more weight, pay more attention to, are more likely to remember what fits with how we want things to be. We often overlook those who don't fit our assumptions. Psychologists call this *confirmation bias*, and it certainly can help keep alive some corrosive and damaging social stereotypes.[24] (Journalist Carl Hulse punningly used the phrase as the title of a recent book, which he subtitled *Inside Washington's War Over the Supreme Court, from Scalia's Death to Justice Kavanagh*.[25] Hulse is looking at the extreme politicization in recent tussles over confirmation of presidential nominees to the Supreme Court.) But especially when we are dealing with human beings with their (somewhat) malleable minds and revisable social structures, we need to remember that some biases can actually be helpful shortcuts that point us in productive directions. If the 'arc of history bends toward justice' (and I'm by no means confident that it does), that could be in part because of tendencies to give greater weight to attitudes toward one another that help us form the alliances necessary to dismantle oppressive social arrangements than to divisive views of dangerous 'others.'

Notes

1. Quote in chapter title is from the Combahee River Collective. Their article appeared in a book with this name and the subtitle *Black Women's Studies*, edited by Akasha (Gloria T.) Hull, Patricia Bell Scott, and Barbara Smith, first published in 1982 by the Feminist Press, Old Westbury, NY, 2nd edition in 2016 by the Feminist Press at the City University of New York (www.feministpress.org),
2. Crenshaw 1989; see also Collins and Bilge 2016; Hancock 2016.
3. See, e.g., Anolli, Zurloni, and Riva 2006, Beukeboom 2014, Maas et al. 1989, Schnake and Ruscher 1998, von Hippel, Sekaquaptewa, and Vargas, 1997, Wigboldus, Semin, and Spears 2000 for an introduction to this research; thanks to David Beaver for sending me these and other relevant articles.
4. To take an IAT yourself on some topic, visit Project Implicit at Harvard, accessed at https://implicit.harvard.edu/implicit/takeatest.html.
5. The encyclopedia article is Brownstein 2019; see also Madva and Brownstein 2018 and Beeghly 2015, 2018 for relevant discussion.

6. Eberhardt 2019.

7. See, e.g., Saul 2018. See also Stanley 2015, esp. pp. 158–160.

8. Earlier I used *conceptual baggage* (McConnell-Ginet 2008, 2012) but I'm following the lead of philosopher Herman Cappelen (2018) in emphasizing the word rather than the concept; he uses *lexical effects* to speak of similar phenomena. I retain *baggage* because I like its suggestion of extra stuff just (sometimes) carried along with a word beyond its meaning when the word is in action.

9. Apfelbaum et al. 2010.

10. Mills 2017, p. 41.

11. On colonial laws, Mills cites Matthew Frye Jacobson, *Whiteness of a Different Color: European Immigrants and the Alchemy of Race* (Harvard University Press, 1998). On expropriation of native lands under the doctrine of 'discovery,' he cites Lindsay G. Robertson, *Conquest by Law: How the Discovery of America Dispossessed Indigenous Peoples of Their Lands* (Oxford University Press, 2005).

12. Audio and transcription of King's famous "I have a dream" speech can be accessed at https://kinginstitute.stanford.edu/king-papers/documents/ i-have-dream-address-delivered-march-washington-jobs-and-freedom.

13. Hobson's 14-minute talk can be heard at www.ted.com/talks/mellody_ hobson_color_blind_or_color_brave?language=en and is reported at https://blog.ted.com/be-color-brave-not-color-blind-mellody-hobson-at- ted2014/.

14. Rickford 2016.

15. *Rest in Power: The Trayvon Martin Story*, on Paramount Network.

16. Karen Grigsby Bates, "A Look Back at Trayvon Martin's Death, and the Movement It Inspired," NPR *Code Switch*, July 31, 2018, www.npr.org/sec tions/codeswitch/2018/07/31/631897758/a-look-back-at-trayvon-martins- death-and-the-movement-it-inspired.

17. In McConnell-Ginet 2012, I discuss some of this literature; Nickel 2016 is an important contribution from a philosopher well versed in the linguistics literature both on the semantic issues and on questions about genericity.

18. This phrase provides the main title for an important book Gelman coedited; see Benaji and Gelman 2013.

19. See Antony 2016 on this point.

20. See Rhodes et al. 2018.

21. See Most 2000.

22. See Saul 2017a for criticism of Leslie's claims.

23. Leslie 2017.

24. Watson 1960 first introduced the notion of confirmation bias.

25. Published 2019.

4   Addressing: "All Right, *My Man* ... Keep Your Hands on the Steering Wheel"

Dr. Alvin Poussaint is an American psychiatrist who has done significant work on the psychological harm that racism routinely inflicts on black Americans.[1] Over fifty years ago, he offered this vivid account of address used to brutally position him as socially inferior, to subordinate him forcibly.[2]

> [A]s I was leaving my office in Jackson, Miss., ... a white police-man yelled, "Hey, boy! Come here!" Somewhat bothered, I retorted: "I'm no boy!" He then rushed at me, inflamed, and stood towering over me, snorting, "What d'ja say, boy?" Quickly he frisked me and demanded, "What's your name, boy?" Frightened, I replied, "Dr. Poussaint. I'm a physician." He angrily chuckled and hissed, "What's your first name, boy?" When I hesitated he assumed a threatening stance and clenched his fists. As my heart palpitated, I muttered in profound humiliation, "Alvin."
>
> He continued his psychological brutality, bellowing, "Alvin, the next time I call you, you come right away, you hear? You hear?" I hesitated. "You hear me, boy?" My voice trembling with help-lessness, but following my instincts of self-preservation, I mur-mured, "Yes, sir." Now fully satisfied that I had performed and acquiesced to my "boy" status, he dismissed me with, "Now boy, go on and get out of here or next time we'll take you for a little ride down to the station house!"
>
> No amount of self-love could have salvaged my pride or pre-served my integrity. In fact, the slightest show of self-respect or resistance might have cost me my life. ... [T]his had occurred on a public street for all the local black people to witness, reminding them that *no* black man was as good as *any* white man. All of us – doctor, lawyer, postman, field hand and shoeshine boy–had been psychologically "put in our place."

The policeman's *boy* humiliated its target with considerable nonlinguistic help. The man doing the addressing was large, armed, and had all the force of segregated 1960s Mississippi and its white supremacist institutions behind him. He also used other available address resources to do his demeaning work. Denying Dr. Poussaint the dignity of being addressed by his professional title and insisting on extracting and using his addressee's first name compounded the demoralizing effect of *boy*, highlighting the push down the social hierarchy.[3]

Vocatives

Boy and *Alvin* are being used as *vocatives* by the police officer. So is *sir* by Dr. Poussaint. A vocative is a direct address form. It targets the person receiving it. It may stand alone. A bare proper name can serve to get attention, to initiate an interaction. "Chris?" A bare endearment can caress. "Darling!" A familiar kin term can protest a bit. "Daddy!" Or address can initiate an exchange with institutionalized roles. "Your honor." To appreciate more fully the possibilities, try performing the examples out loud – the ups and downs of intonation and stress or emphasis contribute a lot. The power of vocatives is by no means confined to the assaultive bludgeoning of the police officer's *boy* or the forced deference of Dr. Poussaint's *sir*. Often what vocatives do is much subtler and not fully noted at a conscious level by either the addressee or the addresser.

Most vocatives are attached to fuller utterances like the policeman's "You hear me?" They designate a person or group (even occasionally a thing) as the intended addressee to whom an utterance is targeted. But this doesn't mean that their calling or summoning function to pull another into interaction is primary. Expressions like *hey* or the more recent *yo* often occur with vocatives, and their main function is indeed what is often called *hailing* – that is, making someone an addressee.[4] But unlike *hey* or *yo*, vocatives like *boy* or *sir* more often close an utterance than open it, and they often continue to occur well after a talk exchange is underway.

Repeated vocatives affirm the ongoing connection and social relationship. If vocatives recur very frequently over the course of an interaction, however, the addressee may feel either assaulted or manipulated, depending on the forms used and the prior relationship of the parties to the exchange. "Why, yes *sir*. I'll be happy to do that, *sir*. … Oh, *sir*, I'll be sure to remember. And, *sir*, don't hesitate to call me if you need anything." The overly helpful self-erasing underling might keep dropping in *sir*. On the other hand, someone who is dominating an ongoing conversation may also use vocatives frequently. "*Lee*, you won't believe what I heard from the guys at the top. They've got plans for us, *Lee*. You and I, *Lee*, we're just peons to them. When you get that pink envelope, *Lee*, don't say I didn't warn you." The repeated vocative reminds the addressee of their status as addressee and of the relationship to them the speaker claims, a relationship that may not be seen in the same light by each participant.

What distinguishes vocatives from the *you* and other forms used to *refer* to the person or group addressed is that vocatives stand on their own. They do not play any of the standard grammatical roles that are crucial for understanding most utterances. The vocative is not a subject, an object, a possessor. Some readers may have encountered a vocative *case* for direct address forms in studying Latin. The dying Caesar said "Et tu, *Brute*" ('And you, Brutus'). Before he was stabbed, he might well have said "*Brutus amicus meus est*" ('Brutus is my friend'). The nominative form *Brutus* is used for subjects as in the second example. It is written differently and sounds different from *Brute*, the vocative for direct address.

Already in Caesar's time, Latin's vocative case was in decline. Most nouns in classical Latin had identical nominative (used for subjects) and vocative forms. The Romance languages descending from Latin like French, Spanish, and Italian no longer have a vocative case marker. As in English and every other language of which I have heard, however, their speakers still use vocatives.

They just do not distinguish them with case markers – that is, mark them formally.

Some languages do still use a vocative case. Vocative case continues to be common in many Baltic and most Slavic languages. Linguist Lillian Parrott observes, for example, that in Czech, direct addresses exclusively in the nominative case strike her consultants "as highly demeaning expressions of power of the speaker over the addressee, as though the addressee did not merit the speaker's recognition as an interlocutor, imaginable only in certain environments, such as the military."[5] In contrast, she reports that in Polish the default case for direct address is nominative. These nominative case forms for direct address are what linguists call *unmarked*, what is expected in the absence of special circumstances. When a direct address form is marked as vocative, that marking indicates that something is being conveyed over and above the standard message associated with the words and address form uttered. Just what that is depends on other features of the speech situation – the vocative case in Polish may convey intimacy or distance, may come off as rude or polite.

Even in languages like English, which long ago stopped marking case on common nouns like *boy* or proper names like *Alvin* (or *Brutus*), vocatives are important tools for building and maintaining social relationships. Or, as we saw in the opening of this chapter, weapons for social oppression.

Power and Solidarity

In 1960, psychologists Roger Brown and Albert Gilman published a groundbreaking analysis of what they called the 'pronouns of power and solidarity.'[6] They focused on second-person pronouns in languages like French, German, and Russian. These and many other languages have historically distinguished so-called 'familiar' or 'intimate' second-person singular pronouns, dubbed 'T' from Latin *tu*, from their 'formal' or 'polite' counterparts, 'V' from Latin *vos*. The second-person pronoun is used to *refer* to the person targeted by an utterance, its addressee, in order to say something about them. A second-person pronoun generally may also be used to *address* that person directly, that is, as a vocative. Contemporary English in most varieties has only one second-person pronoun, *you*, which can occur as a vocative in direct address ("Hey, *you*, come here") or to refer to the addressee ("Where are *you* going?").

Many Indo-European languages have two second-person pronouns useable for addressing a single individual; analysts speak of T/V pronoun systems. The T forms (e.g., *tu* in French) are used only for individual addressees. The V forms (e.g., *vous* in French) were originally only for plural addressees, both as vocatives and in reference. They are still used for multiple addressees and still take plural verb agreement even if the referent is singular. The T/V system, however, began when speakers started using the plural V forms to address high-status individuals. Importantly, it isn't just the pronouns that carry the distinction. The V pronouns remain grammatically plural even when referring to a single individual, that is, semantically singular, a verb in a directive targeting a single individual. These languages have different verb forms for second-person singular and plural subjects. In French, for example, it is "vous mangez" ('you – polite or plural – eat') but "tu manges" ('you – familiar – eat'). In English, directives –"Eat!" – have only an 'understood' and not a pronounced *you* subject. In French uttering "mangez!" ('eat!') signals an unpronounced *vous*, whereas "mange!" points to a silent *tu*. Even though the speaker did not have to choose between saying *vous* or saying *tu*, the form of the verb signals how the speaker is positioning the addressee. In English, speakers can usually avoid signaling how they are positioning themselves and their addressees. In T/V languages, second-person pronouns and agreement markers on verbs in imperatives frequently force the issue, making such avoidance more difficult.

Power and *solidarity* are terms for two very general features of social relationships. Power is an asymmetric relation. If Kim has power over Lee, then Lee does not have power over Kim. Power is one-way only, conceptualized vertically. (Of course power relations are far more complex than this, but the asymmetry is what matters for present purposes.) What Brown and Gilman call the *power semantic* is thus *nonreciprocal*: going down the hierarchy, the form is T, whereas coming up it is V. Solidarity entered the system, Brown and Gilman argue, to differentiate address among equals. Solidarity is symmetric, relations go in both directions. *Reciprocity* is called for. Either both use T to one another or both use V. On the same rung of the hierarchy, solidarity leads to mutual T use, whereas mutual V is exchanged among equals who are not solidary (they may be completely unacquainted).

The (grammatically plural) V forms are sometimes said to show *respect* or to be more *formal* when used to address or refer to a single individual, and the T forms to show *intimacy* or to be more *familiar*. Of course matters are more complicated, at least in part because social relationships are not so simply categorized. But even with this pared-down model, we see multiple things the forms can do. Whereas mutual exchange of V can show respect, a V going up the social ladder that will not be reciprocated can seem deferential, where the deference may be willing (the lower-positioned person acknowledges the higher's authority or entitlement as legitimate) or coerced. Reciprocal Ts can show intimacy and affection, whereas a T going down that cannot be returned may seem condescending, even if its user genuinely values the addressee.

English-speaking feminists and other gender activists have proposed a genderless third-person singular *they* as an alternative to the forced choice between feminine *she* and masculine *he*, the gender 'binary'. (I use singular *they* at many places in this book.) Such moves are sometimes criticized as unwarranted political incursions on 'neutral' grammatical territory and seen as a recent development. Political motives for pronoun choices are, however, far from a new development. (This point is made clearly by Ann Bodine in her 1975 paper on the history and possible future of English *they* with singular referents.[7] We'll return to *they* below and again in Chapter 6.) The French Revolution came hand in hand with calls to abandon V and turn to mutual T for all. Note that it was universal T rather than universal V that was pushed. Because V address was strongly associated with royalty and aristocracy, the groups in which it had first and most strongly taken off as a way to address single individuals, V was seen as inappropriately deferential. As it turned out, V did not disappear from French but continued post-revolution, both among distant equals, particularly those in higher social classes, and up various hierarchies. Things have changed, however.

In France, it is still the case that mutual V is frequent between people who do not see one another as 'alike,' as 'close' in some important way. Nonetheless there is now mutual T in families where children used to address their parents with V (or, sometimes, their father with V and their mother with T). And mutual T among young adults from the same schools and the like is expected. Nonetheless, to use T to a server in a restaurant might seem condescending rather than affiliative, abandoned along with the *garçon*, which can be translated as 'boy,' addressed to waiters in days gone by. Interestingly, a 2019 study found considerable use of T in workplaces to immediate superiors.[8] This was less common in public sector workplaces than in private, and significantly less common if the employee was a woman rather than a man. Indeed, Alex Alber, author of the study, speaks of a *plafond du verbe* 'verbal ceiling' (compare 'glass ceiling') facing women, an obstacle to workplace success created by the norms for 'respectful' speech that constrain women more in using the upward T. Pronominal choice continues an issue in France, though the spots of tension have shifted. Alber suggests that it is not worker empowerment that has promoted upward T but shifts in workplace organization, which now often emphasizes quantitative goals and regular formal evaluations of employees. Such changes lessen the power of the direct supervisor over an employee.

In Québec, on the other hand, mutual T is the norm with people one's own age or younger. Immigrants from France to Québec are often heard by the locals as snobby, putting on airs, when they use V to someone not significantly older, especially if that person has used T to them. The French immigrants in turn are often surprised to learn that the quick move to mutual T among the

Québec citizenry does not always signal the warmth and openness such a shift might in Paris. Not only are there significant differences from one side of the Atlantic to the other. Within each area there is also a multiplicity of addressing practices to be considered, not the uniformity suggested by textbooks. Practices have changed significantly over the past decades, and things keep changing. There is considerable complexity in both the historical developments and in current practices, which the flowchart in Figure 4.1, somewhat tongue in cheek and based more or less on continental French practices, conveys.[9]

A Short Guide to Using Vous and Tu

Figure 4.1   A Short Guide to Using *Vous* and *Tu*

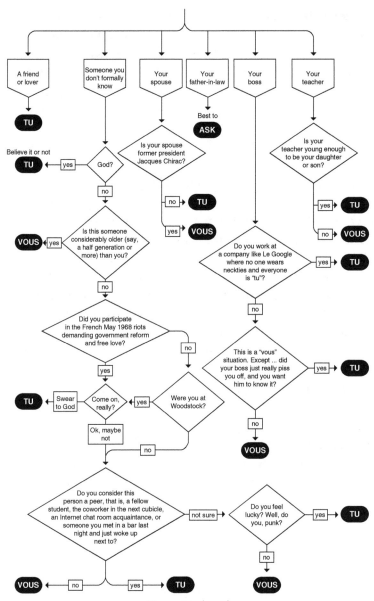

Figure 4.1 (cont.)

From *Flirting with French* by William Alexander ©2014 by William Alexander.
Reprinted by permission of Algonquin Books of Chapel Hill. All rights reserved

Like French, Spanish is now spoken in widely separated areas and quite different, though still mostly mutually intelligible, varieties have developed. Spanish in the Americas comes in many different varieties, and T/V usage norms vary. The basic socially significant choice is between *tú* (singular)/*vos* (plural), both of which are described as 'informal,' and *usted*, the formal second-person pronoun. These are just the subject forms, which stand in for the whole paradigm. As with French, a social message can be conveyed by the form of the verb even when there is no overt second-person pronoun. A language user can hear, for example, and comment on their conversational partner's *usted* even if that form itself has not occurred. Conversation analyst Chase Raymond offers a nice example of one student speaking a Costa Rican variety to another student of Mexican ancestry: the Costa Rican young woman was using verbal forms and pronouns for indirect object and possessor that would go with *usted*. Although she had not uttered that particular word, her Mexican-American fellow student interrupted her with "Usted?," implying that she was being unnecessarily formal, and she switched.

Some varieties of Spanish tend to use the *tú*/*vos* and related forms with strangers, whereas others prefer *usted* for such interactions. Such sweeping generalizations, however, miss the ways in which speakers deploy pronominal and related resources to reposition themselves, even if only temporarily, as Raymond convincingly shows. Although social *status* remains relatively fixed, a speaker can shift social *stance* by exploiting the possibilities in the T/V system. There are several nice illustrations from Raymond's data, all of it from recorded speech not produced for research purposes: 911 phone calls, non-scripted TV political interviews, at-home conversations, phone calls between friends. In one 911 call, for example, the distraught caller responds to the call-receiver's polite *usted* with the non-deferential *tu*/*vos*, placing himself as entitled to the service being demanded. Further into the exchange, when the call-receiver asks him for certain documents and seems to indicate that she is not going to send him the help he is seeking, there is a switch to the more deferential *usted*. This more formal stance appears to be an attempt to stave off the impending refusal and get the result the caller wants, a way of repositioning himself as a respectful and responsible supplicant rather than the demanding loudmouth he might earlier have seemed.[10]

T/V pronominal choices can seem exotic to English speakers. And it is easy to note their exploitation in the service of social oppression. For example, European colonialists using T/V languages typically addressed colonized Africans with T but expected (often effectively, required) V in return. As the reminiscence from Dr. Poussaint opening this chapter shows, however, pronominal forms of address are not needed to subordinate, to assert and enforce social superiority through addressing. Nonreciprocity in address usage is not only possible in English but widespread (though often unnoticed). For Dr. Poussaint to have responded to the request for his first name by asking the police officer for his first name would have probably resulted in incredulity from the police officer, followed almost immediately by a physical assault and, minimally, "a little ride down to the station house" resulting in jail time. Indeed, the result of violating the racial hierarchy through forms of address could be death. At the new National Memorial for Peace and Justice in Montgomery, Alabama, one of the inscriptions reads "Jesse Thornton was lynched in Luverne, Alabama, in 1940 for addressing a white police officer without the title 'mister.'"[11] We can be quite confident that the white police officer in question did not address Mr. Thornton using a title: nonreciprocal address norms are one way that dominance relations are established and maintained.

English Address (and Reference) Resources

English did in fact have its own T/V pronoun distinction well into the seventeenth century. The T form was *thou* (or *thee* or *thy*, depending on the pronoun's grammatical function), and the V form was the plural *you* (or *ye* or *your*). Among strangers, *thou/thee* was used mainly to those whom the speaker saw as social inferiors, whereas *you/ye* was used to those one treated as social equals, one's peers. As the middle class grew, it became more difficult to 'read' people's social status, and the plural *you* began to drive out the singular *thou*, being the 'safer' choice in many contexts. Or at least that's how historians of language often reconstruct the process. The actual process was undoubtedly more complicated and may have been influenced as much by structural linguistic facts (*thou* came with an -*est* verb ending whereas *you* did not) as by social ideology.[12] There are varieties in the north of England that continue the T forms. Somewhat curiously, the T forms are still used in many Christian religious settings, especially for addressing the deity in prayer, probably because of the influence of the King James translation of the Bible. Ultimately, however, *you* has pretty much won out.

There were, however, resisters to the spread of *you* at the expense of *thou* on both political and grammatical grounds. George Fox, one of the founders of the Society of Friends, published his manifesto in 1660, *A Battle Door for Teachers & Professors to Learn Singular & Plural; "You" to Many, and "Thou" to One: Singular "One," "Thou"; Plural "Many," "You."* Fox's coreligionists continued using *thou* and *thee* even though, as he complained in his 1836 *Journal*,

> For Thou and Thee was a sore cut to proud flesh, and them that sought self-honour, who, though they would say it to God and Christ, would not endure to have it said to themselves. So that we were often beaten and abused, and sometimes in danger of our lives, for using those words to some proud men, who would say, "What! You ill-bred clown, do you Thou me?"[13]

Fox did not win the day with his complaints that *you* could not refer to a single individual because it was plural, complaints that evoke recent criticisms of using *they* to refer to a single individual. We will discuss contemporary debates over semantically singular *they* in its various uses later in this book. In thinking about those debates, it is useful to remember that *you* is a grammatically plural form that, primarily for political reasons, has successfully extended its scope to semantically singular uses, many of which are now considered unremarkable. Grammatically, *yourself* is on a par with *themself,* but only the latter form is autocorrected by my word processor.

Although second-person pronouns no longer offer room for English speakers to position themselves and others, we have already seen there are other vocative resources available to English speakers for (re)positioning interlocutors in social space. English address offers a wide array of resources for managing social positions and relations. Figure 4.2 shows some of the personalized choices available to English speakers addressing someone they know. It also shows some more general choices, useable even for those whose identity is not known. These two sets of choices show just a small sample of the many options

Figure 4.2 English Address Options

Personalized

FN:	first/personal name, either in 'official' or shortened or diminutive form (addressee's preferred name variant often depends on addresser and situation)
TLN:	title plus last/family name, either general social title (*Mr* , *Ms* , *Mx* [recently introduced gender-neutral title]...) or professional (*Doc(tor)*, *Professor*, *Reverend*, *Rabbi*, ...)
LN:	last/family name only, perhaps in shortened or otherwise modified form
Bare Kinterm:	*Mom, Mama, Dad, Bubbe, Nana, PopPop, Sis, ...*
Kinterm + N	*Aunt Mary, Grandma Rose, Grandpa Smith, Daddy Steve, Cousin Carl, Spuncle Jacob* (see Bergman 2013), ...

General

Bare T:	*Mister, Doc(tor), Coach, Professor, Teach(er),* ...
Respect Forms:	*Sir, Ma'am, Miss*
Neutral(ish):	*You (guys), Girl(friend), Man, Dude, Lady, Folks, Babe,* ...
Insult/Epithet:	*Bitch, Slut, Bastard, Fatso, Dyke, Faggot,* ...
Endearment:	*Darling, Honey, Love, Sweetie,* ... (often preceded by *my*)

available. Many but not all of the choices in these charts are available not only for *addressing* someone to whom one is speaking but also for *referring* to someone about whom one is speaking, whether or not that individual is present – *third-person* usage.

The differences are slight in address and reference possibilities, but they do exist. In American English, for example, a student can say "Will we have an exam, *Professor*?" Yet "Did *Professor* announce an exam?" to either the faculty member directly (second-person reference) or to a fellow student (third-person) would signal a non-native speaker. Of course, "Did Professor Garcia announce an exam?" is absolutely fine – adding the family name to the title produces a label that works for either address or reference. Similarly, a salesclerk might say "Did you like those trousers, *sir*?" but not "Did *sir* like those trousers?" to either the customer or his shopping companion hovering outside the dressing room. "Did *you* like the trousers?" is essentially the only choice for second-person reference in most contexts. For third person, one might get something like "Did *the gentleman/your friend* like the trousers?"

There are exceptions to these generalizations. English schoolchildren occasionally refer to their teachers using just *sir* or *miss*. And the form *sir* (and also *mistress*) can be used for second-person reference in some circumstances. For example, Jeeves, the valet, occasionally says to Bertie, his employer, things like "Would sir like the red or the blue cravat?" And I have learned that such usages occur in some forms of gay porn. Usage changes. *Professor* was unheard as a vocative from late 1950s college students. We did, however, refer to people in their absence using forms we would not have used to their face. "Did Noam announce a test?" One of Professor Noam Chomsky's students might say that, either to suggest (perhaps falsely) being on a first-name basis with the famous linguist (name-dropping can happen in attempts to boost one's own status), or to indulge, with other students, in mock familiarity.

For our present purposes, however, we can focus on address, including both vocatives and direct reference to the addressee. Many of the same principles we'll discuss here for second-person reference and direct address also apply to third-person reference. Talk of persons not being addressed will, however, become more prominent in the discussion of racial and ethnic slurs and other put-downs in the next chapter.

In the English charts in Figure 4.2, 'T' is not a kind of pronoun but a cover for a title: for example, *Doctor* or *Ms.* or *Reverend*. The hierarchies of the Catholic and Anglican churches (as well as of other religious groups, including many that are not Christian), and of the military, and the vestiges of monarchy and hereditary aristocracy in Britain – these all offer many more English-language titles still in use in some communities. There are even titles bestowed by the British monarch honoring achievement (*Dame* Judi Dench and *Sir* Elton John, for example). My aim here is not exhaustivity: I just want to nudge readers to begin thinking about vocatives they might produce or be addressed by. The contrast between FN – given or 'first' name – and TLN – title plus family name or 'last' name – is often said to be like that between a T pronoun and a V pronoun, but of course matters are much more complicated. (Note that given names do not come 'first' in all languages nor do family names always come 'last.' I will, however, use the FN/ TLN designation because it's so common in research literature published in English.) Not only are there many more options than name choices, but contrasts involving proper names can't be invoked between strangers on the street as the T/V choices can. And most of the English choices in Figure 4.2 convey something about gender categorizing, whereas T and V are not gender marked (although gender relations are certainly highly relevant to their use).[14] This makes things very difficult for those who seek to avoid binary gender categorization. It also complicates things for anyone whose gender identity may be misjudged by others.

As with T/V usage, nonreciprocal address practices sustain power-laden relations. In the segregated South of my childhood, even white people who sincerely thought of themselves as anti-racists participated in nonreciprocal address practices. They often allowed their children to use personal names in addressing adult African Americans while making clear that other adults were to be addressed "with respect." It was "Miz Jones" or "Miz Emily" or "Aunt Emily" (not only for someone in the family but for parents' white friends) but never "Emily" for the mother of a white play-mate. In contrast, the black woman cleaning the house received "Mabel" not only from her employer but also often from children of the household. The house cleaner in turn probably used "Miz Smith" or maybe "Miz Mary," but not "Mary" to her employer, though she may well have called the children by their first names.

Especially in the nineteenth and early twentieth centuries, *Mr. Charlie* or *Mister Charley* was widely used among black people to refer generically to any imperious or exploitative white man. Song titles and literature (e.g., James Baldwin's *Blues for Mister Charlie*) help keep this usage alive. *Mister Charlie* was paired with *Miz Ann*, used widely in the nineteenth century to refer to the wife of the slave owner, the woman in charge of a household, or any white woman whom black people were required to 'serve.'[15] White people who thought Jim Crow laws immoral might sometimes address adult African Americans by TLN and introduce them that way to others. Even they, however, were likely very soon to switch to FN, overlooking whether their black friend reciprocated this 'friendly' gesture. It was not just a matter of overt hostile racism, like that shown by the police officer addressing Dr. Poussaint or the officer who got Jesse Thornton lynched. There were many somewhat more benign but nonetheless deeply problematic asymmetries embedded in everyday address practices. In 1989 African American literary scholar and cultural critic Henry L. Gates, Jr. recalled a childhood encounter where his father was called 'George' by a white man who knew that wasn't his name. The misnamed father explained to his shocked young son, "He calls all colored men *George*."[16] Black people who among themselves spoke of a generic *Mr. Charlie* knew that it would not be wise so to address some random white man. Robert E. Park is a white American sociologist who after retirement from the University of Chicago taught at the historically black Fisk University. It was he who coined the term *racial etiquette* to cover the range of such practices that regularly enforced the subordination of African Americans in the American South.[17]

The racial etiquette governing address of which Park spoke was not made explicit or codified. Institutional settings, in contrast, sometimes have explicit address rules. US elementary and high schools, for example, may require a student addressed by FN to return T+LN or perhaps a bare title to their teacher. Some teachers might prefer for students to address them by FN, but be forbidden by principals or other school authorities from getting kids in their classrooms to adopt that practice. The intermediate T+FN for teachers (*Ms. Lisa*) is sometimes used in schools that are overtly trying to empower students by allowing them some familiarity with teachers, but also wanting overt markers of what is usually described as "respect" from students to acknowledge (and help sustain) the teacher's classroom authority. Ms. Maria and Mr. Ken seem warmer and more approachable than Ms. Gonzalez and Mr. Miller, but also are situated 'above' Maria and Ken. The 'respect' of the title plus some shortened form of the teacher's surname is another intermediate form that can combine respect and familiarity. Ms. Mac or Mr. G, for example, often get so styled without any explicit invitation to adopt those forms. And students sometimes use a bare title: for example, *Teacher, Professor,* or, at least in some British school settings, *Miss,* contrasting with the somewhat more respectful form for men, *Sir.*

Depending on what's common in their out-of-school communities of practice, students may feel uncomfortable using FN without a title to address a teacher significantly older than they are, even if asked to do so. At the college and university level, students are entering adulthood. Such transitions of status can involve delicate negotiation. Half a century ago, some college professors marked their students' farewell to childhood by addressing them as "Miss Miller" and "Mr. Kahn" (or, sometimes just "Brown" for a male student but not for a female). In the US, at least, it is hard to imagine this happening now. These days faculty almost always address and refer to students by first name (or, if their memories fail them, use the zero-address option or something like "you in the back"). Young adult students still, however, may find themselves avoiding vocatives altogether with their instructors, easier to do when there are no pronouns or verb forms involved as in T/V languages.

As in T/V systems, forms used for mutual respect, reciprocal, are also used for deference, one-way, and forms used to show mutual friendship or intimacy are also used to condescend. *Sir* or *Professor Schmidt* may show mutual respect. The same forms may show deference from someone clearly lower in the relevant hierarchy. Respect may also be involved, but need not be. In the military, for example, a deferential *sir* is enforced for male superiors. (Some women officers report occasionally receiving *sir*, presumably because *ma'am* does not carry quite the same recognition of authority.) Respect forms may also curry favor, may position their user as obsequious. Similarly, endearments are sometimes genuinely endearing, especially when reciprocal. A pair of lovers may exchange *sweetheart* or other such expressions. But the male boss who views his *my dear* to his female employee as 'caring' would be quite taken aback and probably annoyed if she began using *my dear* to address him. And a "Hi, sweetheart" addressed to a young woman from a strange man as she walks along a public street can be threatening. Parents regularly use endearments to their offspring but seldom is the pattern reciprocated, even in families where offspring use their parents' first names in address and in reference. Because the relation is usually seen by both parties as mutually affectionate, the asymmetry is not typically seen as condescension from the parent.

Condescension conveyed endearingly is widespread. The elderly, especially if infirm in some way, often receive endearments not only from other family members and acquaintances who might not have so addressed them when they were younger but also from medical personnel and paid caretakers. A young doctor addressing a frail and clearly quite elderly patient with *dear* does not expect that patient to return the endearment. Potential reciprocity is key. To say that such practices involve condescension, are not respectful, is not to deny that they are often prompted by genuine caring. The problem is that the caring is presented in the parent–child mode, essentially infantilizing the elderly recipient.

Social relationships are far more complicated than the power–solidarity model captures. English vocatives can be much more easily avoided than the T/V choice of pronoun or person-marked imperative verb. In situations where relations are changing or are somehow difficult to negotiate, where choices are not clear-cut, English speakers can sometimes sidestep address decisions. And the wide array of choices means that people can devise somewhat distinctive ways of positioning themselves and others, sometimes manipulating the possibility of multiple meanings. But this does not mean that matters are always straightforward. The meaning of any particular form of address or reference depends on who is using it to or of whom – this is where power and solidarity come most clearly into play. It also depends, however, on what else is going on in a given interaction – for example, is an action being asked of someone or is someone offering to act on behalf of someone else – and on patterns of linguistic choices.

Naming, Nicknaming, and Authority

Not just anyone can name anyone else. In the USA, parents are empowered to bestow a name on their child, who may change that name in adulthood, but only with the approval of a court of law. Because personal names are so often gendered, transgender people often seek to change them – and sometimes also, for various reasons, their family names. They have often had to jump through legal hoops not required of others in order to do so. *Deadnaming*, using a pre-transition and wrongly gendered name, is one move some make to delegitimize the gender identity affirmed by a transgender person.

People brought from Africa to be sold into slavery not only got 'family' names from their 'owners' but were typically also given new personal names. (And recall the white man who, in the waning years of the Jim Crow era, felt empowered to call "all colored men *George*.") Shedding the family names that 'masters' imposed on enslaved ancestors (who generally also had had their personal names changed) has been one way that some African Americans have changed the narrative of their own identities. Malcolm X was first named Malcolm Little, Mohammed Ali was named Cassius Clay, and Nzotake Shange was named Paulette Linda Williams.

Naming is also implicated in sexual politics. My own hyphenated family name was an attempt to connect my married self to the earlier me. Still, of course, the name comes from two men – *McConnell* from my father, *Ginet* from my husband. Until relatively recently, Anglo-American law recognized a father's authority over his daughter passing into the hands of a husband when she married, and family names reflected that. (I should say that neither my husband nor my father as individuals ever attempted to exercise such authority. I confess with some embarrassment, however, that our wedding ceremony many decades ago included the question "Who gives this woman to be married to this man?" At the time, we thought my father's answer, "Her mother and I do," showed his and our gender egalitarianism.) More women these days retain their name upon marriage, but it is still the case that children born to heterosexual married couples almost always are given their father's family name. I have a grandson who's an exception; my daughter and her husband gave him the family name *Ginet*, using his father's family name as a middle name. *Mrs Man* is a 1977 book by Una Stannard that explores the history of naming practices and their relation to issues of men's power over women. Of course, it is somewhat dated – the *Mrs John Smith* mode of address is far less common now, though still used, and no states any longer require women to change their name when they marry men (that a woman might marry a woman was not even thought of back then) – but it is packed with useful information. As I have pointed out elsewhere, we cannot say that *Mrs John Smith* is always disrespectful of a woman's individuality. Insisting on such a form has sometimes shielded women of color from being assaulted with their personal names from the mouths of people not entitled to such familiarity. It is easy to assume that nicknames, which do not get regulated by state authorities, have nothing to do with matters of power. Yet like any other potential address forms, they are resources for positioning. Some shortenings or modifications of an 'official' personal name (*Mike* for *Michael, Beth* for *Elizabeth*) become a person's preferred personal name, sometimes used even in formal contexts. The linguist identified as *Geoffrey Nunberg* on an old website (and on books and articles published some years ago) is now known as *Geoff*, not only to friends and colleagues but on his newer professional website and on more recent publications. But such shortenings are by no means always welcomed – salespeople who used *Norm* to my friend Norman were not only seen as inappropriately presumptuous, but were also unlikely to get his business. Sometimes the form that seemed fine in childhood is dropped because of its youthful associations. *Dolly* may become *Dorothy* as an adult professional, and *Ricky* might become *Rick, Rich*, or *Richard*. Among close friends and family, people sometimes tolerate nicknames they would resist from others. Or if the nickname has become the preferred standard personal name (as in the case of Geoff Nunberg, mentioned above), they may tolerate the 'official' name from those who knew them by that in days gone by. Virtually all who met my middle sister in college or later call her *Judy*, but *Judith* comes more easily to me, evoking our early years together. Although she generally prefers *Judy*, she expects (and accepts without complaint) *Judith* from me. (Such tolerance could not always be expected. It would be distinctly unsisterly of me to continue using the familiar childhood name for a sibling who affirmed a gender identity distinct from that assigned at birth and had for that reason discontinued using their childhood name.)

Coining a nickname for someone asserts power over them. The nickname may but need not be imposed: the one named can agree to accept the name. Nicknaming rituals that mark the move of new members from the periphery to full group membership are common in certain kinds of communities of practice – sports teams, for example. I've heard of several Ultimate Frisbee teams where new members put in many months with older teammates observing them, so that someone of longer tenure on the team can eventually settle on an 'appropriate' and distinctive nickname for each individual. These names are then generally used at least during team activities, but sometimes they spread to other contexts as well and may persist long after the nicknamed individual leaves that particular community of practice. Chris is dubbed *Goose* – his family name's last syllable is pronounced 'nay' and gets emphasized and sometimes repeated because many mispronounce it, which reminds someone of the word *nene*, which names a Hawaiian goose – and he has a somewhat long neck. Lee gets nicknamed *Leaf* because she oohed and aahed over the foliage on several autumn team trips – and besides, she has copper-colored hair and the nickname just needs the 'f'-sound tacked on to her standard public name. Next year's new recruits may hear such nicknaming stories – they become part of the team's culture. The nicknames bestowed may tease a bit, but the general spirit is playful, part of what strengthens ties among team members.

Nicknaming, however, is sometimes far more complicated in its effects. And power relations may be less benign than those that structure Ultimate teams. George W. Bush (whom others nicknamed *Dubya*), the forty-third president of the United States, was a prolific nicknamer, bestowing new monikers liberally on those he encountered. He used these newly created names in speaking of and often also to them. He even nicknamed himself at points. Back in his Andover prep-school years, he reportedly pressured others to call him *Tweeds*, after the corrupt but powerful

Tammany Hall boss Tweed. In an article written during Bush's second term,[18] language scholar Michael Adams zeroes in on what he sees as especially problematic in Dubya's nicknaming of others while president. "President Bush's exuberant naming practices," Adams argues, "assert a president's right to put people into their places, as subjects under presidential authority. At the presidential level, nicknaming becomes political because of the office, because a president's authority is executive, not personal." Some of the names Bush bestowed were admiring or neutral, others were critical or at best somewhat 'diminishing.' Advisor Karl Rove was called *Tangent Man*, World Bank President Robert Zoellick drew *The Adding Machine*, senior advisor Israel Hernandez was called *Izzy* or *Altoid Boy* (apparently he carried around breath mints), White House chef Walter Scheib was *Cookie*, Secretary of State Condoleezza Rice got both *Condi* (which she apparently did not mind) and *Guru* (which she did), and Maine Senator Susan Collins was *Sweet Susan*. There were many more. Those nicknamed might nickname Bush in private, but they had to call him *Mr. President* when encountering him in his presidential role, whether or not the press was on hand to observe.

Nicknaming is, in fact, always political. Adams makes this important point in a subsequent article.[19] "Nicknames distribute power within a social group; they can be imposed, or they can be used by agreement between namer and named." A lot of the research on nicknaming has focused on playground or other relatively youthful communities of practice like the sports teams I have already mentioned. Yet nicknames can continue to be important in a wide range of mainly adult communities of practice, ranging from workplace teams to community musical groups to friendship groups.

Nicknames and other features of address choice can matter in service and institutional encounters as well. The police officer stopping Dr. Alvin Poussaint glances at the proffered license and says, "Well, Al, do you know why I stopped you?," asserting their own authority and showing disrespect to Dr. Poussaint. Research on racial dynamics at play in the language used by officers during traffic stops by the Oakland, Cal. police showed the use of first name (in this example, also assuming a familiar nickname) far more common to black than to white motorists. Were Dr. Alvin Poussaint light-skinned, he would have been more likely to hear "I'm sorry to have to stop you, sir." In the next section, I describe that research, which considered not only forms of address but other linguistic features of nearly 1000 exchanges between police and members of the community.

Being (In)Considerate, (Dis)Respectful, (Im)Polite

Many everyday linguistic practices beyond addressing contribute to creating social landscapes, to situating people more or less satisfactorily with respect to one another. Erving Goffman developed the important idea of *facework*: each of us balances our own idea of who we are and want to be with others' acceptance or rejection of our presentations of ourselves.[20] Respect or consideration for another, *politeness* in a broad sense, is in part a matter of helping that other person 'save' face, of supporting their claim to relative freedom of action and to a modicum of positive regard (or at least absence of overt dislike or hostility). It's a matter of considering one another's feelings. If I'm impeded in going about my business, I might expect an apology or the use of 'softening' expressions like *please*. Or I might be mollified by someone's expression of interest in my welfare – "I didn't want you to trip on that curb" – or at least be gratified by a *thanks* or some other expression of appreciation. Politeness or respect in this broad theoretical sense does not require particular 'magic' words or special 'formality' – a shared joke or reference to a shared past experience or even an appreciative burp may, in the right circumstances, show consideration for another. There has been an explosion of research on these topics in recent decades. There have been many articles, books, and conferences about (im)politeness since the early 1970s and there is now even a *Journal of Politeness Research*. There are, of course, nonlinguistic practices that figure in politeness, but my focus here is on linguistic dimensions of attention to one another's 'face' during face-to-face interactions.

I have emphasized that the same linguistic form may have very different effects in different contexts. Addressing someone by first name is friendly and considerate in some contexts and hostile and rude in others – the Mississippi policeman insisting on Dr. Poussaint's first name was deliberately demeaning him. That means, of course, that just observing first-name address in different interactions will not reliably sort those that are respectful from those that are not. You cannot just ignore contexts and count particular forms. But this does not mean that quantitative investigations of politeness are ruled out. It is not easy to develop sensible and reliable measures of respect or considerateness, but it is indeed possible. Measures will change over time, and, crucially, they will need to be adjusted for different kinds of interactions in different sorts of contexts. Linguistic patterns over the course of an interaction and across many distinct interactions in particular *kinds* of contexts can, however, be very revealing if analyzed with care. I ask readers to bear with me as I explain some details of an important study that I think illustrates well how this can be done.

A nine-member team of Stanford linguists, psychologists, and computer scientists have developed one possible approach.[21] The co-Principal Investigators on the MacArthur Foundation grant that provided major funding for the research were Jennifer Eberhardt, a social psychologist whose groundbreaking work on unconscious bias I mentioned earlier, and Dan Jurafsky, a computational linguist, both of whom have received MacArthur 'genius' awards. Rob Voigt, just completing his PhD in linguistics, was lead author of the paper reporting their results.

The team conducted a very careful and revealing 'big data' study of language used by Oakland police to community members in the course of 981 actual traffic stops during April 2014; there were 245 different officers involved and there were 682 black and 299 white motorists stopped. The data set used consisted of anonymized transcriptions of 183 hours of body-camera recordings, transcriptions that included no information on place of the stop or on race or gender of the person stopped; there were a total of 36,738 officer utterances that could be analyzed.

This is a huge amount of material, far more than could be dealt with by human analysts without computational assistance. So the strategy was first to explore assessments of a relatively small set (414) of randomly selected utterances. A group of 70 human raters each read and rated 60 of these utterances, and every utterance got evaluated by at least 10 of the raters. It turns out that human beings rate interactants' speech reliably and consistently on *respect* and on *formality*. (Being polite, friendly, impartial, and respectful all patterned together and were thus bundled together under the umbrella of respect. Formality, which decreased over the course of interactions, was independent of respect.) Using this (relatively limited) data, the research team found that respect shown to white motorists was significantly higher than that shown to black motorists, controlling for the age and (apparent) gender identity of the motorists. But the research group did not stop there.

These initial results and data from the first stage of the inquiry were used to create an accurate model of which linguistic features of utterances contributed to judgments of respect and how much each feature counted, its relative 'weight.' Drawing on previous linguistic research on politeness, researchers examined the 414 sample utterances and came up with such features as *apology* ("sorry to stop you"), *formal title* ("ma'am"), and *introduction* ("my name's Officer …") as counting toward respect and features such as *first name*, *informal title* ("my man"), and *negative words* ("it's showing *suspended*") as counting against it. (The "keep your hands on the steering wheel" injunction quoted in the subtitle for this chapter was the weightiest feature for showing *dis*respect – i.e., it had the highest negative coefficient.) Each feature could be assigned a positive or negative number that constituted its *Respect Model Coefficient*, and then each utterance could be given an overall *Respect Score*, positive or negative, that resulted from adding up all the coefficients in the utterance. Crucially, the scoring system was tested on the 414 human-rated utterances of the first study and refined until computer rankings reliably matched those of the human raters.

Once that stage was complete, the researchers could set computers to assign ratings over the entire corpus, which accounted for over two-thirds of the traffic stops during that particular April. Not only did they repeat the finding that officers were significantly less respectful to black than to white community members. They were also able to show that this result was not a function of the officer's race, nor could it be attributed to disrespect from a handful of "bad apples." As important as the findings from this particular study, the tools the Stanford team have developed can continue to be used. For example, their method can be used to assess the effectiveness of officer training programs aimed at eliminating such race-driven 'respect gaps.'

I doubt if any of the Oakland officers sounded like the Mississippi policeman with his repeated *boy* and his insistence on *Alvin* rather than *Dr. Poussaint*. Nonetheless, like many of us, they used addressing and other everyday linguistic practices to position some community members as less 'worthy' and 'deserving' of respect than others. And, like many of us, they probably were quite unaware of these subtle but significant differences in their linguistic actions.

As we will see in the next chapter, speakers do not only lower (or raise) others' positions when addressing them directly. Speakers may, for example, 'put down' absent others through enlisting their present direct audience as allies when speaking of those absent in negative ways.

Notes

1. The title of this chapter is drawn from Voigt et al. 2017, a study of police talking to community members during traffic stops that is discussed in the final section of this chapter.
2. Poussaint 1991 [1967], pp. 130–131.

3. In a book in progress on addressing practices and their connections to the law, tentatively titled *Call Forth*, legal scholar Richard Brooks has an extensive and insightful discussion of *boy* as an address form for adult men.

4. Kukla and Lance 2009.

5. Parrott 2010, n. 20, 217.

6. Brown and Gilman 1960.

7. Bodine 1975.

8. Alber 2019.

9. Linguist Heather Burnett, herself an immigrant to Paris from Québec, told me that she thinks "a real serious research project going deeper into the use, interpretation and evolution of T/V in [different] varieties of French" is needed.

10. Raymond 2016.

11. Holland Cotter, "A Memorial to the Lingering Horror of Lynching," *The New York Times*, June 1, 2018, www.nytimes.com/2018/06/01/arts/design/national-memorial-for-peace-and-justice-montgomery-alabama.html.

12. Wales 1983.

13. "Why Did We Stop Using 'Thou'?" *Merriam-Webster*, n.d, www.merriam-webster.com/words-at-play/why-did-we-stop-using-thou.

14. See McConnell-Ginet 2003 (reprinted in McConnell-Ginet 2011) for more on gender both in T/V systems and in English-language address and reference.

15. Thanks to Cornell Professor Anne V. Adams for drawing the generic *Mr. Charlie* and *Miz Ann* pairing to my attention. With (white) parents named Charlie and Anne, I found myself confronting this symbolic couple with considerable discomfort.

16. Gates 1989.

17. Cited in Collins 1998, pp. 80–81.

18. Adams 2008. Quote from p. 207.

19. Adams 2009. Quote from p. 81.

20. Especially in Goffman 1967.

21. The research is described in much more detail and more technically in Voigt et al. 2017.

5   Putting Down: "[They] Aren't People – They're Animals"

In the early morning of Saturday, October 27, 2018, a gunman entered the Tree of Life Synagogue in the Squirrel Hill section of Pittsburgh, PA, shouting "All Jews must die" and killed thirteen worshippers, also wounding several other congregants and police officers. On the right-wing social media Gab platform a couple of days before the killing, the young man had indicated that he faulted Trump for failing to identify Jews as responsible for bringing immigrants into the US. "Trump is a globalist [a word historically often used to designate Jews], not a nationalist. There is no #MAGA as long as there is a kike infestation." Shortly before going into the synagogue, the gunman posted on Gab:

> HIAS [an American organization begun in 1881 to aid Jewish refugees and now supporting refugees from many different places] likes to bring invaders [he had elsewhere applauded those who thought of replacing 'illegals' by 'invaders' in referring to people attempting to immigrate to the US] that kill our people. I can't sit by and watch my people get slaughtered, screw your optics I'm going in.

The police who apprehended the gunman at the synagogue reported that he said that "he wanted all Jews to die" and also that he said that Jewish people "were committing genocide to his people."[1] It was gunshots that killed the worshippers, but the gunman's vitriolic anti-Semitic and anti-immigrant rhetoric preceded his gunfire and was used to 'justify' it, rhetoric echoing the increasing flood of such vicious name-calling and smearing by white nationalists.

This virulently anti-Semitic young gunman seemed to think that Donald Trump might be too sympathetic to Jewish people (as Trump points out, his daughter Ivanka and his son-in-law, Jared

135

Kushner, are Jewish). Nonetheless, in 2016 candidate Trump
depicted Hillary Clinton next to a pile of money and a six-pointed
star, familiar tropes evoking Jews, along with the label "most
corrupt candidate ever." The "MAGA" ("Make America Great
Again") slogan his campaign popularized has been intertwined
with increasingly overt anti-Semitic and anti-immigrant language, especially though not only online. Donald Trump is not
personally responsible for the Pittsburgh synagogue attack. Anti-
Semitism and other forms of racism do, however, feed on the kind
of name-calling that he and his supporters (and also some of his
opponents) indulge in.

Such demonizing linguistic practices are often dubbed *hate
speech*, but that notion has proved hard to pin down and has
sometimes been (mis)used to silence journalists or dissidents.
Susan Benesch and her colleagues offer instead a definition of
dangerous speech: "Any form of expression (e.g., speech, text, or
images) that can increase the risk that its audience will condone or
commit violence against members of another group."[2] The
Dangerous Speech Project (DSP) began in 2010 and not only
analyzes what it identifies as dangerous speech from around the
globe but works on developing effective counterspeech strategies
of various kinds to lessen the dangers. Readers may well wonder,
however, whether 'just words' (or even inert images) can indeed
lead to violence.

"Words Will Never Hurt Me"

"Sticks and stones may break my bones but words will never hurt
me." Children, including me, used to chant this in a singsong
when I was growing up. It's been around a long time. An early
citation comes from an American periodical with a largely black
audience, *The Christian Recorder*, March 1862: "Remember the
old adage, 'Sticks and stones will break my bones, but words will
never harm me.' True courage consists in doing what is right,
despite the jeers and sneers of our companions."[3] With a different

audience and for a quite different purpose, the late Justice Antonin Scalia recited a version of the lines during the course of the Supreme Court hearing in the mid-1990s case of *Schenk v. Pro-choice Network*. "Sticks and stones will break my bones, but words can never hurt me ... That's the First Amendment."[4]

The chant is still heard in some schoolyards, I'm told. Since the protective chant often accompanies tears brought on by some bully's taunts, its message is blatantly false. Yet many derisive memes incorporating the slogan circulate, including satirical endorsements that advise throwing a dictionary at those reciting it. Labels like *snowflake* are used to make fun of people expressing concern over name-calling. Snowflakes melt easily and are said to be uniquely beautiful. The metaphor is used to label those, generally on the left politically, expressing hurt or offense at others' words, and to suggest that they are self-preoccupied 'babies.' There is a widespread sense that we should not let others' words harm us, that doing so is a sign of thin-skinned weakness.

Widespread and tempting though this view might be, it is deeply problematic. There are indeed distinctions to be made between relatively minor insults made on a one-off basis and language like that used by the synagogue attacker. In most everyday American English usage, *slur* applies to any insulting or demeaning language that targets either a group or an individual. In recent work on hostile linguistic practices, philosophers of language and linguists have tended to reserve *slur* for expressions that act like derogatory or demeaning labels for particular racial and ethnic groups. On the model of *N-word* as a substitute for one of the most potent and widely discussed of such slurs, I will speak of *S-words* as a special category of slurring language, enforcing and maintaining socially structured subordination.

Like *N-word*, *S-word* allows me to avoid excessive mention of particular offensive forms, although I will mention some in order to illustrate more vividly the phenomena I discuss. As I said in the introduction to the book, linguists and philosophers of language distinguish *mentioning* words, which I do, for example, in quoting others (like the synagogue shooter), from *using* them, as do those quoted (the shooter used a highly offensive S-word designating Jewish people, which I then quoted). As I mentioned in opening this book, there are good reasons for minimizing as much as possible even mentions of these S-words so I will try to do so as well as I can while still being clear.[5]

Many minor insults can readily be laughed off by most targets. Tossing some potential insults back and forth can in fact positively strengthen social ties in some communities. And we will see later in this chapter that even the more deeply corrosive S-words can sometimes be reclaimed or reappropriated by those targeted. Nonetheless words can indeed be potent weapons. Words in and of themselves do not break bones or kill, of course. They do, however, not only often inflict serious psychic damage on their target. They frequently also pave the way for and contribute significantly to non-linguistic actions that may indeed break bones as well as have many other corrosive material effects. This is what the Dangerous Speech Project is about. Name-callers can be emboldened and their linguistic acts can encourage, indeed incite, observers and others not only to join in the name-calling but to escalate attacks on those targeted by the names. Over and over, we find lethal physical assault like that in the October 2018 synagogue mass killing both preceded and accompanied by verbal viciousness.

Malevolent Metaphorical Moves

"Genocidal language games" is how philosopher Lynne Tirrell titled her compelling but deeply disturbing account of the linguistic landscape of Rwanda in the early 1990s.[6] Tirrell is not the first to see language as having played a central role in the mass killings of the Tutsi minority by the majority Hutu. Two powerful quotations open her discussion. "The road to genocide in Rwanda was paved with hate speech."[7] "Words have killed my country."[8] Of course the words were not the whole story, but many have convincingly argued that they played an important role.

Although the focus of Tirrell's account and of my discussion here is the use of subordinating slurs, other less obviously problematic linguistic practices were also vital in sharpening and strengthening the bipolar division of the Rwandan population on which subsequent group-based insults and eventual violence depended. In 1933, Belgian colonialists instituted mandatory ethnic identity cards for Rwandans, rigidifying and emphasizing distinctions between *Hutu* and *Tutsi* that had been far more fluid and invested with much less significance before colonialization. These group labels existed before, but they were less woven into social and political practice. Having to attach an ethnic category label to oneself and to have that category used by the government in various ways heightened the importance attached to that categorization. This emphasis on ethnic labeling made much more difficult the earlier apparent relative elasticity of the boundaries between the groups. André Sibomana, a moderate Hutu journalist and Catholic priest, put it this way. "The differences had always been there. The whites conceptualized and froze them. The extremists turned them into a political program. This was the fatal mechanism on which our country had embarked."[9] Now we will look at the vitriolic metaphorical names that essentially replaced fairly bland labels like *Tutsi* in discourse generated by the extremist Hutu governmental elite.

Before the Rwandan genocide of 1994, a few Hutu extremists began referring to ordinary and apolitical Tutsi using Kinyarwande *inyenzi*, 'cockroach.' That metaphorical label had first been applied to members of the Rwandan Patriotic Front (RPF), a small organized militia of Tutsi seeking to oust the Hutu political leaders who had forced so many Tutsi out of the country as part of the "1959 Revolution." (The RPF used the Kinyarwande *inkotanyi*, 'invincibles,' to dub themselves.) Like the insects invoked by Hutu extremists to name them, the RPF came out at night and were hard to catch. The *inyenzi* label was then extended to all Tutsi in radio broadcasts at the urging of the extremist and virulently anti-Tutsi political elite who dominated the Hutu-led government. Later the term *inzoka*, 'snake,' was also pressed into service.

Initially, these labels were used almost exclusively in all-Hutu contexts, in the absence of their Tutsi targets. They were used, for example, in 'animation sessions' designed by an extremist group within the Hutu leadership to increase the 'us' vs 'them' divide and to spur ordinary Hutu people into murderous violence. Radio and other media also urged the Hutu to wipe out *inyenzi* and *inzoka*, reminding them that they knew exactly how to kill those horrible pests. And indeed the implements for killing neighbors were very often exactly the same as those used for ridding one's home of pests.

Metaphors use language from one domain to talk about another. In this case, hearers were invited to view other people, their Tutsi neighbors, as (if they were) cockroaches or snakes. This was preparation for urging destruction of an entire group, now presented as extermination rather than murder. Using nonhuman metaphors (and also similes comparing people to disgusting or dangerous creatures) is a common tactic for rousing animus against others, for creating and deepening 'us' vs 'them' ill will. They can help turn neighbors into enemies, into threats to one's own well-being. They also suggest certain actions to be taken against these 'enemies,' in this case, the same kinds of actions that might be used to rid oneself of nonhuman annoyances.[10]

It is common to talk about this kind of speech as 'dehumanizing' and to locate its very real and very ugly power in its leading people to see those so labeled as not human. The 'dehumanizing' account of such toxic speech is often accompanied by what philosopher Kate Manne dubs 'humanism,' the optimistic notion that to see others as human, as much more like us than like other kinds of animals, will predispose us to act kindly or at least not viciously toward them.[11] Manne argues, persuasively in my view, that human beings' cruelty toward one another usually crucially depends on thinking of those others *as* humans. The regrettable truth is that humans *do* sometimes seek to subordinate or conquer or punish or shame. Those are actions that really only make sense directed toward humans. Names hurt only humans, the linguistic species among animals. You generally need something more like sticks and stones to hurt nonhuman creatures. The nonhuman metaphorical labels do indeed 'otherize,' emphasizing a view of their targets as 'beneath' the labelers, deserving of contempt. They move them into an enemy camp, not worthy of friendship or respect. The labeler, as it were, dresses the target in snakeskin and says "Beware of this snake-like person out to harm me and mine, eradicate them before they eradicate you." They engage others in allying with them to resist the threat supposedly posed to the labelers and to their 'friends,' their 'in-group,' by the labeled targets. There is undoubtedly much more to be said about how such nonhuman metaphors work and why they are such a frequent feature of dangerous speech. Unfortunately, however, people have demonstrated for millennia all-too-human propensities to harm one another in order to claim or preserve power or privilege. These labels do not so much dehumanize as they subordinate, stoke resentment, and seek to transform others not into *non*humans but into *lesser* humans, fundamentally the same species but of a different and inferior kind.

Nazi rhetoric from the days of the Third Reich and World War II (WWII) offers many examples.[12] Hitler in 1939 says, "We shall exterminate the Jews" and describes Jews as "an inferior race that multiplies like vermin." The term *Untermensch*, 'subhuman,' was common in Nazi rhetoric. In a 1943 speech Himmler declares, "Anti-Semitism is exactly the same as delousing. Getting rid of lice is not a question of ideology. It is a matter of cleanliness." And it wasn't just the Nazis. Chase Clark, then governor of Idaho, joined in the WWII-era vilification of those of Japanese descent. "Japs live like rats, breathe like rats, and act like rats."[13] (*Japs*, of course, was itself already a non-metaphorical slurring label. Truncating a standard label, in this case, *Japanese*, is a common way in which English speakers create forms for name-calling purposes.) Having breathed in some of the anti-German rhetoric of my early WWII childhood, I reportedly scolded someone sneezing near me: "Use a handkerchief or I'll catch your Germans."

Nonhuman metaphors for people continue. In 2016 three Kansas men were convicted of a plot to bomb a mosque and kill Somali Muslim refugees; on tape, the men often spoke of their targets as "cockroaches."[14] On Wednesday, 16 May, 2018, President Donald Trump, speaking to a group of California law-enforcement officials sympathetic to his tightening immigration policy, bluntly proclaimed that (some) immigrants "aren't people – they're animals."[15] As noted by the Dangerous Speech Project, words from the president of the US or anyone with significant power, influence, or charisma are likely to have heightened impact, making their speech potentially especially dangerous. A couple of weeks later, the very popular TV show *Roseanne* was abruptly canceled in response to a tweet from its star, Roseanne Barr. Barr had used *ape* to label Valerie Jarrett, a black American woman who had worked closely with former President Barack Obama. Nonhuman metaphoric labels remain particularly powerful for separating 'them' from 'us.'

What is clear from Rwanda and from many other contexts is that designating people using labels primarily reserved for unpleasant nonhuman organisms can not only assault and injure the people so labeled, subordinate them as inferior kinds of people. It can, importantly, also display contempt for them, whether or not they are present, to an audience being potentially recruited as allied haters – and sometimes, ultimately, as agents who will carry out mass destruction of the targeted group.

Of course it is also true that those labeled are often seriously harmed when nasty labels are attached to them. Tirrell recounts a story from a Tutsi father whose three-year-old daughter was extremely upset when she heard someone speak of her using *inzoka*, 'snake'. Such appellations don't bother only children. They can and do inflict significant harm on targets of any age. I will talk a little more later about these direct harms to targets, of which there are many first-person accounts.[16] What I want to emphasize here, however, is what I'll call the "infectious" character of such name-calling, the social contagion it fosters. (Tirrell herself has spoken about "toxic" speech in the contemporary US, and a 1985 paper on effects of slurs beyond their targets is sub-titled "How to Spread a Social Disease."[17]) It is not only unpleasant metaphors like those used for the Tutsi that can have such infectious properties.

Escalating Language Games

"Befehl ist Befehl," said many German soldiers when accounting for their role in the mass murder of some 6 million Jews and of many others, including some 25 percent of Europe's Roma people as well as many people stigmatized as gay men or lesbians. English speakers have used the equivalent "an order is an order" to evade responsibility for heinous actions they have been ordered to perform.

Ordering is one of many *speech acts*, things people do with words in their utterances.[18] Not just anyone can order anyone else to do anything at all. In spite of my agreeing with Kate Manne that human beings do indeed lash out at one another as other human beings, I do think they usually only do so if they have what strike them as justifications for their actions or if they are lashing out in rage or fear. Most human beings do not randomly rape or torture or kill others. They do so to show their power over the other, to express anger at the other, to discipline, to intimidate. But it need not be the individual 'other' who provides such motives – it can be the 'other' as a member of a social identity group. Being ordered or even just strongly encouraged to harm another human being usually requires those issuing the directives to be in positions of significant power or authority over those being directed – or to provide them with motives. Unless I'm already predisposed to inflict the harm being proposed, seeing it perhaps as deserved revenge, I am not likely to set off to do so just because someone suggests I do. Of course, if I'm in the military and a superior is issuing a directive to me, I will probably obey – and if I do not, there will almost certainly be a cost to me, some kind of punishment. Other institutionalized relations also often carry enforcement potential: parent–child, teacher–student, employer–employee, or bureaucrat–citizen provide examples. Virtually any asymmetric relationship can do the trick. Sheer size and strength can intimidate and help people succeed in getting orders obeyed.

The most effective way to get help in harm-inflicting projects, however, is to get potential helpers to adopt those projects as 'their own.' War and genocide are usually made to happen by leaders' enlisting many willing participants to attack those targeted. Ordering as such becomes unnecessary, or at least of minor importance. There are many linguistic practices that support such efforts – for example, propaganda campaigns – but name-calling is an important one. In the Rwandan case, the names themselves urged the ordinary Hutu to see their Tutsi neighbors in a new light, as human enemies of whom they needed to rid themselves by killing them 'as if' they were snakes or cockroaches. The widespread use of these metaphors helped make that inherently murderous perspective seem 'normal' to many ordinary Hutu, who began to find orders to kill their neighbors, often completely implicit ("You know how to rid your territory of cockroaches"), all too easy to obey.

Nasty nonhuman metaphors, though highly effective, are not essential for transforming the relatively neutral indifference of one social group to another targeted group into dislike and often contempt. Any social identity label can become poisoned. Link dislike with fear, and it becomes easy to move on to loathing and blame for imagined ills. What may begin as essentially nonengagement can all too quickly transmute into potential deadly assault if fanned by those standing to benefit most from decisive subordination or even elimination of the targeted group. Names for social groups that start life as relatively innocuous category labels can accrue a large and dangerous baggage through histories of problematic deployment.

As I noted earlier, Tirrell draws on a game metaphor in her account of the linguistic practices that contributed to the

Rwandan genocide. In doing so, she notes that philosopher Ludwig Wittgenstein introduced this way of thinking and talking about linguistic interaction. Interrelated linguistic actions like "giving orders and obeying them" are the sorts of practices that Wittgenstein considers language games. Name-calling practices, as Tirrell demonstrates, can also be considered language games. "[T]he term 'language-*game*' is meant," Wittgenstein said, "to bring into prominence the fact that the *speaking* [and, of course, also the *hearing*] of language is part of an activity, or of a form of life."[19] Some analysts have drawn not just on the informal Wittgensteinian idea of language games but on mathematical game theory to talk about various kinds of linguistic practices, including the use of slurring group names, of S-words.[20]

As part of a larger work on addressing, legal scholar Richard Brooks argues that "cursing" in the sense of hurling racial epithets may help solve what game theorists call a 'coordination' problem.[21] As he explains, someone considering an act of nonverbal violence knows there is less risk involved if others join in. Their public *verbal* violence, the name-calling, not only diminishes the target's status in beholders' eyes but also indicates to those beholders that they would not be alone in attacking. If a potential physical attacker's verbal violence goes unchallenged, is perhaps even copied, then the potential attacker has more reason to think that an actual physical attack can be mounted with impunity. Empirically, Brooks shows, verbal violence often precedes nonverbal violence. To do so, he draws on data gathered by the Atrocities Documentation Survey conducted among refugees in Chad who had experienced attacks in Darfur from Janjaweed militia or Sudanese government forces, sometimes both. Reports included detailed accounts of racial epithets preceding and often during rape and other kinds of sexualized violence, beatings and knifings, whippings and brandings, setting people afire, and similar acts aimed at wiping out the Darfuri.

Word 'games' pour fuel on the sticks and add weight to the stones.

S-Words Nearer to My Home

In the US these days the highly offensive *nigger* is the most widely discussed and publicly censured of the S-words. It is often called the N-word or the N-bomb, or written n****r, or supposedly disguised in some other way. The disguised versions are used in order to mention the strongly tabooed word, to avoid even *seeming* to use it. Even the disguised versions, however, readily evoke the word and for many, especially those who might be targets, they also evoke its deeply difficult history and its often corrosive effects. There are a number of publications, including several books, devoted to discussing the long history of the N-word, its diverse uses, and controversies surrounding it.[22] And in late 2018 the *Washington Post* launched the N-Word Project,[23] inviting a number of pairs of people to discuss different questions that have been raised about the word. (Some of the pairs are interracial but most have two black or two white people; all the discussions I have watched and listened to were very thoughtful.) According to the online site for the N-Word Project, the N-word was tweeted 500,000 times daily in 2014, and in 2018 the National Football League (NFL) proposed banning its use on the football field.

I have spoken of *the* N-word, but sociolinguist Arthur Spears argues that there are two distinct words, one of which is spelled (and pronounced) without an 'r,' either *nigga* or *niggah*. The latter form is frequently used among members of black communities, the targets of the N-word, often in address, for something like bonding. In these uses, it is much like *bro* or *dude*.[24] (Sociolinguist Geneva Smitherman distinguishes a number of different senses with which this latter r-less form is used among African Americans.[25] It is sometimes used negatively, she suggests, and in such uses can target people of any race.) The bonding address is sometimes used among white people or from white people to their black friends. Some people, however, argue that only in very special circumstances are white people licensed to use the form. As philosopher Luvell Anderson puts it, white people lack the necessary community standing to claim full 'addressing' status.[26] That status derives from personal community ties and from connections to the relevant social and linguistic history. Such ties and connections are rare indeed for people who are not socially identified as black. (They do occur. For example, black football players sometimes build ties with white teammates that allow for reciprocal use of the 'bonding' variant, at least in locker-room and some on-the-playing-field contexts.) For convenience, however, I will call this 'bonding' form the *target* variant, because its primary use is among those who are targets or potential referents of the N-word. I will call the 'demeaning' usage with the (written but often unpronounced) *r*, the *slur* variant. It is usually the target 'bonding' variant that occurs in rap and hip-hop.

Given that both forms can have the same pronunciation and originate from a common source, many are understandably reluctant to speak of two different words. A sizeable number of people, both black Americans and white Americans, would like to see both variants disappear. They argue that the target variant is inevitably tainted by the slur use and its oppressive history. They are skeptical that target uses really are insulated from the corrosive effects so evident in the slur uses. Some note that other racial and ethnic epithets do not have target uses like those of the N-word. (It is quite true that there are none with such widespread and well-known target-group uses, but there are instances of appropriation of other social slurs for some purposes. I discuss some cases in a later section.) I quite agree that it can be very difficult to separate uses, but it also seems evident that, especially among younger people, what I'm calling the target variant often has positive value.

In their wonderfully informative *Articulate While Black: Barack Obama, Language, and Race in the US*, sociolinguists H. Samy Alim and Geneva Smitherman set out some of the sources of controversy about the target variant among African Americans.[27]

> Whereas *nigga* has a long history of use within the confines of the Black community, a new generation has boldly made this language

> reclamation project a matter of public record. . . . Few, if any,
> Blacks, regardless of age or social station, would claim that the
> term has not been widely used in Black social contexts. Their
> objection is that a new generation has taken the community's term
> to the public, in prime time, and to the furthest corners of the
> globe.

There is, of course, much more to be said both about the target
variant and about its increasing public presence. What I focus on in
the rest of this section, however, is the slurring variant of the N-word.

With the *r*, whether pronounced or not, the slurring N-word is
certainly not only associated with highly negative stereotypes of
black people. It is also very closely tied to a history of name-calling
practices embedded in social structures and practices that keep
institutionalized racism alive and all too well in the US. Calling
someone that name now brings into play, makes highly salient, an
incompletely acknowledged history of slavery, lynchings, Jim
Crow laws, continuing discrimination in housing, education,
jobs, incarceration, and more. As one of the discussants on the
N-Word Project noted, this was the last word many heard before
dying at the hands of a lynch mob. And that history is coupled
with the kind of everyday racism experienced by black people in
the US that leads to the police being summoned when black
people are simply going about their business but somehow inspiring fear in white observers: waiting to meet someone at Starbucks,
barbecuing for a family picnic in a public park, leaving an Airbnb
carrying luggage in a middle-class neighborhood, napping. Phillip
Atiba Goff notes the danger of a police officer's being "deputized
as a personal racism valet" by the white complainant who thinks
with no evidence other than problematic assumptions that these
black people are up to no good.[28] It is no wonder then that finding
the N-word spray-painted in front of a church with an African
American congregation, or on the door of a black sorority, is not
only profoundly disturbing. Such (slurring) N-word uses also fit
into and help support the broader continuing subordination of
black Americans.

Black Americans who call white Americans by names like *cracker* or *honky* or *redneck* can certainly succeed in insulting or offending. They cannot, however, thereby subordinate their targets, force those targets below themselves. Such terms used by other white people can and sometimes do subordinate their targets. Institutionalized racism, however, limits the kind of putting down they can do to white targets when issued by black people. There are a number of linguistic actions that can only achieve their goals if speakers are properly positioned institutionally. A couple in front of me actually becomes legally married when I say "I now declare you legally married" only if I have the proper kind of license from the appropriate governmental authorities. On the other hand virtually anyone can say "I'm sleepy" and thereby describe their current state. Whether they achieve additional desired effects such as being offered a comfortable bed in which to lie will depend on various factors, including their relation to the addressee and other features of the context in which they commit themselves to the proffered description. Name-calling that subordinates works more like marrying than like describing. That is, subordinating insults, S-words, require systematic social support.

Some of the few empirical studies available suggest that slurring N-words and other racial and ethnic S-words are used more often in the absence of those who are their potential referents than hurled directly at targets.[29] S-words used in speaking of people of a particular social group can function to ally people who have some inclination to view themselves as properly 'above' members of that group and sometimes to turn those perhaps relatively faint inclinations into stronger dispositions. S-words typically carry with them a history of the sometimes casual, sometimes rabid, bigotry that their primary users have embraced. As use of the Kinyarwande terms in Rwanda illustrates so vividly, these epithets help fuel fear and hatred of those targeted by the epithets among the group who uses them. There is a kind of contagion effect as language publicizes affiliation with those who see themselves as properly superior to the target group, making such down-putting stances less risky to embrace for others who might have been waiting to see how sentiments were tending.

Using an S-word, even in the absence of potential targets, allies the user with the community of those who use that S-word and with their distinctive subordinating perspectives,[30] their often supremacist ideologies,[31] and their contempt for those targets.[32] S-words that are widely used may have a much more diffuse range of perspectives and ideologies associated with them than those used only within relatively small communities. Linguist Geoff Nunberg notes that there are, for example, many quite different slurs for black Americans, some now very out-dated.[33] Their nonequivalence, he argues, needs to be explained. He proposes that their distinctive significance derives from the distinctive attitudes and practices among the community of those who use (or did use) them. Those using an S-word are self-affiliating with a restricted community of its users, who share certain derogatory attitudes toward the word's target group. (Such self-affiliation is not attributed to very young children or nonnative speakers who mistakenly think the S-word the default.) We interpret an S-word as demeaning its targets because we recognize the community of those using it as contemptuous of those targets in some way or other and recognize the user as thereby affiliating themselves with that contempt-bearing community. As Nunberg puts it, "In a nut-shell: racists don't use slurs because they're derogative; slurs are derogative because they're the words that racists use."

Nunberg suggests that S-words are not special in announcing their users' affiliation with a community of like-minded folk on some issue where there is disagreement. For example, whether one says *pro-life* or *anti-abortion* lines one up on one side or the other of the debate over abortion. He calls all such words *pre-judicials*. Just using them announces a speaker's point of view, their ideological stance. Viewing S-words and other slurs in this way makes it clear why their damage is by no means confined to pain they cause their targets.

In emphasizing the potential 'infectious' properties of slurs, I do not want to minimize the direct harm they can inflict on their targets, especially though not only when they are called by such names. "These epithets come down to our generation weighted with hatreds accumulated through centuries of bloodshed." These words came from Justice Robert H. Jackson, dissenting from a federal court's refusal to recognize the need for protection from racist speech.[34] Langston Hughes pointed to that history and to its continuing effects in his 1940 memoir *The Big Sea*.

> The word *nigger* sums up for us who are colored all the bitter years of insult and struggle in America: the slave-beatings of yesterday, the lynchings of today, the Jim Crow cars . . . the restaurants where you may not eat, the jobs you may not have, the unions you cannot join. The word *nigger* in the mouths of little white boys at school, the word *nigger* in the mouth of the foreman at the job, the word *nigger* across the whole face of America! *Nigger! Nigger!*[35]

And lest we think such responses to the N-word are just historical artifacts, here is what fifteen-year-old Chet Ellis, son of writer Trey Ellis, had to say in the spring of 2017 about hearing another student just 'mention' and not even 'use' the word in one of his classes.

> She said that on the sign [being held by a student from another school] was written "Warde High School has N******s," except she used the actual word. In US History class. In our 92.6% white Fairfield County suburb. My body froze. Time stopped. I never did hear the end of her story. The air became viscous and the tension in the room felt palpable. . . . I knew the student hadn't used the word in a malicious way, but the response from my body was primal. The N-word is a word that takes African Americans back to 1619 on the tobacco fields of Jamestown and the very beginning of the tragedy of human enslavement. It reminds us of Jim Crow, of the senseless beating of Rodney King, and of the killings of 258 black people by the police in 2016. Nevertheless, several of my white friends want to use the N-word in recounting their favorite lyrics. Others even claim that keeping them from saying it is some

form of reverse racism. They, like the student in my class, don't
understand how the word takes my breath away.[36]

So it is quite clear that the (slurring) N-word continues to have
visceral effects on potential targets, even if it is mouthed by someone quoting another, just 'mentioned.' There are substantial bodily
effects that are part of the general psychological damage the N-
word (and other potent slurs) can inflict.

At the same time, investing the N-word as such with magically
evil powers is deeply problematic. Not only has this led to absurd
moves like removing *Huckleberry Finn*, written in a far different
era, from library shelves or firing teachers who tried to engage
their students in discussion of the word like the exchanges filmed
by the N-Word Project. It has also encouraged people in positions
of power to leap on and immediately fire – with lots of public
fanfare accompanying dismissals – any and all of their underlings
who might utter the word, no matter what the circumstances.
Don't misunderstand. Firing might well be an appropriate
response in many situations. The real difficulty is that those so
responding often use swift punishment of the N-bomb hurler or
other such high-profile actions as irrefutable evidence of their
own committed anti-racism and more general moral uprightness.
They then view themselves as having loudly and clearly signaled
their anti-racism. They don't notice or see any need to look for
and try to dislodge more mundane kinds of racism (and sexism
and other kinds of unfair social arrangements) – an all-white
group telling and laughing at racist jokes, different handling of
Jamal's and Erik's applications and promotions, assuming that the
office cleaner's work is worth only a fraction of a percentage as
much as the executive's, and on and on. And, of course, few if any
of the white Americans crusading to wipe out N-word production
understand the complexities and varieties of uses among African
Americans.

In an opinion piece published in the *New York Times* on
September 7, 2019, Walter Mosley, a novelist who was also one
of the writers for *Snowfall*, an American crime drama series, tells

readers about his experience shortly after he had signed on to write scripts for another show on another network.[37] He had recounted to his colleagues stories of an LA cop he'd met who said that he "stopped all niggers in paddy neighborhoods and all paddies in nigger neighborhoods, because they were usually up to no good." One of those colleagues later complained to the Human Relations Office that Mosley's uttering that word in telling that story of his experience made them "uncomfortable." When HR called Mosley to say that they'd been told he'd "used the N-word in the writers' room," he responded "I *am* the N-word in the writers' room." But he was told he could not utter the word, only write it in a script. "I couldn't use that word in common parlance, even to express an experience I lived through. There I was, a black man in America who shares with millions of others the history of racism. . . . If addressed at all, that history had to be rendered in words my employers regarded as acceptable. There I was being chastised for criticizing the word that oppressed me and mine for centuries." The discomfort of a fragile white colleague trumped Mosley's right to describe his experiences effectively. He resigned.

The N-word matters. It matters, however, because both use and mentioning of the word are embedded in a complex array of social practices, many of which continue to sustain race-based privilege and advantage for white people. And just how it matters has changed over time and depends on who is using or mentioning it in which contexts.

Native American Team Names and Mascots: "In Whose Honor?"

Many Americans are probably aware of the ongoing controversy over the use in sports of names and other cultural references from the history of indigenous people of the Americas. The highest profile case has been the ongoing attempt to get the professional Washington, DC NFL team to stop calling itself the *Redskins*. The name still had not changed in the summer of 2019, nor did it seem likely that the name would soon be retired. There are other professional sports teams with names evoking Native American history, for example, the Kansas City *Chiefs* and the Cleveland *Indians*. And there are many university, college, and high school sports teams with such names or mascots, though their numbers have significantly declined.

Protests over these team names and mascots are often associated with so-called 'political correctness' (PC), seen as oversensitivity of 'snowflakes' to linguistic choices. PC was supposedly introduced into American life beginning in the late 1960s by activism centered on social identity groups, so-called 'identity politics.' (In Chapter 7, I briefly discuss 'political correctness.') In this particular case, opposition has been led by tribal leaders and by a variety of indigenous-rights organizations.

Fred Veilleux, a Chippewa Indian from the Leech Lake band in Minnesota, published a powerful short piece in 1995 called "Indians Are a People, Not Mascots."[38] Veilleux offers a short introduction to the genocide perpetrated by European settlers on the indigenous peoples whose land they wanted. The term *red skins*, he notes, was originally quite literal, used to designate the scalps of native peoples, for which large rewards were offered. Veilleux also very effectively shows how the face-painting, costumes, and 'war dances' in which fans engage constitute parody and even sacrilege to Native Americans. As he notes, there would be loud protests if fans dressed up in papal regalia and "Ave Maria" was played on stadium organs whenever there was a score. He and others working with him did indeed succeed in getting many schools in Minnesota and beyond to abandon the Native American names, mascots, fake tomahawks, and the like they had been using. All too many, however, continue to ignore the testimony of Veilleux and other Indians of the extreme offensiveness of these fan practices, not only to adults but even more corrosively, in their effect on children.

Team owners and others who have resisted calls for change still frequently claim that these contested symbols are intended "to honor" Native Americans and celebrate their history. Whatever the intent might be or have been, the central question is the effect. *In Whose Honor?*, a 1997 award-winning documentary aired on PBS and still widely screened, focused on Charlene Teters, a Spokane Indian and then University of Illinois graduate student.[39] Teters clearly did not see these widespread practices as honoring her and her family. She launched a campaign to retire Illinois mascot Chief Illiniwek, who was officially ousted in 2007 but has continued unofficially (and apparently with at least some secret aid from university employees) to be a presence on the Champaign–Urbana campus. The NCAA (National Collegiate Athletic Association, to which any US-based college or university that wants to be involved in intercollegiate athletic competition must belong) had insisted that such symbols be retired, but later, in recognition of tribal sovereignty, allowed exceptions if, and only if, a school's namesake tribe approved.

In this case the Peoria, now located in Oklahoma, constitute the only federally recognized tribe of the Illinois (not, in fact, the Illini as sport fans at the university once thought). Jay Rosenstein, who produced *In Whose Honor?* and who has continued to be involved in the ongoing campus debates, recounts the story. In May of 2018, two trustees supporting the Chief's official return went to Oklahoma, seeking the blessing of the Peoria. They were faced instead with ringing condemnation.

> The image portrayed by Chief Illiniwek does not . . . honor the heritage of the Peoria Tribe . . . and is a degrading racial stereotype that reflects negatively on all American Indian people. The Peoria Tribe of Indians does not endorse or sanction . . . Chief Illiniwek as mascot for the University of Illinois, nor do they have any future plans to rescind the tribal resolution, which was approved by a unanimous vote.[40]

Redskins, in contrast to *Chiefs* or *Indians*, has been widely considered a slur since at least the 1940s. And beginning in the 1960s, some Native Americans began trying to get the DC team to change its name. Signing on as a pro bono expert in the 1990s in support of this movement was none other than linguist Geoff Nunberg, whose work on slurs I have already cited.[41] In the 1990s he did painstaking work in dictionaries, novels, and other sources to compare uses of *redskin* to those of the far more neutral (and far more frequent) label *Indian*. He found clear evidence that it was used "in contexts suggesting savagery, violence, and racial inferiority." In the early twenty-first century, however, it became possible to use computational tools and digitized source material for much larger-scale studies. These strengthened the earlier conclusions: "for every 'friendly redskin' there are 289 references to 'friendly Indian' but for every 'pesky/wily/crafty redskin' there are only 4.5 references to 'pesky/wily/crafty Indian.'" Given the far greater frequency of 'Indian' in the various sources he used, this is striking indeed.

Native American complainants got the TTAB (Trademark Trial and Appeal Board) of the US Patent Office to rule in June of 2014 that, as a derogatory word, *redskins* had to be canceled in the Washington, DC team's federal registrations. The team appealed but, in part because of access to considerable additional data in a 165-page document submitted by Nunberg, the ruling was upheld. That ruling was rendered null and void, however, in 2017 because of a decision in a different case.

In *Matal v. Tam*, the Supreme Court of the United States (SCOTUS) ruled that the Asian-American musical group The Slants could retain its name in spite of the fact that the name is used slurringly for Asian-American targets. SCOTUS unanimously concurred with a lower court's ruling that the Lanham Act's prohibition of disparaging names in trademarks constituted an unconstitutional infringement of freedom of speech. It was the Lanham Act provision on which TTAB relied in its decision against the Washington team's right to patent its name.

Interestingly, both the Slants case and a similar 2014 case from Dykes on Bikes turned on slurring words that the patent-seekers sought to reclaim as members of the targeted and derogated group. That was certainly not the case with the name of the Washington football team. Although polls of the general American public as well as of respondents who claim Indian identity show respondents against changing the Washington team's name or indifferent to it, many indigenous people continue to fight against the name. And in focus groups, four out of five native people object. In an interview after launching a campaign to get the team to "change the mascot," Oneida nation leader Ray Halbritter put it this way.[42]

> They say having a team named after a slur is not harmful. Well, it is harmful. Language and symbolism are very important. People who are not on the receiving end of this, I can understand why they don't see it. They don't feel a connection because they are not the ones being harmed. That's why we're standing up. This is not just about having a politically correct way of speaking. We have children and we are saying enough is enough ... If Roger Goodell [NFL Commissioner] were in a room full of Native Americans, he would not say: "Hello Redskins, nice to see you." If Roger Goodell met my children he would not say, "Nice to meet you little redskins." So it stands to reason that if a term is not acceptable for casual conversation, it should not be marketed to America through a sports team.

Goodell, however, continues to defer to Dan Snyder, the Washington team owner. Snyder has reiterated many times that he will NEVER change the name ("and you can put that in caps," he told one publication).[43]

There is evidence of significant psychological harm to young native Americans not only from the R-word but from the web of practices associated with less slurring 'Indian' names and mascots – body painting, 'war cries,' brandishing 'tomahawks,' dressing up in 'Indian' regalia, 'ceremonial' dancing. In 2005, the American Psychological Association endorsed a resolution urging the retirement of these practices because of their harmful effects. As then APA president Ronald F. Levant put it, "These negative lessons are not just affecting American Indian students; they are sending the wrong messages to all students."[44] Indeed, although direct effects on native targets are indeed troubling, perhaps the worst part of these practices is what they do to others. Native American team names and mascots help normalize the stereotyping and 'othering' of indigenous peoples. They deepen rather than mitigate the ignorance of most Americans about the peoples who were living on the

land they now consider theirs when their ancestors arrived from
Europe.

Slurs Targeting Women

Not all slurs are S-words and not all focus on racial or ethnic
identities. Systematically exploring how words can actually inflict
serious hurt really got rolling in the 1970s. Feminist linguists and
philosophers began, for example, to investigate how words that
designate women have tended to acquire negative and often heavily
sexualized meanings even if they started out as quite neutral.[45] That
is, they become pejoratives and thus available for insulting (and
thereby often constraining) women – *hussy*, for example, once just
meant 'housewife,'[46] *mistress* did not carry sexual meaning, *witch*
was parallel to *wizard* (a status to which J. K. Rowling's *Harry
Potter* series has done much to return it), and so on.

Long histories of sexism and misogyny have, however, given
English speakers a wealth of resources for demeaning women *as*
women: *slut, bitch, hag, harridan, hussy*, and many, many more.
Such words differ from most of the canonical racial and ethnic S-
words in having semantic content beyond designating a particular
group: they fault a woman's appearance, her sexual behavior, her
assertiveness, or the like. In addition, these expressions cannot
generally be used to designate women as a general group irrespec-
tive of any other properties they might have. (*Bitch* may be an
exception here, and I discuss that case below.) They have, however, certainly functioned oppressively in policing women and
keeping them "in their place."

Women traditionally have felt pressured to behave so as not to
have such labels attached to them, but in recent decades there has
been considerable resistance to these pressures.[47] For example,
during a 2011 York University session on preventing campus rape
Toronto police officer Michael Sanguinetti said: "I've been told
I'm not supposed to say this – however, women should avoid
dressing like sluts in order not to be victimized." As news of this

comment spread, many were outraged. And then a month or so later, Robert Dewar, a Manitoba judge, gave a 'conditional sentence' (no time served) to a man convicted of rape. He criticized the raped woman for her "suggestive attire" and giving off other signals that "sex was in the air." He expressed sympathy for the rapist, whom he described as a "clumsy Don Juan." These two high-profile cases were instrumental in the decision by Sonya Barnett and Heather Jarvis to work on redefining *slut* as a woman in charge of her own sexuality. They and other young women began working to dislodge views like those expressed by Sanguinetti and Dewar, which cast women as responsible for sexual assaults on them. With that objective in mind, they organized the first "SlutWalk." The event was on April 3, 2011, in Toronto and, to the amazement of organizers who expected at most a few hundred participants, drew some 3000 people. Many women showed up dressed in very short skirts or bikinis and revealing tops, wearing stiletto heels and lots of makeup. They carried signs with messages like "My clothes are not louder than my voice" and "My being a slut does not give you a license to rape me" and "We ♥ Sluts." Since that first event, SlutWalks have been held around the world.

Not without controversy, however. Resistance to SlutWalks has come from different directions. There have been powerful indictments from black women. The Crunk Feminist Collective had a particularly eloquent response.[48] That response was prompted in part by a sign held by two white women at the first NYC SlutWalk, "Woman is the N****R of the World" (the sign had the N-word spelled out as in the title of the John Lennon and Yoko Ono song):

> If we thought of the history of feminist movement building as a
> battle over terms, what we would find is that every major battle
> over terms and the rights and identities attached to them has
> always had the same damn problem: the racial politics, like the
> Black women implicated in them, have been fucked. "Suffrage"
> didn't include all women. (Just ask Ida B. Wells how she felt about
> marching at the back of the 1913 suffrage march.) "Woman" is not
> a universal experience. (Sojourner Truth anyone?) "Nigger" is not

a catchall term for oppression. (Ask Pearl Cleage.) Feminism is not a universal organizing category. (Ask bell hooks, Audre Lorde, Barbara Smith, Fran Beale, and on and on.) And "slut" is not the anchor point of a universal movement around female sexuality, no matter how much global resonance it has. (Ask a Hip Hop Generation Feminist.)

The blog continues:

> [S]lut-shaming has particular resonance for white women, whose sexuality has largely been constructed based upon middle-class, often Christian, heteronorms of proper chaste womanhood. The positive referent about chastity against which slut becomes the negative referent has never been universally available to Black women. A Black woman who "freely enjoys her own sexuality" [a definition of *slut* the blog takes from Alice Walker] has been called "jezebel, hoochie, hoodrat, ho, freak, and perhaps, slut." In other words, "slut" is merely part of a constellation of terms used to denigrate Black female sexuality; it is not at the center of how our particular sexuality has been constructed. But "sluttiness" and "slut-shaming" around sexuality are in fact, central to white women's experiences of sexuality. So to start a movement around that word is inherently to place white women and their experiences at the center.

The word *slut* and its partner *slutty* have also been deployed to enforce class privilege. Ways of dressing and presenting oneself common among the (white) upper crust traditionally have not gotten those who could afford them labeled sluts. Women trying to move up the social hierarchy have often been told that certain clothes or makeup styles made them look 'cheap,' often essentially equivalent to 'slutty.' The label *lady*, still in some uses associated with social privilege, is frequently the alternative to *slut*. Some of this is changing, but there are still often class dimensions in labeling someone *slut*.

Opposition also came from feminists who have repudiated the pressure on women to make themselves attractive to heterosexual men. Even though they might agree with the SlutWalk organizers that blaming victims of sexual assault is wrong, many feminist women have no interest at all in displaying themselves in the ways that heterosexual male culture apparently finds especially titillating. They are concerned when large male audiences attend SlutWalks in order to comment suggestively on the bodies of scantily clad participants. So reclaiming *slut* is far from a general feminist goal.

In certain hip-hop-influenced communities, *bitch* can be used for any woman without attributing to her the usual distinctive nastiness associated with demeaning uses of the term. That is, such speakers would deny that bitches are inevitably *bitchy*, that is, somewhat ill-tempered and quite willing to display openly their annoyance to those who displease them. Whether the speaker-affiliation with these communities signaled by this generalized use of *bitch* inevitably signals misogyny is very much debated. The expression *my bitch* does seem closely associated with a view of women normatively 'belonging' to men whom they serve, certainly placing them in a subordinate position. (When *bitch* targets men, as can happen, the message of serving and subordination often accompanies it.) Women who use this generalized *bitch* for one another may be appropriating and trying to reclaim it or something else may be going on. It is likely that there is no straightforward and simple story to be told about these linguistic practices, and I certainly am too much of an outsider to the communities in which they flourish to shed light on their gender politics.

Boys and men still can be insulted just by being called *girls*, *ladies*, or the like – and retorts that counter these stances are not easily found. Philosopher Rae Langton illustrates this point with the following "light-hearted and high-decibel exchange,"[49] which she reports witnessing in 1990 at a football (US *soccer*) game played in Melbourne, Australia:

> St. Kilda supporter to sluggish player: "Get *on* with it, Laurie, you *great girl!*"
> Alert bystander: "Hey, what's wrong with a girl?"
> St. Kilda supporter: "It's got *no balls*, that's what's wrong with it!"

And Langton tells us, "In case of doubt, the sluggish player is a man, and 'great' is an intensifier, not a compliment." Although Langton's Australian example is some three decades old, it could have happened yesterday. The bystander brought out explicitly the tacit assumption that labeling the player 'girl' was disparaging. But, as Langton points out, the heckling fan enthusiastically embraced that assumption. Their quick (and cleverly punning) retort to the protesting bystander shows how difficult resistance to such practices can be. Counterspeech is seldom easy.[50]

In most of the English-speaking world, the "radical notion that women are people"[51] has gotten considerable traction in the past few decades. But even people who might overtly endorse such a sentiment are far from fully onboard. Slurs targeting women, including transgender women, remain commonplace, though the particular linguistic practices involved are shifting, and there is considerable disagreement on strategies for resistance.

Other Insults and (Apparent) Name-Calling

Not all nasty things one might say about or to people constitute pushing them down as members of particular social groups. Some insults draw on negative attitudes toward particular characteristics to express a negative view of an individual whose social identity is generally beside the point: *spaz*, *retard* (source of the more recent political putdown, *libtard*), *dumb*, *bastard* (*son of a bitch*), *lame*, and *gay* (as in schoolkids' derision of those not 'with it') are a few of these in current or recent American English. Some deride appearance – *fatso*, *four-eyes*, *baldy* – and others seem to slam intellectual ability or educational achievement – *idiot*, *moron*, *dumbbell*, *illiterate*. Still others mock those seen as currying favor with superiors – *teacher's pet*, *brownnoser*, *asslicker*, and the like. Some seem quite mild – *jerk*, *fathead*, *klutz*, *nincompoop* – and others just seem nasty – *piece of shit*, *fucker*, and many more that I encounter when reading comments sections online. Such insults can constitute a targeted expression of the speaker's reaction to what's just been said or done non-linguistically. For example, to your admission that you've broken my favorite cup or to your doing just that in my presence I can respond with just "klutz" or "you klutz" or, more wordily, with something like "you're such a klutz." (And of course I could use much stronger insults.)

The same Geoff Nunberg whose theoretical work on slurs and whose research role in support of eliminating the R-word name for the Washington, DC football team I have already mentioned, has also had a lot to say about insults and insulting in contemporary American culture.[52] His witty and erudite *Ascent of the A-Word*, subtitled *Assholism: The First 60 Years*, was published in 2012. There is a fascinating account of the rise of the word, which seems to have started its career during WWII, and Nunberg's presentation of that career is compelling. He is very good on carving out the boundaries of assholism, linking it to a kind of self-aware arrogant self-entitlement. Young children, no matter how bratty, don't have the A-word applied to them. Interestingly, the A-word does not carry with it strong moral censure. There is the sense of violating social norms, but it is often married with the idea that doing so ultimately has beneficial effects – makes one a strong leader, effective in the courtroom, and the like. One of Nunberg's hypotheses is that assholism has a special resonance with our times.

It is especially striking that, writing back in 2011, Nunberg characterizes Donald Trump as the ultimate asshole. And, yes, he is indeed speaking of the Donald Trump elected president of the USA in 2016. Trump was then best known as star of *The Apprentice*, a very popular 'reality' show. As Nunberg's book was being written, Trump was becoming a prolific user of Twitter. Trump's tweets were spreading his discredited 'birtherist' views that then President Barack Obama had not been born in the US. They were also broaching the idea that Trump would run for president in 2012 himself.

> Donald Trump comes closer than anyone else to being the
> archetype of the species [asshole, that is]; crossing genres, he
> exemplifies all the ways an asshole can capture our attention . . .
> Trump's preeminence in this line testifies to his mastery of the
> mechanisms of publicity. Apart from [comedian Stephen]
> Colbert, no one in public life understands better than he how
> engaging assholism can be, both in real life and in its broadcast
> simulacra. "The Apprentice" [the TV show which made Trump
> famous] epitomizes the genre of reality television built around
> situations in which people can be abusive to others who have
> willingly consented to take part in return for money or celebrity.
> Every episode arcs towards a finale that gives the viewers the
> opportunity to watch a powerful man acting like an asshole
> towards his supplicants . . . the format keeps the "reality" close
> enough to the actual so that the asshole's behavior is distressing
> to his targets without ever reaching so deep into their lives that it
> becomes genuinely disturbing to the viewer. They allow us to
> enjoy the spectacle of social aggression without experiencing any
> vicarious moral risk.

Nunberg quotes Trump supporters who acknowledge or
even embrace such designations of Trump. "Trump may be
an arrogant asshole but he says what he thinks." "I will vote
for Trump, precisely because he is a jerk, but a jerk who
knows when he's getting screwed on a deal, and will make
sure it is America that comes out on top." The A-word is
potentially more offensive than *jerk*, but it also carries with it
more suggestion of power or dominance. The *loser* label is
much more likely to accompany *jerk* than *asshole*. The Trump
fan quoted here may be using *jerk* as a milder, less offensive,
substitute for the A-word.

Overt insults are not new to our age, as Nunberg is well aware.
What is new is their widespread circulation via mass media. This
includes not only TV and video use of insults to entertain but
social media like Facebook, Twitter, Instagram, comments sections on blogs, and the like, where insults are often anonymous.

Reclamation: A Success Story?

Sometimes S-words can be reappropriated, reclaimed, and defanged by targets for self-assertive positive uses. Under what conditions can this happen? What sorts of moves and language games are involved? And when can those who are not targets join in?

Linguist Heather Burnett raises these questions in discussing affirming uses of *dyke*.[53] In many contexts, *dyke* is taken as a slurring or derogatory way to speak of lesbians, an S-word. This is why, as mentioned earlier, the US Patent Office refused to register the name of the organization, Dykes on Bikes. And yet members of that organization so called themselves, proudly and without apology. Although they recognized the widespread negativity associated with the label, they inverted that devaluing, made *dyke* a positive form. Burnett suggests that they were conveying their identification with (or perhaps aspiration to become) a certain distinctive social persona: a woman with a stereotypically masculinized self-presentation who is sexually attracted to women and who embraces a generally countercultural lifestyle and radical politics. To embrace that social persona is to reject identification with another social persona, which Burnett labels *mainstream lesbian*. The mainstream lesbian presents herself in a more conventionally feminine way, is less focused on the sexual component of the woman–woman bonding she celebrates, and generally more eager to fit into mainstream capitalist society. And she may well be somewhat hostile toward those who label themselves *dyke* or at least may be uncomfortable with their lifestyles and politics. These are *gradable* notions – one can be more or less dykey or dykish, for example, and Burnett's semantic model incorporates this gradability. They are larger-than-life stereotypes – few claim to be, or think of other real people as, at the extremes on all components. Homophobes who might use *dyke* to label all lesbians indeed draw on the *dyke* persona, which they disdain, but they do not recognize the *mainstream lesbian* persona. They are still circulating the slur.

There may be non-homophobes who would value diversity within lesbian communities and would view themselves as neutral on the political and other differences between the (stereotypical) dyke and (stereotypical) mainstream lesbian. Some of these people might even use *lesbian* to identify themselves; others might accept labels like *gay* or *straight* but not *dyke*. Can such people enter into the reappropriated positive use of *dyke*? I think Burnett would answer "no," the reason being that only those who recognizably identify with that social persona can reasonably expect others to realize that they do not share widespread negative attitudes toward it. But I'm not sure that's the whole story. I can imagine contexts in which I am confident that my hearers clearly recognize that I do not attach negative value to the dyke social persona, indeed that I positively value it even though I do not identify myself with it. I am indeed moderately confident that I have been in such contexts in real life. Nonetheless, I would be reluctant to so label others because I do not see myself as 'licensed' to do so. There is still the sense that I do not have the community standing to use *dyke* to label others, that it remains off-limits to all but those who so label themselves. Yet I do not need special standing to use the relatively neutral *lesbian* or the once slurring *queer*.

The best-known apparent success story for reappropriation of a slur is that of the word *queer*, now widely used in many contexts friendly to those now frequently designated as LGBTQ in mainstream US sources. The word *queer* provides the last catch-all initial in the 'alphabet-soup' label. (There's a long story to be told about the proliferation of identity labels that has produced such strings to collect everyone outside strictly hetero and gender-binary categories. Not trusting Q to include everyone who does not identify as lesbian, gay, bisexual, or transgender, some add *I* for *intersex* and *A* for *asexual* and then perhaps a + or something else to indicate that more distinctions may prove important.) AIDS activists who formed the organization "Queer Nation" in the 1990s found *queer* useful as a straightforward term that was more inclusive than other options. The extract from the "Queer Nation Manifesto" in the box in Figure 5.1 explains.

In NYC, San Francisco, and elsewhere chants of "We're here, we're queer, get used to it" were heard in marches and other protest events of the early 1990s. And in the streets of London's Soho just after the June 2016 mass shootings in the Pulse night-club in Orlando, FL, there were still echoes of that earlier resistance: "We're here, we're queer, we will not live in fear." Reclaimed, *queer* was and has remained a powerful tool for practical politics – the ready rhymes and the familiarity helped a lot.

As the "Queer Nation Manifesto" notes, the word *gay* could not have done the same work. Not only did it have a much stronger

---

Queer!
Ah, do we really have to use that word? It's trouble. Every gay person has his or her own take on it. For some it means strange and eccentric and kind of mysterious. That's okay; we like that. But some gay girls and boys don't. They think they're more normal than strange. And for others "queer" conjures up those awful memories of adolescent suffering. Queer. It's forcibly bittersweet and quaint at best – weakening and painful at worst. Couldn't we just use "gay" instead? It's a much brighter word. And isn't it synonymous with "happy"? When will you militants grow up and get over the novelty of being different?
Why Queer . . .
Well, yes, "gay" is great. It has its place. But when a lot of lesbians and gay men wake up in the morning we feel angry and disgusted, not gay. So we've chosen to call ourselves queer. Using "queer" is a way of reminding us how we are perceived by the rest of the world. It's a way of telling ourselves we don't have to be witty and charming people who keep our lives discreet and marginalized in the straight world. We use queer as gay men loving lesbians and lesbians loving being queer. Queer, unlike **gay**, doesn't mean **male**.
And when spoken to other gays and lesbians it's a way of suggesting we close ranks, and forget (temporarily) our individual differences because we face a more insidious common enemy. Yeah, **queer** can be a rough word but it is also a sly and ironic weapon we can steal from the homophobe's hands and use against him.

"The Queer Nation Manifesto" was originally distributed to onlookers by marchers in the ACT UP contingent of the 1990 New York City Gay Pride Day Parade. The full text is at www.historyisaweapon.com/defcon1/queernation.html

Figure 5.1 The Queer Nation Manifesto (excerpts)

assumption of maleness, but it did not have the same kind of slurring history. *Gay* was a self-designator that then spread into wider usage in the 1970s, becoming so accepted that it is now more or less neutral. Its use among children to derogate all manner of stuff – "that scarf's so gay" – undoubtedly got going from their having heard the word *gay* used negatively of men sexually attracted to other men. But the children picking up on homophobic-fueled negativity of some adult uses of *gay* were almost certainly not linking *gay* to matters of sexual preference. Their usage is relatively recent and plays at most a minor role in social subordination of those deviating from heterosexual norms. In contrast, although *queer* was a preferred self-designator for many gay men in the early twentieth century, it also was consistently used outside the target group to derogate, and it had not moved into widespread non-slurring use. It was in part precisely because it was an active and still potent slur that *queer* was available as a retaliatory weapon to be wielded in pushing back against heterosexism, in asserting the rights of gay men, lesbians, bisexuals, and others outside normative boundaries in matters of sexuality and gender.

It is not just in shouted slogans, however, that *queer* was reclaimed. The word *queer*'s other meanings (e.g., 'peculiar,' 'odd,' 'eccentric,' 'strange') have seemed especially apt to many academics and others thinking about the complex nature of sexual and gender identities and politics. Many of these thinkers endorse a kind of 'dis-identity' politics that tries to unsettle traditional boundaries and ways of thinking, that 'queer-ies' (puns are much appreciated!) not only 'straight' norms but also many assumptions operative in LGBTQ communities as well. Self-styled 'queer theorists' have established and teach in 'queer studies' programs at many colleges and universities. They organize 'queer theory' conferences and write for and edit 'queer theory' journals. On June 5, 2018, Edmonton in the Canadian province of Alberta launched a 'queer history app' for iPhones and Androids, an app designed primarily to educate the city's schoolchildren.[54]

So *queer* might seem fully rehabilitated, no longer allying its users with a community of homophobes like those who widely used it during my youth. But appearances can be misleading. Though *queer* was generally considered 'politer' than some other sexuality-oriented slurs, those targeted by it in their school days were and still are often upset by activists' push to embrace what they still experience as a slur. Linguist Anne Curzan in her wonderful book, *Fixing English*, has a very insightful discussion of reappropriating slurs. *Queer* is one of her main examples, and she draws on comments made in August 2000 by Gabriel Rotello. Rotello was founding editor of *OutWeek*, an activist publication of the late 1980s and early 1990s that not only embraced *queer* but actively and self-consciously promoted its use.

> I needed a word that could encompass everybody's crowding under the rainbow flag. . . . When a new activist group dubbed itself Queer Nation, the die was cast. Queer was definitely here. . . . The trouble was that lots of older activists hated it. They argued that queer was a term of oppression and that to use it was to endorse the dictionary's verdict that there was something "odd and suspicious" about homosexuals. They had spent their lives fighting that idea, they argued, and this represented a huge step backwards. . . . [A] term I had hoped would bring everyone together did exactly the opposite – it divided the hip, cool younger activists from their unhip, uncool elders.[55]

Rotello, as had others, predicted the demise of reclaimed uses of *queer*. Those predictions proved wrong. It is not just in academia but in popular culture that *queer* has found a welcoming home: *Queer as Folk* and *Queer Eye for the Straight Guy*, later just *Queer Eye*, do not sound like slurs or even offensive to many people both within and outside the target group. That many entertainers have openly embraced queer identities is undoubtedly one of the factors that has supported reclamation.

Queer is, however, still sometimes used slurringly, probably most often out of the hearing of its targets. It can still subordinate, especially if used as a noun ("There are so many queers in that class") rather than as an adjective ("Queer teens face less hostility from their peers than they did even just a couple of decades ago"). (At the end of Chapter 1, I discussed the different categorizing potential of nouns, used for labeling, as opposed to adjectives, used for describing.) So even this "success story" has limits. Nonetheless, *queer* has shifted ground quite significantly over the past half-century. It is not only or perhaps not even primarily used as a weapon anymore. Rather, it serves as a tool both for battling oppression and for exploring and expanding concepts of sexuality and gender.

Notes

1. Alex Amend, "Analyzing a Terrorist's Social Media Manifesto: The Pittsburgh Synagogue Shooter's Posts on Gab," *SPLC (Southern Poverty Law Center)*, October 28, 2018, www.splcenter.org/hatewatch/2018/10/28/analyzing-terrorists-social-media-manifesto-pittsburgh-synagogue-shooters-posts-gab.
2. See Benesch et al. 2018, accessed at https://dangerousspeech.org/guide/.
3. See "Sticks and Stones May Break My Bones," *The Phrase Finder*, www.phrases.org.uk/meanings/sticks-and-stones-may-break-my-bones.html.
4. See Brison 1998, p. 29, for details.
5. See n. 1 in "Getting Started" about philosopher Cassie Herbert's unpublished work on this matter.
6. See Tirrell 2012 for a much fuller account than I give below.
7. Quoted from Schabas 2000, p. 144 in Tirrell 2012, p. 174.
8. Naasson Munyandamutsa; speaking at "The Language of Genocide" symposium, Harvard University, March 27, 2007; quoted in Tirrell 2012, p. 174.
9. Quoted from Sibomana 1999, p. 92, in Tirrell 2012, p. 181.
10. Camp 2017.
11. Manne 2016. Thanks to Matt Shields for reminding me of the relevance of Manne's work here.
12. These quotations come from "The Holocaust: Nazi Officers on the 'Jewish Question,'" *Jewish Virtual Library*, n.d., www.jewishvirtuallibrary.org/nazi-statements.
13. "Anti-Refugee Rhetoric and Justifications for WWII-Era Mass Incarceration: Is History Repeating Itself?", *Densho Blog*, November 20, 2015, https://densho

.org/5-alarming-similarties-between-anti-syrian-refugee-rhetoric-and-justifications-for-world-war-ii-era-mass-incarceration/.

14. Roxana Hegeman, "3 Men Convicted in Kansas Plot to Bomb Somali Refugees," Associated Press, April 18, 2018, www.chicagotribune.com /news/nationworld/ct-kansas-bomb-plot-verdict-20180418-story.html.

15. Brett Samuels, "Trump on Immigrant Gang Members: 'These Aren't People,' They're 'Animals,'" *The Hill*, May 16, 2018, http://thehill.com /homenews/administration/388026-trump-on-immigrant-gang-members-these-arent-people-theyre-animals.

16. In, e.g., Matsuda 1989, the most frequently cited article in the history of the *Michigan Law Review*.

17. Greenberg and Pyszczynski 1985.

18. Austin (1975 [1962]) launched the study of speech acts to which many philosophers and linguists have contributed. There has been a recent resurgence of important work on this topic, some of it inspired by interest in the relation of language use to matters of social justice. See especially Fogal, Harris, and Moss, eds., 2018; the editors' introductory essay is very useful although quite technical.

19. Wittgenstein 1958, Part I, 23., p 11b.

20. See, e.g., Asher, Paul, and Venant 2017, Burnett 2019a and 2019b, and Roberts 2015 for samples of different uses of games to model precisely certain aspects of conversational interaction.

21. I thank Richard Brooks for sharing with me a draft of this material, which is part of a book on address practices that he is writing, tentatively titled *Call Forth*.

22. See, e.g., these books, Asim 2007 and Kennedy 2003, and these articles, McWhorter 2016 and 2018, and Allan 2015; see also discussions in Smitherman 2006 and in Smitherman 2000 [1994] and in Alim and Smitherman 2012.

23. "The N-Word: An Interactive Project Exploring a Singular Word," *The Washington Post*, n.d., www.washingtonpost.com/wp-dre/features/the-n-word.

24. Spears 2006.

25. See, e.g., Alim and Smitherman 2012, especially pp. 112–114 and note 47 on p. 128.

26. Anderson 2018.

27. Alim and Smitherman 2012. The quotation is from p. 118.

28. The Goff quote is from an article by Jamilles Lartey, "Oppression in America: 'To Root This Out We Need a Movement Against Racist Policies," *The Guardian*, June 6, 2018, www.theguardian.com/us-news/2018/jun/06/ everyday-racism-in-america-how-to-fix-it?utm_source=esp&utm_medium =Email&utm_campaign=GU+Today+USA+-+Collections+2017&utm_

term=277303&subid=21668292&CMP=GT_US_collection; this appeared in a section of the *Guardian* devoted to issues of racism in the US.

29. Embrick and Henricks 2013 is a workplace study of N-word uses; Nunberg 2018 provides this and many other useful references.
30. Camp 2013.
31. Swanson in press.
32. Jeshion 2013.
33. Nunberg 2018, p. 244.
34. Quoted in Matsuda 1989; quote appears on p. 46 in Matsuda et al. 1993.
35. The Langston Hughes quote appears in Nunberg 2018, p. 286.
36. "Meet Chet Ellis, the 15-Year-Old Who Wrote a Moving Essay on the Cost of White Privilege," *The Undefeated*, https://theundefeated.com/features/meet-chet-ellis-the-15-year-old-who-wrote-a-moving-essay-on-the-cost-of-white-privilege/. Chet's prize winning essay on the cost of white privilege is reproduced in this April 21, 2017 essay by Kelley D. Evans.
37. Walter Mosley, "Why I Quit the Writers' Room," *New York Times*, September 6, 2019, www.nytimes.com/2019/09/06/opinion/sunday/walter-mosley.html. All quotations in this paragraph are from this article.
38. Veilleux 1995; thanks to philosopher Mary Kate McGowan for alerting me to this important essay.
39. http://jayrosenstein.com/pages/honorlinks.html is the website of filmmaker Jay Rosenstein, which has links to reviews of the film and the article Rosenstein wrote in 2018 reporting on the Peoria's absolute rejection of Chief Illiniwek.
40. See note 39.
41. The Nunberg quotes here come from Frances Stead Sellers, "When Is a Word a Slur? One Linguist Argues Big Data Can Help Tell," *Washington Post*, April 7, 2015, www.washingtonpost.com/news/arts-and-entertainment/wp/2015/04/07/when-is-a-word-a-slur-one-linguist-argues-big-data-can-help-tell/?utm_term=.2bbdf38e0b48.
42. Dave Zirin, "Oneida Nation Fights to Change the Name of the Washington Football Team," *The Nation*, September 13, 2013, www.thenation.com/article/oneida-nation-fights-change-name-washington-football-team/.
43. Erik Brady, "How Long Is 'NEVER'? NFL Team Owner Dan Snyder at Five Years and Counting," *USA Today*, December 15, 2019, https://eu.usatoday.com/story/sports/columnist/erik-brady/2018/05/09/dan-snyder-redskins-mascot-never-five-years-later/596491002/.
44. "Summary of the APA Resolution Recommending Retirement of American Indian Mascots." American Psychological Association website, n.d. Quoted at www.apa.org/pi/oema/resources/indian-mascots.

45. See, e.g., Baker 1975, Lakoff 1973, Schulz 1975, Stanley 1977.
46. McConnell-Ginet 1989 discusses this shift.
47. See "SlutWalk," *Wikipedia*, n.d., https://en.wikipedia.org/wiki/SlutWalk, for a wealth of references.
48. "I Saw the Sign But Did We Really Need a Sign? SlutWalk and Racism," *Crunk Feminist Collective*, October 6, 2011, https://crunkfeministcollective .wordpress.com/2011/10/06/i-saw-the-sign-but-did-we-really-need-a-sign-slutwalk-and-racism/.
49. Langton 2018, p. 145.
50. But visit the DSP website (dangerousspeech.org) for ideas, including forming alliances, using humor, and others.
51. Definition of *feminism* due to Marie Shear; see Deborah Cameron's January 26, 2019, blog post on Shear, "Radical Notions," https://debuk .wordpress.com/2019/01/26/radical-notions/.
52. See Nunberg 2012; my quotation comes from the extract from that book that was published at salon.com, "Trump, Jobs, Zuckerberg: We Idolize Jerks," August 12, 2012, www.salon.com/2012/08/12/trump_jobs_zuckerberg_ we_idolize_jerks/.
53. Burnett 2020.
54. Emily Mertz, "Teaching Edmonton's Queer History: App Aims to Fill Gaps in School Curriculum," *Global News*, June 5, 2018, https://globalnews.ca /news/4251365/edmonton-queer-history-app-alberta-curriculum/.
55. See Anne Curzan's 2014 chapter on this topic and her long quote from Gabriel Rotello, pp. 154–155.

6   Reforming/Resisting: "It's Like a Kind of Sexual Racism"

Linguists continue (rightly) to be impressed by the highly structured nature and essentially unlimited expressive capacity of all human languages, including sign languages used among communities of deaf people and disparaged varieties of spoken language like African American English. If languages are all essentially equal, then how could some speakers legitimately complain that inadequate or problematic linguistic resources contribute to their social oppression? Additionally, as linguists (again rightly) observe, much linguistic change happens below the level of conscious attention. Isn't it pointless to push for linguistic reform?

Given this background, it's not surprising that linguists lagged behind many other academics in recognizing that linguistic resources readily available at any given time might not equally serve the interests of all members of a particular linguistic community. And academics generally lagged behind political activists on language matters, at least in part because so many were in dominant social groups and did not find themselves bumping up against what seemed problematic linguistic practices.

But times have changed. Linguists, especially but not only sociolinguists, increasingly recognize that linguistic practices are far less uniform across speakers and communities than they might seem. Variation is the norm and to a considerable extent it is socially driven, a valuable resource for people that helps them adopt diverse social personae and maneuver in the social landscapes they inhabit, their diverse communities of practice, and their travels among them. It is not just pronunciation or syntax that varies – it is both the inventory of lexical items, words, and other meaningful units, and also the ways in which they are deployed in linguistic practice. And it is not just the lexicon of content words that reformers seek to change.

Linguistic reform of the lexicon can involve creation of new forms (*Ms.* as a social title for women that does not indicate marital status) or shifting of familiar forms in order to help change the phenomena they label (e.g., extending *marriage* so it is no longer confined to unions consisting of a woman and a man forming the core of a family). Sometimes there are efforts to eliminate forms deemed problematic because of the baggage they carry (*dumb*), perhaps replacing them with alternatives (*mute* or *without speech*) or perhaps trying to retire them altogether. And reform can target more abstract elements of language. In this chapter I will talk about gendered pronouns in English. In other work I have discussed socially motivated uses of grammatical gender in languages like French and Hindi.[1]

Few attempts at reform sail through without encountering pushback of various kinds. Along the way, I will mention resistance to reform attempts. Resisting can take many forms: offering alternative changes, trying to show the reformers that their mission is misguided, or open mockery. And of course attempted reform fails if it is ignored, if no community embraces it and joins with the reformers.

The Birth of *Sexism*

In principle, it should be easy to add new words as needed for new things or new ideas, ways of organizing our experience. Human languages all benefit from the design feature that linguist Charles Hockett dubbed *dual articulation*. That is, the meaningful units of language are composed from a small set of recurring units that do not in themselves carry meaning. In spoken languages these are units of sound that can easily be put together in new ways to form new words. (Signed languages, too, can and do readily add new expressions.) When there is need to express new content, we can always create a new word to designate the new content. The problem dissolves. Or so it might seem.

The feminist psychologist Sandra Lipsitz Bem, a good friend, spoke to me on more than one occasion about her struggles in the mid-to-late 1960s to find a name for what she and other pioneers in the 'second wave' of feminism were addressing as part of what became known as the women's movement. "It's like a kind of 'sexual racism' – a 'sexism' – that, like racism, infects not only attitudes and assumptions but also a wide range of cultural discourses and social institutions." That's the sort of thing she remembered saying in various talks she gave. On page 1 of her 1993 *The Lenses of Gender*, she offers the following. "Beginning in the 1960s, the second major wave of feminist advocacy raised social consciousness ... by exposing – and *naming* (my italics) – the 'sexism' in all policies and practices that explicitly discriminate on the basis of sex." Notice that in creating this name, she did not just put together sounds in some arbitrary fashion. Rather she used components like *-ism* and *sex* that were already in circulation, carrying some content and also some useful lexical baggage.

It is highly likely that a number of different people came up with *sexism* and the related *sexist* independently. In a 1985 article in *American Speech*, Fred R. Shapiro, a legal scholar and librarian interested in word histories, does not mention Sandy Bem when discussing the introduction into public discourse of *sexism* and *sexist*. He cites instead a 1968 talk by Pauline M. Leet at Franklin and Marshall College for the earliest usage of *sexist* he was able to locate. Leet explicitly develops the parallel of sexual and racial oppression: "both the racist and the sexist are acting as if all that has happened has never happened, and both of them are making decisions and coming to conclusions about someone's value by referring to factors which are in both cases irrelevant."[2] Shapiro cites the 1968 book *Born Free* by Carolyn Bird for the earliest printed uses of *sexism* and *sexist*, uses that credited the mimeographed speech by Leet.

Later that same year, apparently without knowing of Leet's and Bird's uses, Sheldon Vanauken, who taught history at Lynchburg College in Virginia, published a small pamphlet called *Freedom for Movement Girls – Now.* Vanauken uses *sexism* and *sexist* throughout that book. In a "Note on Words," he explains his choice.

> The parallels between *sexism* and *racism* are sharp and clear. And just as a *racist* is one who proclaims or justifies or assumes the supremacy of one race over another, so a *sexist* is one who proclaims or justifies or assumes the supremacy of one sex (guess which) over the other. But the meaning of *sexist* is obvious. And that's the whole point. It's a better word than *male chauvinist*, which is bulky, usually mispronounced, and imprecise in meaning. . . . *Sexist*, on the other hand, is short, precise, instantly understandable. It has a short, vicious sound, and it inherits the ugly overtones of *racist*. It is potentially a word of power.[3]

Male chauvinist and *male chauvinism*, which began being used in the 1950s and which Vanauken advocated dropping in favor of *sexist* and *sexism*, were undoubtedly inspired by the leftist *white chauvinism*, which had been in use for some time with much the same coverage as *white supremacy*. But *white chauvinism* was mainly used by a small political elite, and the wider public were not familiar with the expression. Shapiro also points out that the expression *male chauvinist pig* was often used quite mockingly in the press, and *male chauvinism* focused on beliefs and attitudes and was less readily useable for systemic issues that disadvantaged women. In other words, *sexism* brought more welcome and less objectionable lexical baggage than its competitors.

Since the late 1960s, the suffix *-ism* has been widely used in the US to draw attention to systematic disadvantaging of people on a variety of bases: *ableism* (Merriam-Webster dates usage in advocacy for rights of those with disabilities to 1983), *ageism* (coined in 1969 by gerontologist Robert C. Butler), and *audism* (coined by Deaf Culture scholar Tom Humphries in 1975) are a few examples, all of which have been around for decades now. But for a variety of reasons, including the size and impact of the social

movements involved, these other -*ism* words have not gotten the
wide traction of either *racism* or *sexism*. They are mostly used in
communities of advocates for the groups in question. This does
not mean that they have been useless. DeafBlind writer and
activist John Lee Clark writes that adding a new word "can change
the way we see everything."[4] Clark talks about how *audism*,
though introduced as noted above by a deaf intellectual, only
really gained traction after hearing and sighted psycholinguist
Harlan Lane used it in his 1993 book, *The Mask of Benevolence:
Disabling the Deaf Community*. As Clark observes, "Sighted Deaf
people had always known that hearing society discriminated
against them, but the new word suddenly made it much easier
to identify and analyze." For blind people, including those who are
also deaf, the term *vidism* has been coined to add specificity
beyond the generic *ableism*. But Clark sees a need for something
over and above combining *audism* and *vidism*. He wants another
term to help think about the special ways in which the DeafBlind
community has been disempowered by the active discouragement
of full use of various different tactile modes of sensing. Much of
the hearing–sighted world (to which most of our globe's people
belong) has an array of practices that discourage gathering tactile
information. People in many cultures do not readily touch most
other people, other living things, or even inanimate stuff in their
environment. Clark has recently proposed *distantism* for these
attitudes and practices. Distantism, he argues, puts bubbles
around people. These bubbles interfere with the kinds of physi-
cally close connections needed to develop and exploit people's
potentially quite substantial capacities to learn about one another
and the world tactilely. Words like *distantism* and other -*ism*
coinages can be useful even if they remain restricted to relatively
small communities of practice.

   Nonetheless, only *racism* and *sexism* are widely known and used.
And only *racism*, at 3988, ranks among the 5000 most common
words of English as determined on wordfrequency.info. Google hits
on the last day of February in 2019, though an imperfect guide, gave
these approximate results: *racism* 322,000,000; *sexism* 64,900,000;

ageism 3,520,000; *ableism* 2,520,000; and *audism*, which my word processor wanted to correct to *autism*, came in at a very distant 159,000 (about 2 weeks later, *vidism* got 7980 and *distantism* got 1450). These numbers reflect a phenomenon that feminist scholar Miranda Fricker has dubbed 'epistemic injustice.'[5] What this means is that groups that are socially disadvantaged by oppressive institutions and practices or even mostly by small numbers are also at an 'epistemic' disadvantage. They are handicapped in their pursuit of knowledge, of understanding. An important component of this handicap is linguistic, as has been pointed out with many examples by black women thinkers, other feminists, and a host of activist scholars involved in trying to understand and combat various kinds of injustice. Labels and meanings that are most widespread and readily available tend to make existing social arrangements far easier to speak of than alternatives.

In the next section I will talk about attempts to redefine *racism*, to reshape its content so that it better covers the various kinds of factors that operate to sustain racial inequality. Before that, I will say a bit more about the checkered career of *sexism* (and also the related but much older terms *feminism* and *feminist*).

Given that second-wave feminism got a major boost from the experience of women working in the anti-racist civil rights movement in the early 1960s, it is not surprising that *sexism* took off as an all-encompassing name for a variety of matters those women and others were identifying. It is ironic, however, that, just like first-wave feminism in both the UK and the US, which pushed for suffrage and for political status for relatively affluent white women, the focus of second-wave feminism was on improving things for that same group. Betty Friedan's *The Feminine Mystique* focused on the malaise that many well-educated full-time mothers and homemakers in the US felt, "the problem that has no name." She urged them (us – I was in her target group) to hire nannies and housekeepers and find 'fulfilling' careers, neglecting the exploitation of low-waged domestic workers, virtually all women and many of them black women.

The feminine mystique, an ideology that presented women's all-consuming goal in life as caring for (and sexually satisfying) husbands and bearing and nurturing children, was not a problem for most black women. These women were overwhelmingly in waged labor of one kind or another. They were generally not suffering from the excessive chivalry or other constraining practices that are part of what psychologists Susan Fiske and Peter Glick have dubbed *benevolent sexism*,[6] which involves notions of 'protecting' and 'cherishing' women. There really is no such phenomenon as *benevolent racism* and, though benevolent sexism may have played some role in some black women's experience, it was hardly major. Any protection or cherishing they might get from lovers, husbands, brothers, or sons could be experienced as welcome respite from the indignities heaped on them in their workplaces and in so many public spaces.

A major difference between sexism and racism is that most people have intimate and often loving connections throughout much of their lives to others whose gender identity is different from theirs – offspring, parents, siblings, spouses, and lovers (for those in mixed-sex relationships). Relatively few (American) people have such connections to someone bearing a different racial label, and for even fewer do such connections persist through their lifetimes.

Feminism and *feminist* were terms of much longer standing than *sexism*, but they immediately came into use to label the anti-sexism efforts and those involved in them that got going in the 1960s and 1970s. Activists and intellectuals involved with both gender and racial issues within black communities, however, often found Alice Walker's *womanism* and *womanist* more appealing. "Womanist is to feminist as purple is to lavender," proclaimed Walker. *The Womanist Reader* first appeared in 2006, and was followed six years later by *The Womanist Idea*, both important collections of womanist scholarship edited by Layli Maryapan (the first volume under the name Layli Philips).[7]

Social theorist Patricia Hill Collins has insightfully explored the debates among black women over the labels *womanist* and *black feminist*, each of which carries its own lexical baggage and each of which can be mobilized for different purposes. She points to a tension between, on the one hand, focusing on differences among black women both now and over time and, on the other, developing social institutions and political strategies that can support a collective 'voice' for black women that emerges in part from conversations over time. "Whatever African-American women choose to name a Black women's standpoint, womanism and Black feminism encounter the issues confronted by any knowledge that aims to 'talk back' to knowledges with more power."[8] Collins insists on the critical importance of a "visionary pragmatism" that couples grand ideas of how the world should be with strong commitment to practical actions that might bring that world nearer. She cites black feminist anthropologist Johnnetta Betsch Cole, former president of Spelman College: "While it is true that without a vision the people perish, it is doubly true that without action the people and their vision perish as well." In part because the words *sexism* and *sexist* were so often used in contexts that clearly did not include most black women's experience, other coinages like *gendered racism*, introduced by sociologist Philomena Essed, have had considerable currency among black women intellectuals.

Recently digital media specialist and Black feminist scholar Mona Bailey came up with the portmanteau *misogynoir*, which she began using in writing by 2010.[9] The word, which Bailey emphasizes she intended "to describe the unique ways in which Black women [and not just any 'women of color'] are pathologized in popular culture," has become relatively widely used (on February 18, 2019, *misogynoir* slightly lagged the far older *audism* in Google hits with 125,000 but by February 19, 2020, it registered 286,000 and *audism* only 152,000). Trudy, self-styled womanist and creator of Gradient Lair, a digital space for Black women, has also played a large role both in spreading that word and theorizing about its significance.

One highly visible component of white mainstream anti-sexist activism was, of course, linguistic. Many feminist activists, not only in the US but elsewhere, identified a significant range of linguistic expressions and practices as sexist and worked, with considerable success, to eliminate them. I'll have more to say about campaigns against so-called sexist language later, what they've accomplished and what they have not. It is clear, however, that launching the new labels *sexism* and *sexist* and, not long after, labels like *sexual harassment* and *date rape* and eventually *intersectionality* had enormous impact. Such linguistic reform was essential to doing both the analytical and the practical political work involved in what became known as the women's movement. It is not that there were clearly developed concepts and related publicly observable phenomena just waiting to get linguistically tagged. Rather, 'naming' areas of interest then created a publicly available space for further socially shared work on the phenomena, sometimes collaborative and sometimes contentious.

New expressions do not matter much if at all when they just lie on a shelf. They can and often do, however, give people instruments they need in order to accomplish collective social and intellectual work, and to develop concepts that can help in understanding (and changing) the social world. Of course what the words do keeps shifting and may often be contested. To see examples of this, we will look at some of what has happened and is happening to the racial ancestors of *sexism* and *sexist*.

Reshaping Existing Linguistic Resources: The Case of *Racism* and *Racist*

Most standard American English dictionaries explain the categories labeled by *racist* and *racism* in both race-neutral and individualistic terms. The noun form of *racist* is defined by *Oxford Online* this way: "A person who shows or feels discrimination or prejudice against people of other races, or who believes that a particular race is superior to another. Example: *'the comments have led to her being called a racist.'*" And the adjective, which can be used to categorize not only people but also actions, institutions, and more, including words and their uses, has this entry: "Showing or feeling discrimination or prejudice against people of other races, or believing that a particular race is superior to another." Example: *'we are investigating complaints about racist abuse at the club.'*[10] Collins does not rely on words like *discrimination* or *prejudice*, saying that "if you describe people, things, or behavior as racist, you mean that they are influenced by the belief that some people are inferior because they belong to a particular race."[11] For a number of online dictionaries, entering *racist* brings up only definitions of *racism*, implying, perhaps, that a racist person is one who believes in or supports racism as they define it. And those definitions in standard dictionaries overwhelmingly focus on individuals' beliefs and actions. There is little if any attention in most established dictionaries to social practices and institutions that give systematic advantage to some at the expense of others on the basis of assignment to different racialized groups.

Activists in the civil rights movement recognized clearly that eliminating racism was not just a matter of "changing hearts and minds" but required changing laws and social practices. From the 1970s on, social theorists began arguing that to understand racism requires going beyond individuals' actions, beliefs, and attitudes to social and cultural factors. It is not that conscious ideas about one another, racially insensitive interactions, and racially charged emotions of individuals play no role in racism. Obviously they do. Rather, the point is that to tackle racism, we also need to attend to problematic social structures and practices that continue to support advantage on the basis of skin color. Here's the start of a sample definition of *racism* from that wider perspective, which readers might find useful. "Racism refers to a variety of practices, beliefs, social relations, and phenomena that work to reproduce a racial hierarchy and social structure that yield superiority, power, and privilege for some, and discrimination and oppression for others."[12] Of course such definitions do not really settle questions about what counts as racism or how to deploy the word.

There is a large philosophical literature on defining *race*, *racism*, and *racist*. Sally Haslanger, for example, has discussed some of the issues involved, including why discussions of the terminology matter. And in a number of widely read papers, Jorge Garcia has argued for a focus on individual 'vice,' on morally reprehensible hatred or contempt or disrespect based on perceived racial identity. Charles Mills and others have criticized Garcia's focus on what is in people's 'hearts,' and discussion continues. Certainly the sociocultural framework that dominates social science discourse as well as much of the philosophical discussion can make assigning moral responsibility to individuals far more complex than views that focus on individual hearts and minds. Even though I suggested in Chapter 3 that combatting racism often requires institutional policies that, for example, keep track of links between racial categories and certain sorts of outcomes, I would not want to say that the woman at the post-Charlottesville rally I attended who said she did not "see color" was racist or even that what she said was racist. Nor would I want to apply the label *racist* to everyone who dresses up in pseudo-Indian costumes to cheer on their high school football team or uses some kind of makeup to darken their face for some sort of costume party, even though such practices do, I think, help perpetuate racially unjust social arrangements. White parents who seek 'good' schools and 'wholesome' friends for their children avoid neighborhoods with a sizeable black population. In doing so, they shore up segregated living and educational systems that help foster continued racial oppression, yet characterizing such actions or the people engaging in them as racist on that basis may seem problematic.[13] Hearts and minds, motives, do sometimes seem morally relevant even though they tell only part of the story.

   What 'social' notions of racism do is focus attention on the pernicious *effects* of racism on those oppressed by it. Individual people's beliefs, affect, and motivations certainly contribute to but do not produce all, perhaps not even most, of these effects. In the US, such effects for African Americans include diminished self-esteem, increased police surveillance and incarceration, poverty and heightened stress levels, impaired physical and mental health, de facto housing and school segregation with lowered educational resources, diminished opportunity for intergenerational accumulation of wealth, and so on. And because this broader understanding of racism links ideologies – beliefs, both acknowledged and tacit – to hierarchy and to structurally based privilege, it is not symmetric. In many ways, racism in the USA could accurately be called *white supremacy*. That term, however, is closely tied to the overt extreme bigotry and hatred promoted by the Ku Klux Klan and similar groups.

No matter what it is called, however, racism is not symmetric. In other words, the term *reverse racism* makes little sense if we are thinking of racism in social terms. People of color can (and sometimes do) negatively stereotype white people or yell insulting names at them. Doing so demonstrates what might be called *reverse racial prejudice*. It does not, however, invert existing racial hierarchies and their seriously damaging effects. But there is widespread belief that practices such as affirmative action constitute reverse racism, that they give unfair advantage to black people over white people. (There is substantial evidence that this is not so.) Eduardo Bonilla-Silva, whose work I mentioned in Chapter 3, argues that the widespread use of a somewhat shifted norm of *colorblindness* is part of what supports racism in a new guise.

The word "reproduce" in the expanded definition I gave above points to the stubbornly persistent nature of racial hierarchies. In the US and elsewhere, these hierarchies are supported and sustained by what sociologist Philomena Essed dubbed *everyday racism*. Actually, that's misleading. Essed, herself a woman of color born and educated in the Netherlands but now based in the US, first coined the Dutch expression *alledages racisme*. That was the title of her 1984 book, which was translated into English less than a decade later. Everyday racism involves routine practices that reinforce racist biases and that in various ways work to elevate one group over another. Such routine practices often involve linguistic practices. Anthropological linguist Jane Hill has explored what she calls the "everyday language of white racism." She includes the use of terms like *squaw* that target native Americans, the use of 'Mock Spanish' in media and in lighthearted banter ("no problemo," "hasta la vista"), and the repetition and wide circulation of racial slurs and stereotypes in the 'moral panic' that ensues when some public figure comes out with something overtly racist.

Virtually everyone living in the US, no matter what racialized group label is assigned to or claimed by them, engages in some of these arguably problematic practices. The point of the broader social perspective on racism is to help better understand the persistence of racial inequality so as to increase the chances of success in collective anti-racist projects. The goal is not to assign guilt or cast blame on a wider group of individuals, to broaden the pool of those labeled *racist*. Yet the (partial) shift in much public discourse to a somewhat broader conception of racism (and of sexism and other ways in which social power relations confer advantage on some at the expense of others) is often experienced as morally castigating all whites (or men or members of other 'ascendant' social groups).

As we have already seen, matters are complicated by the fact that people live in intersecting hierarchies of power and privilege. Black women have brought out very clearly the frequent casual racism of many of the white women who identified themselves/ourselves as feminists, including their/our all-too-frequent neglect of the experiences, lives, and perspectives of women of color. This intertwining of feminism and racism began in the nineteenth century with the suffragists and continued throughout the next century. Although twenty-first-century feminists mostly acknowledge this problematic history and at least "talk the talk" of anti-racism, it would be naïve indeed to think that all such problems have vanished. Class and economic status are also dimensions that rank people and accord them differential privilege. Although people of color are statistically far less affluent than their white counterparts, there are some very wealthy black people and there are many impoverished white people. Education too ranks people in the US, and it intersects with economic status, with race, and with sex.

The social broad-based understanding of racism was first articulated by activists and scholars of color and then influenced the work of a number of other politically engaged intellectuals (including those working on sexism and related issues). What people not committed to such projects often heard were sweeping critiques of familiar practices in which they participated and 'gotcha' applications of the *racist* label (or *sexist* or *male chauvinist*). It is not surprising that the favored entry for *racist* on the *Urban Dictionary* site,[14] reproduced in the first entry in Figure 6.1, is a rant against the author's interpretation of an expanded social approach to understanding racism and a plea for what the author calls the 'real' definition, something like what many standard dictionaries give. The second-ranked entry has substantially more 'thumbs up' (or 'likes') than the top definition but a slightly lower ratio of likes to dislikes; it just hurls invective at the whole notion of racism. The third insists that not all racism is directed at blacks, and the fourth and fifth basically try to present their authors as non-racist.

Urban Dictionary contributors do not, of course, constitute a representative slice of Americans, whether whites or people of color. Their entries do, however, illustrate, the widespread panic about being labeled *racist*, especially in certain contexts. Some of that panic is the product of what sociologist Robin DiAngelo has dubbed 'white fragility.'[15] White fragility fosters (often deliberate) 'white ignorance,' the notion of which was articulated and named by philosopher Charles Mills.[16] This fragility stems from fear that we whites, including those of us who call ourselves progressive and take pride in proclaiming our commitment to racial equality, will be exposed for our role in maintaining the deep hypocrisies of American history and of persisting racial stratification and injustice in "the land of the free." Some panic, however, stems both from misconstruing the expanded notion of racism (which leads

Figure 6.1 *Urban Dictionary* Definitions of *Racism* (in order of rankings)

1. racism (posted December 20, 2005)

A term that used to mean **prejudice** towards one or more races.

In modern use, this word is used by people to explain the behaviour of people of other races, whether race is called into **the issue** or not.

Also: racism can now include having good race **relations**. If you try to be friends with someone of a different race, someone will call you a racist.

ME: *Dude I met this black guy when I was ...*
IDIOT: *RACIST!*
ME: *How is that racism? I was going to say that I met this **black dude** when I was going to see my best friend, who's asian.*
IDIOT: *You're **just friends** with that asian because you think that makes you a good person for not being racist. You must feel sorry for him, you goddamn racist!*
ME: *Race doesn't come into it. But **people like you** force race issues into everything.*

Like: 1423   Dislike: 424

2. racism (posted January 26, 2008)

Pure Bullshit. *Fresh out* of *the bull's arse.*

Like: 4640   Dislike: 1580

3. racism *(posted April 20, 2004)*

something people cant understand **doesnt** just happen against **blacks** from **whites**. *On an example **earlier** people keep using **black people** as **the only** people discriminated against*

Like: 2889   Dislike: 977

4. racism (posted May 26, 2004)

It's **Stupid**, we are all **amazing**, so **chill**. *white, black, hispanic, asian, indian, arabic, does it matter? Racism is messed up, all of our races have done good and bad.*

Like: 684   Dislike: 221

5. racism (posted May 4, 2003)

An excuse given by one 'race' of people to abuse another person's **rights**. Usually created by **blind ignorance**.
Racist: "All black people lie, steal and cheat – its in their genes."
Actual: "All people lie, steal and cheat – its in their genes."

Like: 1777   Dislike: 744

From www.urbandictionary.com/define.php?term=racism (accessed August 5, 2019) some to think that speaking of race at all is racist) and from the weaponizing of the label *racist* for purposes that have nothing to do with anti-racist motives. For example, given official proclamations of anti-racism at many corporate headquarters and the like, labeling a coworker *racist* can be an effective way to get them in trouble, perhaps removed from the payroll.

Here is one real-life example of such malicious labeling told to me by an observer. (I'm eliminating identifying information to protect the privacy of those involved.) A young black man employed in a large store was telling his white manager about a comment he'd heard from a white stranger he happened to encounter at a country music concert. She looked startled by his presence and said something like "Your people don't listen to this kind of music, do they?" "I reminded her," he reported in his conversation with his manager, "that 'my people' have the vote now." The manager laughed appreciatively and said "Did she remind you that it was just 3/5 of hers?" They went on working together companionably. A new young white employee, already at loggerheads with the manager, observed this interaction and later reported in a public meeting that "I don't like working under a racist." How he described the exchange to the higher-ups is unclear but their response was to suggest that the manager accept a transfer to another store, which he did not want to do, or resign. Using *racist* to label others can be a way of claiming virtue, of distancing oneself from all responsibility for continuing racism. Such labeling also focuses on individuals rather than on larger social patterns and arrangements. And the management response illustrates the kind of 'moral panic' that can overrespond to racially charged incidents while neglecting genuine persisting problems.

Back in October of 1991 Clarence Thomas provided a master class in evacuating *racism* of real content in order to weaponize it. A year later Toni Morrison edited *Race-ing Justice, En-gender-ing Power: Essays on Anita Hill, Clarence Thomas, and the*

Construction of Social Reality. Among the articles is "Doing Things with Words: Racism as Speech Act and the Undoing of Justice" by Claudia Brodsky Lacour, whose theoretical writings often draw on philosophical thought. In this case, she uses aspects of philosopher John Austin's theory of speech acts, articulated in his *How to Do Things with Words,* to analyze Thomas's deployment of the word *racism.*[17]

> Anita Hill's words were silenced not by any conflicting testimony, nor certainly by anything that could be passed off as evidence, but by a word, the very word that, unspoken, had previously safeguarded Clarence Thomas from rigorous investigation. It was in "response" to Anita Hill's testimony that Thomas said the word "racism," and in proclaiming himself a "victim" of "racism," an apparently enraged Thomas disarmed his interrogators .... [I]t was "racism" the *word* [italic added], not the thing, that rendered Anita Hill's words effectively meaningless by rendering deaf those for whom those words were intended. From the Senate hearing room, to the press room, to the living room, the word "racism" cut off a mental channel of communication.

When Thomas used the word *racism* to discredit Anita Hill's testimony, which no one really believed was motivated by racism, then, Lacour suggests, he told the public that the word was empty, that racism was not a real thing. The word replaced any real response and "aimed blame in melodramatic gestures at no one in particular and at everyone ... With a calculated ripple effect the word 'racism' took everyone supposedly surrounding Anita Hill into its scope. ... [T]he attack worked. Thomas drew sympathy from blacks and whites alike and 'racism' was universally deplored." Members of the congressional hearings committee, all men, piled on to join in loudly deploring the racism that Clarence Thomas and his black family had faced. They implicitly acquiesced with Thomas's implication that it would be racist to even consider the charges of Anita Hill, a black woman, against him, a black man.

Disputes over applicability of *racism* and *racist* continue. They are often part of ongoing debates over how best to understand and confront issues of race, especially the position of black Americans, in the USA. In turn, these arguments about the meanings of words stand in for (unacknowledged) debates over issues like school busing in order to desegregate schools, which are 'color-conscious,' vs so-called 'colorblind' policies in many arenas of life. And much more. In his brilliant *Keywords*, social theorist (and word historian) Raymond Williams cautions against attempting to push for "one 'true' or 'proper' or 'scientific' sense and dismissing other senses as loose or confused."[18] He speaks here of the word *culture*, but what he says is, I think, applicable to the word *racism*. Competing senses reflect in part competing understandings of how individual beliefs and actions as well as everyday practices relate to larger-scale institutions and social structures. There is clearly interaction between 'hearts and minds' and social and cultural systems. For some purposes – intellectual, political, even moral or ethical – it can be both useful and appropriate to push for one rather than another understanding. Philosophers recently have given considerable attention to delineating interpretations with particular purposes in mind.[19] My emphasis here, however, is on different understandings of words like *racism* and *racist* that are advanced and deployed by ordinary people in the course of their social lives.

Given the different understandings, the different meanings associated with *racism* and *racist*, should we say that disputes over their applicability in which the different meanings play a part are 'merely verbal,' that those arguing with one another are really just talking past one another? No. At least most of the time, such arguments are really about what the words *should* mean. And that linguistic dispute is part of the nonlinguistic argument about what social relations and arrangements tied to racialized groups should be and also about what strategies might be needed for change. There are no easy answers here but the disputes are substantive, not 'just semantics.'

Is It About Language? Redefining *Rape*

In some cases language gets reformed with little or no talk about words as such but only about their content. The case of *rape* provides a good example. Many are unaware that the word *rape* in English usage several centuries ago simply did not apply to penile–vaginal intercourse forced by a husband on his wife. The crucial issue was that of consent. Sir Matthew Hale's seventeenth-century formulation is widely quoted: "The husband cannot be guilty of a rape committed by himself on his lawful wife, for by their mutual matrimonial consent and contract the wife hath given up herself in this context unto her husband, which she cannot retract."[20] Hale's Law, as this 'marital exemption' principle was called, operated in many Anglo-American jurisdictions well into the 1970s.

In her 2013 book *Redefining Rape: Sexual Violence in the Era of Suffrage and Segregation*, historian Estelle Freedman offers a wide-ranging historical account of evolving understandings of *rape* in the United States.[21] She notes that despite the continued rule of Hale's Law in courtrooms, nonconsensual sex within marriage was seen early on by some feminists as importantly like other kinds of nonconsensual sex in inflicting harm on the women assaulted. In the 1870s and 1880s, for example, Lucy Stone and Henry Blackwell detailed husbands' assaults on wives in their "Crimes against Women" column in the *Women's Journal*. Although Stone and Blackwell did not protest the general tendency to cast black men as rapists of white women and to ignore white men's rapes of black women, they did hold white husbands responsible for sexual violence targeting both their wives and their servants.

Like wives and servants, sex workers also have generally been presumed to be unable to withhold consent. In the spring of 1986,

Pasadena Superior Court Judge Gilbert C. Alston dismissed rape allegations brought by a thirty-year-old Hispanic sex worker, declaring "A woman who goes out on the street and makes a whore out of herself opens herself up to anybody." Alston's decision was widely criticized, but many others were also unwilling to acknowledge that a person may consent to some sexual encounters yet nonetheless withhold consent for others, even if they are with the same person. Interestingly, even in the nineteenth century not all viewed a woman's chastity as essential to finding that she had been raped. Writing in 1864, a Vermont justice said, "It is no defence that she was a common strumpet, if a rape was actually committed upon her."

Black women during reconstruction and the subsequent Jim Crow era did not shrink from calling attention to the racial politics of talk about rape, which was sometimes dubbed "The Negro Crime." Not only were black men often accused of rape on the basis of no more than looking a white woman in the eye, and then murdered by lynch mobs, but black women were portrayed as sexually promiscuous and thus always consenting to, indeed even welcoming, sexual attentions from white men. The idea that a white woman might enter consensually into a sexual relationship with a black man was considered unthinkable. A white woman who did so could later with impunity label her black partner a rapist. False accusations of this kind were sometimes the result of strong pressure on the woman from white family or friends, sometimes the result of the woman's changed attitudes toward the man.

Beginning in the early 1880s, journalist Ida B. Wells was unflinching in exposing the many false rape accusations made against black men that led to lynchings. Often, she wrote, the lynchings gave an "excuse to get rid of negros who were acquiring wealth and property," and "to keep the race terrorized."[22] Carefully studying news reports she found that fewer than one-third of lynchings actually involved accusations of rape, and of these many of the accused were in fact innocent. Blacks were sometimes lynched, as she observed, just "because they were saucy" – that is, not adequately deferential, obsequious. Wells also pointed to false accusations of rape that did not come from the white woman whose 'honor' was supposedly being protected. She noted that a white reporter had found that a black man lynched for alleged rape of a young white woman in Chestertown, MD was innocent. "The girl herself maintained that her assailant was a white man. When that poor Afro-American was murdered, the whites excused their refusal of a trial on the ground that they wished to spare the white girl the mortification of having to testify in court."[23]

At the same time, Wells noted that black women had a long history of sexual assault on themselves and their daughters by white men, a history that began with slave-owners raping enslaved women to increase the number of human beings in their possession. Emancipation did not end white men's sexual abuse of black women without fear of consequences, a situation that was exacerbated by the hypersexualizing stereotypes of those women. Ida B. Wells was perhaps the most outspoken and direct in her analysis of the role of rape, purported and actual, in helping shore up white power over black people. She noted that it was only white women whom southern white men seemed eager to protect and she did not shrink from criticizing the hypocrisy involved. "Virtue knows no color line, and the chivalry which depends upon complexion of skin and texture of hair can command no honest respect."[24] Wells and other black women gave reasoned and insightful analyses of interracial rape and accusations as about racialized power rather than sexual desire or proclivities. Although they sometimes wrote for publications with white audiences, their ideas got little currency beyond black communities. Their work did, however, play some role in the eventual creation in the twentieth century of interracial coalitions to stop the practice of lynching. Rape myths in the service of racism continue: Donald Trump characterized Mexican immigrants as "rapists."

Nearly a century after Ida B. Wells wrote, white feminist thinkers like Susan Brownmiller began articulating a similar view that rape was about power and not desire.[25] Their emphasis, however, was on men's power over women, mostly ignoring racial dimensions. Nearly a century after Lucy Stone and Henry Blackwell detailed and labeled "crimes" sexual assaults on wives by husbands, this latter group of feminists began to use *rape* to talk about such crimes. They realized that this linguistic move could be a powerful way to hold such husbands morally and legally accountable, to move toward making their actions criminal and not simply distasteful or unfortunate. Applying the label *rape* to a husband's sexual assault on his wife, whether or not a court validates the labeling, can have profound effects.

Although change came slowly in this matter, the marital exemption, Hale's Law, had disappeared from rape laws in the United States by the end of the twentieth century as a direct result of the work of anti-rape activists. There continues to be some pushback, but Anglo-American courts (as well as courts in many other jurisdictions around the world) now hold that a man's being married to a woman does not mean he cannot rape her. Indeed, for any man, whether or not he is someone with whom a woman has at some point consented to have sex is generally no longer held relevant to whether he raped her on a particular occasion. It is no longer just women who can be raped, and there has been growing public awareness that boys and men can also be victims. Readers of the *NY Times* in 2011 chastised the paper for avoiding the word *rape* in its reports of sexual assaults on young boys by Jerry Sandusky, an assistant football coach at the University of Pennsylvania. The public editor responded with an interesting article on *rape* as a word "in flux."[26] As announced by then Attorney General Eric Holder on January 6, 2012, the FBI now uses a new gender-neutral definition in collecting data on rape: "The penetration, no matter how slight, of the vagina or anus with any body part or object, or oral penetration by a sex organ of another person, without the consent of the victim."[27] The generally prevailing norms and conventions for labeling sexual contact *rape* have changed significantly as part of our general understanding of what counts as consent to sexual contact. But there continue to be debates.

Work like that of discourse analyst Susan Ehrlich helps us understand how, even though the boundaries of the word *rape* have expanded and continue to expand, there is an array of ongoing social and linguistic practices that help sustain sexual violence by constraining what gets counted as *rape* or even as the less seriously sanctioned *sexual assault*.[28] The law may say that a woman's sexual history, the clothes she wears (or doesn't wear), or whether she puts up a 'fight' should not be considered in deciding whether she has been raped. That does not, however, keep lawyers, juries, less formal investigative panels, and sometimes judges from taking such factors into account. Their questions to a female accuser often assume she is on trial, and their questions to a male defendant often assume that he has simply 'misunderstood' her lack of enthusiasm for his advances. She can be blamed for insufficiently vigorous objections, with her expressed fear of the man ignored.

Philosopher Susan Brison argues that the whole idea that being raped is just having had sex but not consenting to it is profoundly confused and misleading. As she notes, we don't treat being robbed as a nonconsensual gift or murder as nonconsensual assisted suicide. She proposes that we understand rape not as a kind of sexual interaction to which one party has not consented but as "gender-based sexualized violence." And, she suggests, rape of boys and men or of nonbinary people are also tied to wider systems of genderized power relations and do not just constitute objectionable individual actions. Part of the difficulty, as Brison sees clearly, is that familiar ways of talking (and thinking) about heterosexual activity not only ignore gender inequality but foster assumptions about women and men that contribute to sustaining that power differential. "The language of consent assumes a double standard in heterosexual relations. It is assumed that the man – the strong, active, sexually aggressive, partner – takes the initiative, seeking consent from the woman – the weak, passive, sexually submissive, one."[29]

Sexualized violence, or the threat thereof, is part of what supports continued gender hierarchies. Thus there are significant vested interests at play in trying to limit the scope of what can be labeled *rape*. These topics continue to be explored in the era of the #MeToo movement. For instance, there is beginning to be talk of *gray zone sex*, which may not constitute rape, sexual assault, or even sexual harassment but is in some real sense not fully consensual and far more than a "bad date." There are also, of course, occasional cases of false accusations of rape. But the myth of rape as a heinous crime committed only by vicious monsters, by 'brutes' who jump out and attack defenseless virtuous young maidens, is one reason why both women and men, often understandably, hesitate to apply the label to what they both recognize as nonconsensual sexual encounters, as coerced.

What is far harder to understand is the extreme reluctance to use the *rape* label even in cases like assaults on unconscious women. In her very instructive blog on feminist language issues, linguist Deborah Cameron reports that virtually all media sources expressed what she aptly labels "unreasonable doubt" in early 2019 reports on a case in Arizona. A severely brain-damaged woman who had been essentially comatose in a healthcare facility for many years (reports ranged from "over a decade" to "27 years") surprised her caretakers when she gave birth on December 29, 2018, her moaning finally drawing attention to her condition.[30] Even in the (unlikely) event of artificial insemination, there had to have been an assault on this woman, a crime committed. Virtually all the news reports, however, spoke of "alleged" or "possible" or "apparent" assault or rape. Why? As Cameron points out, some of this might have been just reflexive wording to ensure that the perpetrator was treated as "innocent until proven guilty" and not convicted by the press. But she also argues that this obviously excessive reluctance to label what happened a crime is likely to stem as much from systemic devaluation and widespread ignoring of the difficulties facing disabled women (and perhaps also Native American women – it later emerged that the woman was

Navajo) as from trying to protect a potential defendant against criminal charges.

Legal journalist Dahlia Lithwick reports that Jeffre Cheuvront, a Nebraska district judge, barred the word *rape* from proceedings in the fall of 2006 in which a complainant (*complainant* has replaced the word *victim* in many courtrooms) was alleging that she had been raped.[31] Cheuvront approved a motion from the defense that the words *rape, victim, sexual assault, assailant,* and *sexual assault kit* all be forbidden. And then in preparing for a retrial in 2007 the prosecution asked for a ban on words like *sex* and *intercourse,* a motion that was denied. As Lithwick puts it, "The result is that the defense and the prosecution are both left to use the same word – *sex* – to describe either forcible sexual assault, or benign consensual intercourse. As for the jurors, they'll just have to read the witnesses' eyebrows to sort out the difference." The defense lawyer had raised the worry that use of *rape* would prejudice the jurors. "It's a legal conclusion for a witness to say, 'I was raped' or 'sexually assaulted.'" But as Lithwick and legal scholar Robert Weisberg point out, there really is no neutral language for the prosecution and its witnesses to use. Lithwick puts it this way. "The real question . . . is whether embedded in the word *sex* is another 'legal conclusion' – that the intercourse was consensual . . . If the complaining witness in a rape trial has to describe herself as having had 'intercourse' with the defendant, should the complaining witness in a mugging be forced to testify that he was merely giving his attacker a loan? . . . [O]ne can still say *murder* or *embezzlement* on the stand."

At this point one might well want to protest that the changes and ongoing debates I have been discussing are not about language or what we call things at all. They are about sexual consent and coercion. Certainly such debates are not only about language. They are, however, in part about language, particularly about the applicability of certain words and expressions like *consent, rape, assault,* and *have sex.*[32] In the case of the word *consent,* debates are often doubly about language, given that there are norms of linguistic practice (e.g., those that make 'no' a frowned-upon move in many contexts) that can lead to what looks like 'assent' but may well be less than full 'consent.' Those words figure in informal practices of accusing and denying as well as in institutional contexts such as congressional hearings and judicial processes. Sexualized power relations and sanctions, not only those legally imposed but those operative in corporate cultures and elsewhere, play out in part through linguistic practices.

Preferred Gender Pronouns

English speakers have long taken it to "go without saying" that people can be readily sorted into women and men, girls and boys. We have also presumed that, once sorted, an individual's gender category remains constant. These assumptions of gender binarism and constancy are by no means the province of English speakers. They are pervasive. What is true of English and a number of other languages (but far from all) is that we rely on those assumptions whenever we speak of a particular individual other than ourselves or our addressee(s).

The standard English personal pronouns for singular third-person reference are gendered. English speakers learn very early to use *she* (and the rest of the paradigm: *her*, *hers*, and *herself*) for specific individual (presumptively) female referents and *he* (and *him*, *his*, and *himself*) whenever speaking of those we take to be male. There continues to be a limited use of *he* where there is not a specific referent and the point of what is said is general (e.g., "an English major chooses his words very carefully"). As noted in Chapter 2, such usages are declining, and singular *they* (along with *them*, *their*, *theirs*, *themself*) now often appears, even in formal written contexts. In such generic cases there has long been the practice of using singular *they*, kept in check only by the concerted efforts of many English teachers, editors, and the like. There is a website detailing many places in Jane Austen using singular *they*; the site also gives many more recent examples of singular *they*.[33]

In many cases where gender identity is unknown or the speaker would rather not specify, *they* (along with the rest of the paradigm) comes to the rescue: "someone left *their* computer in 106" or "my friend is going to lend me *their* unicycle so I can try it out." But we still tend to resist *they* in such contexts as those where the individual has just been referred to by a proper name. "Lee lost *their* bike" seems to suggest that the bike Lee lost belonged to a group (to which Lee might or might not belong), although such uses are increasing, helped by automated messages on social media ("Lee has changed their status"). Could we just repeat Lee's name? For many, the difficulty here is even greater. "Lee lost Lee's bike" strongly suggests two different people named Lee being spoken about. There's almost certainly a better chance of getting ourselves used to interpreting "Lee lost their bike" as a non-gendered equivalent of "Lee lost her bike" or "Lee lost his bike" than going the two-*Lee* route, a strategy that would only work in any case where an individual's name is known. And nearly equivalent sentences with *they* or the other members of the paradigm already sound perfectly OK in everyday encounters. Two people meet in a parking lot near the trail where they plan to hike. One points to a person off in the distance and says "That person told me just before you got here that they lost their bike here yesterday so be sure to lock yours." Easy. Admittedly this would be much harder if the person who gave bike advice is still on the scene, and the speaker points to that person and says "They just told me . . ., " no matter how androgynous their appearance might be. Yet people are beginning to be accustomed to such usages, and singular *they* is definitely increasing its reach.

Of course much of the time people successfully talk about non-addressees using the familiar gendered pronouns. But even those who do not question either gender binarism or gender constancy and rarely if ever knowingly encounter people who do raise such questions sometimes find themselves in a position where a non-gendered singular third-person pronoun would be useful. In addition to the many general cases that have been widely discussed, the gender identity of the person one wants to speak of may be unknown or irrelevant.

Increasingly, especially for younger people, speaking of those who might identify as transgender or nonbinary raises live and not just theoretical pronoun issues. It is not really difficult to speak of transgender women or transgender men. Most appreciate being referred to by the pronoun that matches the gendered identity they affirm. (It can be a little trickier speaking of transgender people before their transition. Some, but not all, adopt the policy of using the pronoun that would have been used of them at that earlier time.) That is not to say that all who know they are speaking of a transgender woman use *she* in speaking of her. Misgendering by using *he* to speak of a transgender woman can be a deliberately hostile act and does happen. The wrong pronoun may, however, sometimes slip out from a speaker who knew the person well before transition and is still struggling to change old linguistic habits. (Those old friends and family may also sometimes forget and use a former misgendered first name; if done with deliberate malice, as does happen, the practice is often called *deadnaming* by members of transgender communities and their allies.) Misgendering can also and sometimes does occur when someone simply mistakes another's affirmed gender (and that happens not only to transgender people). When a speaker is not sure of gender identity (or rejection thereof) of people of whom they are speaking, it would be useful indeed if *they* (and its mates) were always considered acceptable. We are certainly not there yet in most English-speaking communities of practice.

But what should be done if a speaker wants to talk about someone whom they know rejects gender binarism, identifying as neither female nor male? My own default is to try to go with singular *they*, even though it still sometimes feels quite odd. That oddness is not only because of the (relatively minor) issues discussed above in contexts where a proper name has just been used or where the person is present with those speaking to one another. It is also because choosing *they* can highlight my avoidance of the more usual gendered options, something that could on occasion interfere with other things I'm trying to accomplish in the particular context. Nonetheless, singular *they*, which the American Dialect Society (ADS) chose in 2015 as the Word of the Year, was recognized again by ADS at the beginning of 2020 as the Word of the Decade precisely because of "its growing use to refer to a known person whose gender identity is nonbinary."

Some universities and other educational institutions now routinely ask students for their "preferred gender pronouns" (widely abbreviated as PGPs) and send these to instructors, asking them to respect students' preference for how others should speak of them. Occasionally, meeting venues provide name tags allowing attendees to indicate their PGPs, and a very few people offer their PGPs when introducing themselves face-to-face or online. "Hi, I'm Sally, and my PGPs are *they*, *their*, and *them* though I expect and am perfectly happy with the *she/her* option." At a meeting designed to increase awareness of gender-identity issues, I actually said something along these lines. I was the only person still affirming the gender identity assigned me at birth – that is, the only cis person – who chose the non-gendered option. The others at the meeting giggled a little but no one, even among these open and active transgender and nonbinary supporters, used *they* to speak of me. My attempt to model singular *they* as a general-purpose default option to familiar gendered forms was a resounding failure. Even more recently, I attended a party to welcome the out-of-town cast and director for an upcoming play at a local theater. One of the theater staff asked us to give our pronoun preferences when introducing ourselves. Most people forgot or just mumbled them – a couple of interns asked for *they*, *them*, and *their* (probably this known preference was what prompted the staff member's suggestion). I was one of the last and this time I said "I'm Sally and I write about pronouns – I prefer *they*, *them*, and *their* as defaults but I don't mind people using *she* and *her* to talk about me." Well, it was a party, and the wine-fueled laughter just upped the enjoyment level.

Not surprisingly, the vast majority of English speakers (and perhaps many readers of this book) have not even heard of PGPs and still assume that choosing between the *she* and *he* options is always appropriate. They may occasionally be slightly perplexed when someone's appearance is a little hard to read (and may sometimes use *they* in such situations), but pronouns are not a huge concern for them. When I drafted this section in early spring 2019, offering or requesting PGP information was a relatively rare occurrence in my own experience and, according to my informal poll of friends still teaching at colleges and universities, not terribly common even for those more closely in touch with young people. Interestingly, by January 2020, volunteering one's PGPs in person or online with the expression "my pronouns" had apparently become highly salient to members of the ADS, many of whom are in university settings. They voted in "my pronouns" as 2019 Word of the Year. Along with Word of the Decade "singular *they*," recognition of Word of the Year "my pronouns" highlights developing linguistic practices in many communities of practice that make it easier for people to control how others assign them gender.[34] But this does not eliminate the need for default options. Even if it becomes standard in introducing oneself to offer, along with a name, "my pronouns are . . .," there will still be situations in which a pronoun is needed to refer to someone with unknown and unavailable PGP. For such reasons, I strongly advocate widening the use of singular *they* as a default non-gendered option.

Many protest that the pronoun's plurality should rule it out. But remember the discussion in Chapter 4 of the development of *you* to address individuals and not just groups. As we saw, *you* began as the plural of *thou*, and we now find its use to refer to single individuals as well as groups unproblematic. Keep in mind that *you* continues to take plural verb agreement in mainstream varieties of English even when designating a single individual yet it also has a singular reflexive form, *yourself*. ("If you are [not *is*] unhappy, treat yourself [not *yourselves*] to a massage.") On this model, it would seem easiest to retain plural verb agreement for *they* but adopt the singular reflexive form. (Speaking of someone using the non-gendered option would then yield sentences like "If

they are feeling stressed, they should treat themself to a massage.")
In addition, there are many people around the world who use
English regularly but have some other native language (or even
several other languages they use for work and at home). Some
non-native speakers whose own language does not gender pronouns frequently make what native speakers and the person
spoken of take as the "wrong" choice of gendered pronouns. For
such non-native speakers, a non-gendered default like *they* might
also be welcome.

Having *they* as a default is quite consistent with using other
options if preferred by the person of whom one is speaking. Some,
for example, ask others to refer to them using *ze* (with either *zir*,
zirself, *zirs* filling out the paradigm or *eir*, *eirself*, *eirs*). Others opt
for the so-called Spivak pronouns, which were relatively widely
used on LambdaMOO, an online community launched in 1990
and very popular for some years. These also have variants: either *e*
or *ey* instead of the subjective *she* or *he*, *em* instead of the objective
her or *him*, *eir* instead of the possessive adjective *her* or *his*, *eirself*
for the reflexive -*self* forms, and *eirs* instead of the possessive
pronouns *hers* or *his*.

As I was writing this section in the spring of 2019, I heard about
a conference slated to be held in June 2019 in Kingston, Ontario,
"They, Hirself, Em and YOU: Nonbinary Pronouns in Research
and Practice." Organizers posted a notice on LinguistList that
called for linguistic work on this topic and indicated that there
would also be contributions from educators, activists, and scholars outside linguistics, and a wide range of other discussions. Just
a day or two earlier I had learned that the Lesbian Gay Bisexual
Transgender Resource Center at the University of Wisconsin,
Milwaukee, planned to host a celebration on October 17, 2019
of International Pronouns Day. The point of their event: to
promote not only finding out the pronouns others prefer but
respecting those preferences by using them. Here is their statement of purpose: "Referring to people by the pronouns they
determine for themselves is basic to human dignity. Being
referred to by the wrong pronouns particularly affects transgender

and gender nonconforming people. Together, we can transform society to celebrate people's multiple, intersecting identities."[35] Both the Canadian conference on nonbinary pronouns and the Wisconsin celebration of respecting people's pronoun preferences show that nonbinary pronouns and personal pronoun preferences are quite consequential issues within certain communities.

There appears to have been concern about nonbinary pronouns in English many hundreds of years ago, but the worry at that point was the possible loss of gendered pronouns. Our current familiar 'feminine' *she* only came into English when the contrast between *hē* (the Old English ancestor of the modern so-called masculine *he*) and *hēo* (the OE so-called feminine pronoun) was vanishing because the unstressed final syllable of *hēo* was so often dropped. Had *she* not been pressed into service, we would have had only one personal pronoun in English by Chaucer's time, and the current concerns over nonbinary pronouns might not ever have surfaced. About a millennium ago some of those speaking what is now called Old English, a Germanic language from which modern varieties of English descend, apparently were so eager to retain a gender binary in the pronoun system that they may well have brought in a new pronoun from a Scandinavian language to do the job. We don't of course know very much at all about what went on in the various communities in which *she* and *hēo* competed with one another. We do know that taking a function word from another language – an article, preposition, pronoun – is relatively rare. This is in sharp contrast with the ease with which languages adopt content words from other languages. In English, examples of content words that were originally non-native, modeled on words in another language, abound: *beef* from French, *algebra* from Arabic, *glitch* from Yiddish, *patio* from Spanish, *toboggan* from Miqmaq (an Algonquian language of North America), *tsunami* from Japanese, *tomato* from Nahuatl (once called Aztec, varieties of which are still spoken widely in Mexico), *bungalow* from Urdu (spoken in India and Pakistan), and on and on. Borrowing of *she* from Icelandic or some other Scandinavian language is not the only possibility, and we may never really have the full story on the history of *she*. What we can certainly infer, however, is that many of those tenth- and eleventh-century speakers cared a lot about keeping the binary split, the split that causes so many difficulties in our own times, especially for transgender or nonbinary people.

I noted earlier that the ADS has singled out singular *they* and "my pronouns" as helping English speakers escape the familiar forced binary of *he* and *she*. In part because of the unusual and interesting history of *she* and in part because of the increasing frequency of its occurrence in the late twentieth century as feminist analysis and activism made clear that *he* was not so generic as had often been proclaimed, the ADS has also honored *she*. In the year 2000, ADS selected *she* as the Word – not of the Year, Decade, or Century – but of the (immediately past) Millennium.[36] Back in 2000, escaping forced gender binaries was still not something widely discussed. The ADS announcement did not talk about the fact that *hēo* might have quietly vanished and left English with a single personal pronoun, thus one with no gender content, erasing the forced binary choice.

The pronoun *she*, however, is by no means yet a fully equal partner of *he* – it remains marked. Nearly two decades after *she* was selected as Word of the Millennium, MIT linguist Roger Levy and colleagues at Potsdam and at the University of California at San Diego decided to use the 2016 US presidential elections as a naturally occurring experimental situation to study gendered pronouns. What they found was that, even among people who both expected and wanted Hillary Clinton to win, there was considerable reluctance to use *she* to refer to the (then as yet undetermined) "next president." Singular *they* was the favored choice and gender hedging was also used (e.g., *he or she*), but *he* was preferred to *she*. And reading *she* in contexts where it was not stereotypically expected that the referent would be female led to comprehension difficulties compared to *he* or *they*. A year later the research team conducted similar experiments using the UK parliamentary elections, where Theresa May was not only the incumbent prime minister but her party was heavily favored to win (and did win). The pronoun *she* was produced more often in the UK study for "the next prime minister" than *he*, but not at the expected rate, and without the expected comprehension advantages for *she*.[37] Although the authors do not put it this way, there still seems to be reluctance to embrace *she* as able to refer to just an ordinary human being. Femaleness still contrasts with maleness in being seen as specially distinctive, a condition that bars those having it from being fully representative of 'normal' humans.

Many current speakers of English are dismissive of pronoun concerns. Language users mostly talk and write or text with little explicit attention to their pronoun choices. Most of the time pronouns, which are more tied into language structure than content words, get slotted into what we say almost automatically, with no explicit attention to the process at all. Being forced to weigh pronoun choices feels "weird" to many and makes them (us) uncomfortable. The parenthetical "us" is my admission to my own occasional discomfort about pronoun choices, discomfort with many sources. For some speakers, such discomfort can lead to noticing the privileges derived from never having questioned gender identities. People nudged out of their comfort zones sometimes become allies of those whose own position has not allowed them the luxury of comfort about these matters.

Most people like to think of language as just 'there,' as neutral. They do not enjoy being reminded that some familiar linguistic practices may become unsustainable as social practices become more sensitive to the interests of a wider range of people, including those outside standard gender/sexual binaries. Changes are underway, but those involving pronouns are especially challenging. This is in part because pronouns are more deeply embedded in linguistic structure than content words like *girl* or *boy*. It is also in part because issues of gender, sex, and sexuality are very deeply embedded in social structure – and many, perhaps especially older people, would rather not think about them much at all.[38]

Euphemism vs "Identity-Affirmation" or "Correction"

There is a substantial literature on euphemisms, which linguists
Keith Allan and Kate Burridge dubbed 'shields.'[39] A euphemism is
used as an alternative to other 'dispreferred' expressions in an effort
to shield language users from harmful effects that use of the dis-
preferred alternatives, often 'blunter' or 'more direct' or even
'tabooed,' might bring. Feared harm could be to the speaker:
perhaps avoiding the distasteful alternative seems thoughtful or
polite, saving the speaker from potential social disapproval. And
speakers do not only try to shield themselves. The reason for
avoiding alternative expressions is often fear that their hearers
may be harmed by them. Perhaps direct criticism will damage a
hearer's self-esteem, so the speaker shields the hearer by substitut-
ing some euphemistic comment for the criticism they would otherwise give. Some of what its critics call "PC language" might qualify
as euphemism, but certainly not all. I'll discuss language policies
and guidelines, including some of those labeled "PC" and debates
around them, in the next chapter.

Do euphemisms actually 'improve' language? There is a vast
array of areas in which euphemisms are regularly introduced:
death, sex, bodily functions, money, religion, governmental actions,
and many kinds of taboos. Linguists are fond of pointing to what
cognitive scientist Steven Pinker dubbed the "euphemism treadmill."[40] Gravediggers and embalmers give way to undertakers who
become morticians who become funeral directors. A water closet
becomes a toilet becomes a bathroom becomes a rest room
becomes the facilities. When a dog can "go to the bathroom on
the living room rug," "go to the bathroom" needs another euphemism – it can no longer "shield" us from the immediate image of
smelly bodily wastes spilling into the outside world. The original
indirection has vanished because of the very heavy use of the new
term. The distasteful lexical baggage carried by earlier forms has
been firmly reattached to what is now essentially their replacement.
Some euphemisms persist *as* euphemisms, generally because they
have not crowded out terminology that denotes more directly.

Few if any believe that changing terminology will in and of itself change other aspects of the world, including social arrangements. Relabeling garbage collectors "sanitation engineers" will not bring them respect or higher wages, nor will it free them from dirty, smelly, heavy physical labor on the job. And it is hard to imagine that anyone doing such work ever thought so. In many cases, the new labels are not initiated by those being renamed. There are certainly cases of those in power – bosses or politicians, for example – offering terminological window dressing to groups they control in lieu of improved working conditions and genuine respect. Such insincere 'merely verbal' moves have given a bad name to linguistic activism.

Are frequent shifts in identity labels like those we saw in the first chapter signs that the euphemism treadmill is operating? Steven Pinker seems to think so. "Names for minorities will continue to change as long as people have negative attitudes toward them. We will know we have achieved mutual respect when the names stay put."[41] But people did not begin adopting *black* or *African American* rather than *Negro* to shield anyone from pain or embarrassment. They were not advocating alternatives to *Negro* in a misguided attempt to veil racist attitudes, to lessen bigotry. They were, I contend, far more concerned about naming themselves and fostering new positive associations within black communities than in obscuring negative ones that outsiders might have (or that even those so labeled might have internalized). Those who offer new identity labels for themselves and those with whom they share that identity are not proposing yet more euphemisms. Rather they are trying to strengthen ingroup ties, to use positive self-definition as one (though certainly not the only) component of group mobilization, part of a strategy to improve the group's standing. Such shifts can be seen as identity-affirmations from within, which take different forms at different times. Motives and source matter enormously in deciding whether a particular linguistic innovation is a euphemism.

ASL (American Sign Language) scholars Jami Fisher, Gene Mirus, and Donna Jo Napoli make this important point in their recent paper on some cases of (sub)-lexical changes being proposed and adopted within ASL-using communities.[42] Many signs in ASL (and in other sign languages) originate as highly iconic – that is, the appearance of the sign in some ways resembles its content. For example, the sign for SMOKE looks a lot like someone holding a cigarette (a V-shape made by the index and middle fingers held near lips, other fingers folded down), and the sign for DRINK looks a lot like someone holding a glass and moving it up from mid-chest to near lips, ending with thumb at mouth and palm outward and slightly curved fingers.[43] Over time iconicity is often reduced as new signs stabilize but may nonetheless remain, a process that is more evident to some than to others. Spoken languages too have iconicity – for example, words like *eek* and *boom* 'sound like' their content. Iconicity is far more pervasive, however, in sign languages than in spoken languages because the three-dimensional space used in signing offers more potential than speech sounds for creating signs that 'resemble' their content. (The difference in medium means that sign languages differ in other ways from the languages with which hearing people are familiar. Most hearing people are unaware that sign languages have complex and distinctive structures of their own and are not 'signed' versions of ambient spoken languages.) Iconicity often brings with it what I've called lexical baggage – that is, associations beyond the content of a lexical item. What reformers (my term, not theirs) propose is to 'correct' a sign – that is, to change it in order to remove baggage that seems at odds with how the reformers understand what is being talked about. They want to 'align' the form with the meaning, to make the sign 'truer' to the world or to their experience, less potentially misleading or distorting.

Not all form–meaning mismatches get 'corrected.' Much as English continues to use 'films' long after film-free digital photography has taken over in Hollywood and elsewhere, long after cell phones have taken over, ASL mostly continues to use a sign for TELEPHONE inspired by handsets that the user holds to ear and mouth. (There is a newer sign especially for cell phones, but it is not widely used.) This misalignment of form and meaning goes uncorrected because there are no serious interests at stake, no potential unwanted problematic meanings conveyed. For many, the sign is probably now completely arbitrary, no longer iconic at all. There does not seem any need for correction.

Here is a case where the authors of the study mentioned above find evidence that a felt need for correction has indeed pushed change. The earlier BLIND sign involved a bent-V handshape, pointed directly toward the eyes. The newer sign preserves the handshape but moves the hand to the cheek on the same side as the hand. This shift reduces the iconicity and thereby is better aligned with views that being blind, as an identity, involves more than absence of vision just as being deaf involves more than matters of hearing. In discussing this change, a number of their deaf consultants reminded the authors of an ASL sign for AUDISM used some decades ago. That sign graphically indicated a similarly simplistic essentializing by many hearing people of deaf people. Such essentializing is an important component of audism, which is systematic privileging based on audiological status. The sign used B-handshapes above, below, and on the ear, suggesting problematic 'boxing in' of deaf people by many hearing people on the basis of their audiological status. (Finger-spelling is more commonly used for AUDISM nowadays.) Correcting the BLIND sign, deaf consultants explained, helped avoid suggesting that blind identity is just about people's eyes, about the status of their vision.

Not all the cases discussed in this study are connected to identity. They all, however, are instances where some deaf signers have seen the forms as problematic from their perspective as members of deaf communities. (Not all signers agree, in part because iconicity is in the eyes of the beholder and in part because not all recognize a misalignment.) The suggested corrections in the cases discussed are not offered or adopted as 'shields' to protect against something unpleasant or impolite or tabooed in some way. Rather, they are designed to remove problematic visually suggested messages, including those that assume the universality of the perspectives of hearing people.

Linguistic awareness, the authors suggest, is especially acute in deaf communities, given that ambient spoken languages are not fully accessible and entry into signing communities is often hard-won. Modern technology, including posting videos, has allowed deaf communities more readily to discuss and to change their shared languages. 'Correction' of signs not only eliminates what the reformers see as misalignments of form and meaning. Correction also helps spread newly emerging 'sensibilities' within deaf communities. It can be an important part of the process of supporting and promoting the new attitudes and stances.

Euphemisms can be useful linguistic innovations. Some even escape the lure of the euphemism treadmill. But calling a proposed linguistic change a euphemism often constitutes resistance to that change, dismissing the possibility that it might be helpful to language users pursuing certain interests. Self-affirmation and correction are metalinguistic moves that can be useful components of social action and change.

Notes

1. See McConnell-Ginet 2014.
2. Quoted in Shapiro 1985, p. 6.
3. Quoted in Shapiro 1985, p. 7.
4. John Lee Clark, "Distantism," *Tumblr*, August 3, 2017, https://johnleeclark .tumblr.com/post/163762970913/distantism.
5. See Fricker 2007; she uses the term 'hermeneutical injustice' for this particular kind of difficulty in improving understanding that faces those who lack social power. As Mary Kate McGowan reminds me, there is a vast literature from black women thinkers and other feminists on the ways problematic assumptions are often 'built into' readily available linguistic labels.
6. Glick and Fiske 1996, 2001.
7. See Phillips 2006, Maryapan 2011. Thanks to Mary Kate McGowan for suggesting I mention these important collections.
8. Collins 1998, pp. 70–71. Pages 61–76 are all highly relevant to the issues underlying debates among black women intellectuals on *womanism* vs *black*

feminism. The reference to "visionary pragmatism" and the quote from Cole are on p. 188.

9. See Bailey and Trudy 2018 for discussion, especially of their contention that their work in developing and applying this new concept is often ignored.

10. "Racist," *Oxford Dictionaries*, n.d., https://en.oxforddictionaries.com/definition/us/racist.

11. "Racist," *Collins Dictionary*, n.d., www.collinsdictionary.com/us/dictionary/english/racist.

12. Nicki Lisa Cole, "Defining Racism Beyond Its Dictionary Meaning," *Thoughtco.com*, July 14, 2019, www.thoughtco.com/racism-definition -3026511.

13. See, e.g., Haslanger 2012 [2010], Garcia 1999, Shelby 2002, Mills 2007, Faucher and Machery 2009.

14. Emerging Technology from the arXiv, "The Anatomy of the Urban Dictionary," *MIT Technology Review*, January 3, 2018, www.technologyreview.com /s/609871/the-anatomy-of-the-urban-dictionary.

15. DiAngelo 2018.

16. Mills 2007.

17. Lacour 1992. First quote from p. 132, second from 138. For Austin's foundational work on speech acts, consult Austin 1975 [1962], the second edition, which includes emendations from editors J. O. Urmson and Marina Sbisà.

18. Williams 1983.

19. Haslanger 2012 [2000], Cappelen 2018, and Shields 2019.

20. See, e.g., Russell 1990, p. 17.

21. Freedman 2013 is my source for the material in this and the next four paragraphs.

22. Freedman 2013, p. 107.

23. Freedman 2017, pp. 107–108.

24. Freedman 2013, p. 104.

25. Brownmiller 1975.

26. Arthur S. Brisbane, "Confusing Sex and Rape," *The New York Times*, November 19, 2011, www.nytimes.com/2011/11/20/opinion/sunday/confusing-sex-and-rape.html.

27. "Attorney General Eric Holder Announces Revisions to the Uniform Crime Report's Definition of Rape," US Department of Justice, January 6, 2012, https://archives.fbi.gov/archives/news/pressrel/press-releases/attorney-general-eric-holder-announces-revisions-to-the-uniform-crime-reports-definition-of-rape.

28. Ehrlich 2001, 2007.

29. From Susan Brison's unpublished 2018 Dartmouth Presidential Lecture, "Sexual Violence, Social Meanings, and Narrative Selves," available at www.youtube.com/watch?v=OYLN5K6ISrc.

30. "Unreasonable Doubt," *Language: A Feminist Guide*, January 13, 2019, https://debuk.wordpress.com/2019/01/13/unreasonable-doubt/.

31. Dahlia Lithwick, "Gag Order: A Nebraska Judge Bans the Word Rape From His Courtroom, *Slate*, June 20, 2007, https://slate.com/news-and-politics/2007/06/a-nebraska-judge-bans-the-word-rape-from-his-courtroom.html.

32. I have written elsewhere about debates over applicability of *have sex*; see, e.g., McConnell-Ginet 2018b.

33. "Jane Austen and Other Famous Authors Violate What Everyone Learned in Their English Class," The Republic of Pemberley website, n.d., www.pemberley.com/janeinfo/austhеir.html.

34. See www.americandialect.org/wp-content/uploads/2019-Word-of-the-Year-PRESS-RELEASE.pdf for the ADS press release on both "my pronouns" and "singular *they.*"

35. "Gender Pronouns," LGBTQ+ Resource Center, University of Milwaukee. https://uwm.edu/lgbtrc/support/gender-pronouns/.

36. The ADS announcement of that choice can be found at the following URL, www.americandialect.org/1999_words_of_the_year_word_of_the_1990s_word_of_the_20th_century.

37. For a concise and clear account of the research see Anne Trafton, "'She' Goes Missing from Presidential Language," *Phys.org*, January 8, 2020, https://phys.org/news/2020-01-presidential-language.html, which reports on von der Malsburg, Poppels, and Levy 2020.

38. After this book was already in production I read the review at www.nytimes.com/2020/01/21/books/review/whats-your-pronoun-dennis-baron.html. (Joe Moran, "English's Pronoun Problem Is Centuries Old," *The New York Times*, January 21, 2020.) Judging from the meticulous scholarship in Dennis Baron's earlier books on gender-neutral pronouns in English and related topics, I am confident that reading Baron 2020 will greatly enrich the reader's knowledge of the history and current situation of English personal pronouns.

39. Allan and Burridge 1991; Allan and Burridge 2006 and Allan 2018 continue their work.

40. Pinker 2002, p. 212.

41. Pinker 2002, p. 213.

42. Fisher, Mirus, and Napoli 2019.

43. See Cristina Baus, Manuel Carreiras, and Karen Emmorey, "When Does Iconicity in Sign Language Matter?" 2012, NCBI website, www.ncbi.nlm.nih.gov/pmc/articles/PMC3608132/ for discussion of iconicity in sign languages and pictures of some iconic and some non-iconic signs.

7 Authorizing: "When I Use a Word It Means Just What I Choose It to Mean . . . [But Who] Is to Be Master?"

> "[T]hat shows that there are three hundred and sixty-four days
> when you might get un-birthday presents –"
> "Certainly," said Alice.
> "And only **one** for birthday presents, you know. There's glory
> for you!"
> "I don't know what you mean by 'glory,'" Alice said.
> Humpty Dumpty smiled contemptuously. "Of course you don't –
> till I tell you. I meant 'there's a nice knock-down argument
> for you!'"
> "But 'glory' doesn't mean 'a nice knock-down argument,'" Alice
> objected.
> "When **I** use a word," Humpty Dumpty said, in rather a scornful
> tone, "it means just what I choose it to mean – neither more nor
> less."
> "The question is," said Alice, "whether you **can** make words mean
> so many different things."
> "The question is," said Humpty Dumpty, "which is to be master –
> that's all."
>
> Lewis Carroll, *Through the Looking Glass*

Humpty Dumpty's view of meaning is usually held up for ridicule. He is not as far off, however, as Alice and most others have thought. He articulates the important insight that there can be power struggles over what a word means. Humpty Dumpty sees a struggle between the language user and a possibly recalcitrant word. The word *glory* resists his effort to use it to mean "a nice knock-down argument" because that word comes with a history of uses that do not support such a use. And though Humpty Dumpty could indeed stipulate its meaning on this occasion,

Alice is quite right to think that in doing so he is not playing by the rules. Stipulations of one's meaning are sometimes appropriate, but bizarre when they seem to diverge completely from familiar uses. Even when stipulation is appropriate, its success is often limited. People's familiarity with previous uses and prevailing current norms for use does let them make small shifts, especially if they can see a purpose to them. Even small shifts can be hard to sustain, however, and the stipulator risks being misunderstood. Becoming master via just stipulating rarely works well.

Still Humpty Dumpty is onto something important. Power and authority – mastery – are indeed important for what words can be used to mean, what they can do. Though words themselves certainly do constrain their users, struggles for mastery over them arise primarily from conflicts of interest among language users. Different ways of using a word typically serve somewhat different interests, and users in different social positions and with different available resources may well be at odds over which interests to pursue. Who is to be acknowledged semantic master of this word? On what basis? In what contexts? In principle, semantic mastery could potentially always be at issue, arising simply from tugs-of-war between similarly placed individuals with divergent interests. Although we do see localized disagreements, struggles for semantic mastery are typically more global, sometimes within a community of practice and often between communities.

What I call *semantic authority* involves socially structured relations and institutions within a community of language users, social practices of authorizing (or de-authorizing) various linguistic practices, what words mean and which words to use. Some semantic authority is institutionalized, some is less formally claimed, and there are often contests.

Dictionaries

For many, including me, the term *semantic authority* initially conjures up memories of being told to consult a dictionary to see whether our own or someone else's attempted use of an expression has been endorsed by the revered volume. Looking things up in 'the' dictionary was a frequent activity in my childhood home. Talk of 'the' dictionary, however, ignores the multiplicity of dictionaries and their being compiled by human beings, both facts often forgotten by those who hold them in awe.

The best mainstream dictionaries draw on extensive lexicographical research, which, until recently, was based largely on print materials selected as representative of 'respected' usage of their time. Not surprisingly, the compilers making sense of these limited samples of actual language use have themselves generally been from socially dominant groups, mostly affluent white men. In the 1970s and 1980s, feminists published a number of alternative dictionaries that trenchantly criticized and often wittily exposed the biases in mainstream dictionaries: the sexist (and generally also elitist) assumptions in definitions, illustrative quotations, choice of source material, and the like.[1] But arguably these volumes also did much more.

In her 2018 book, *Women and Dictionary Making*, Lindsay Rose Russell has an excellent discussion of these second-wave feminist dictionaries, their predecessors, and some of their descendants.[2] "[F]eminist dictionaries," she argues, "while chronically vulnerable to minimization – as light satire, utopian pipedream, or less-than-rigorous lexicography – are a robust resource for understanding not only how dictionaries enact sexism and androcentrism [male-centeredness] but also how they might yet become more egalitarian in the interest of all English speakers." Russell proposes that feminist dictionaries embody three distinctive fundamental principles. First, they not only "disclose" but they "foreground their circumstances of production." This demystification of dictionary-making helps block assumptions of something like divine revelation dictating dictionary entries. Second, they encourage active (and "opinionated") dictionary use. Third, they "highlight the meanings they create and circulate as salient only within and because of certain contexts, contests, persons, and perspectives."

Among the second-wave feminist dictionary projects was *Websters' First New Intergalactic Wickedary of the English Language,* authored by lesbian feminist philosopher and word-loving academic Mary Daly "in cahoots with" Jane Caputi. The "Websters" in question are not part of Noah's family but "word-weavers," whom Daly invites to join her in playing with word histories and reclaiming words like *hag* and *crone* for proud self-labeling. This frequently cited entry summarily dismisses traditional dictionaries: "**Dick-tionary, n.**: any patriarchal dictionary: a derivative, tamed and muted lexicon compiled by dicks." I was reminded of Daly's acerbic definition when linguist Deborah Cameron cited it in "Dictionaries, dick-tionaries, and dyketionaries," a posting on her blog, *Language: A Feminist Guide* dated June 30, 2015. (For eminently readable, sane, and often witty discussions of linguistic politics, go to debuk.wordpress.com.)

Cameron's beautifully lucid essay was prompted by reactions she encountered to the decision in 2015 to add an entry for *cisgender* to the *Oxford English Dictionary.* Some were dismayed and others delighted, but both responses see the OED as authorizing this relatively recent coinage to designate the overwhelming majority of people who are not transgender, who see themselves as belonging to the gender that matches the sex assigned them at birth on the basis of their bodies. Cameron explains clearly what contemporary mainstream dictionaries aim to do: document actual patterns of usage across a wide range of users. At the same time, Cameron is under no illusions that this goal is actually achieved. She notes that mainstream dictionaries rely on often problematic past scholarship. She goes on to observe that, though lexicographic and editorial practices have improved in past decades (including the employment of more women even in mainstream dictionary-making), biases still persist in these sources. Like Russell, Cameron sees feminist dictionary projects as important resources both for reducing such bias and for developing dictionary-making practices that are less vulnerable to 'mastery' by those in dominant social groups. At the same time, she emphasizes that inclusion of a word in a respected mainstream dictionary does not count as endorsing that word or the projects and interests of those using it. As Cameron notes, however, dictionary users will probably continue taking inclusion as endorsement, treating dictionaries as authorizing rather than as trying to report on trending usage.

Although they are commonly interpreted as endorsing norms, contemporary mainstream dictionaries do not present themselves as semantic authorities. In contrast, language mavens like the late William Safire, who wrote often witty and frequently informative blurbs for popular consumption about current usage of various expressions, sometimes do offer authoritative pronouncements. Usage is often criticized, sometimes lauded, sometimes simply analyzed or explained. Metalinguistic activities like these are certainly socially situated, and they do sometimes play a role in claims of semantic authority, but few such pundits acquire the authority of dictionaries.

In spite of the serious limitations of dictionaries, many still turn to these sources to authorize their own preferred meanings or to de-authorize competing ones. Citation of dictionary definitions, we saw in the preceding chapter's discussion of changes in the meaning of *racism*, is a common move made in trying to establish disputed claims of semantic authority. We'll see that dictionaries also figure in continuing disputes over authorizing gender-neutral understandings of *marriage*, disputes that have also involved other institutional authorizing sources like courts. The authority of dictionaries has been important in disputes over whether Donald Trump's continued ownership of an enterprise that on occasion does business with foreign officials would violate the 'foreign emoluments' clause of the US constitution. Before his inauguration in January 2017, the president's legal team relied on two dictionaries from the period in which the constitution was drafted to argue that ordinary business dealings would not be covered. These two dictionaries did each include a sense of *emolument* that limits it to something like salary or similar compensation for particular services. Legal scholar John

Mikhail and some colleagues, however, then conducted an exhaustive study of the nearly 200 English language and legal dictionaries from 1523 to 1806. They found only 8 percent even specified such a sense. They also found that all of these dictionaries, including the two cited by the lawyers on whom Trump relied, also included a much broader sense of profit, gain, or benefit. And they provided other evidence from documents written by or familiar to those involved in drafting the constitution that the word was overwhelmingly used then in the broader sense that would indeed count hotel rooms or dinners for diplomats as emoluments.[3]

Appeal to a dictionary might well have tempted Alice in her exchange with Humpty Dumpty. Although Lewis Carroll has not recorded her doing so, she could have directed Humpty Dumpty's attention to something like the definition in Figure 7.1 of many

plural **glories**

1a: praise, honor, or distinction extended by common consent: renown

b: worshipful praise, honor, and thanksgiving
    giving *glory* to God

2a: something that secures praise or renown
    the *glory* of a brilliant career

b: a distinguished quality or asset
    The *glory* of the city is its Gothic cathedral

3a(1): great beauty and splendor: magnificence
    the *glory* that was Greece and the grandeur that was Rome – E. A. Poe

(2): something marked by beauty or resplendence
    a perfect *glory* of a day

3b: the splendor and beatific happiness of heaven;
    broadly : eternity

4a: a state of great gratification or exaltation
    when she's acting she's in her *glory*

b: a height of prosperity or achievement
    ancient Rome in its *glory*

5: a ring or spot of light: such as

a: aureole

b: a halo appearing around the shadow of an object

Figure 7.1 Definition of *Glory* from MerriamWebster.com

different senses of *glory*. Pointing out to Humpty Dumpty that nothing remotely resembling 'nice knock-down argument' is to be found there might have given Alice satisfaction. It would probably not, however, have led to her emerging victorious in their exchange.

Division of Linguistic Labor: Expertise

Although he doesn't speak of 'authority,' philosopher Hilary Putnam posits the widespread existence of what he calls a "linguistic division of labor."[4] Noting that most of us use words like *elm* and *beech* without ourselves being able to tell whether a particular tree is one or the other, Putnam suggests that some language users know enough about relevant differences among kinds of trees to let the rest of us use tree names without having full access to conditions for applying them correctly. We can outsource responsibility for regulating usage, deferring to the *semantic authority* of professional tree specialists and informed amateurs.

People often 'know' and use a word without access to criteria that determine its applicability. This doesn't mean they need have no ideas at all about how the word might function, the realm in which it does its thing. If, for all you know, *elm* designates some kind of animal rather than a kind of tree, then, to paraphrase Putnam, "there's no point talking elms with you." You're not yet part of the linguistic community in which *elm* can be used to make linguistic moves. So you do seem to need to have some ideas about elms to talk about them, but those ideas need not even be accurate so long as they serve to align you with the rest of the *elm*-using community. You've delegated responsibility for keeping track of the semantic links that tie *elm* to particular kinds of trees to people who are experts about tree matters: their semantic authority derives from their epistemic authority in this field. It's only knowledge of language in a limited sense that is necessary for this kind of semantic authority. The same background that is used to distinguish *elm* from *beech* also works to distinguish *orme* from *hêtre*. An essentially monolingual English-speaking arborist could be a semantic authority for the French words so long as they knew that *elm* translates as *orme* and *beech* as *hêtre*.

Expertise seems relatively straightforward in the case of tree names. But even in apparently 'objective' arenas, conflicts can and do arise over semantic authority.

Dueling Experts: The Pluto Wars

Recent discussions of the word *planet* illustrate. The word *planet* comes into English from ancient Greek πλανήτης (*planētēs*) 'wanderer.' Observers of the skies in ancient Greece had noticed that some heavenly bodies seemed to have fixed positions whereas others seemed to change their positions, to wander. Early on, *planet* designated the sun that dominates daytime skies on earth (they saw more of it in the Ithaca of Greece than I do in often rainy Ithaca, NY), the earth's moon, asteroids, and directly observable 'stars' like Venus that appeared in different places in the sky at different times. Usage changed as we learned more about astronomical objects, including, for example, that the earth moves around the sun rather than vice versa. By the end of the nineteenth century, the term *planet* had settled down and applied only to the eight bodies then known to orbit our sun. They included our own Earth plus the five others visible with the unaided eye – Mercury, Venus, Mars, Jupiter, and Saturn – along with two discovered with telescopes and mathematical calculations – Uranus (found in 1781) and Neptune (found in 1846). In 1930 tiny and distant Pluto was added to the list, and my schoolmates and I learned about the nine planets in our own solar system.

In the last decade of the twentieth century, however, dissatisfaction began growing among some scientists with applying the word *planet* to exactly those nine objects. Not only were there planet-like bodies found orbiting other suns but even in our own solar system a variety of objects emerged with at least as good claims to planetary status as Pluto. Like most everyday words, *planet* had no precise definition but on August, 24, 2006, the International Astronomical Union (IAU) held a vote at its meeting in Prague on the following explicit definition: "A celestial body that (a) is in orbit around the Sun, (b) has sufficient mass for its self-gravity to overcome rigid body forces so that it assumes a hydrostatic equilibrium (nearly round) shape, and (c) has cleared the neighborhood around its orbit." (Condition c sounded like 'tidiness' to me when I first read it but I have learned that it is a matter of 'dynamical dominance,' which means it doesn't keep colliding with other objects in its orbit, and is mainly a function of size.) The definition, which excludes Pluto (dubbed a 'dwarf planet' – fitting the first two criteria but not the third), was approved, though by no means unanimously. Many members vowed publicly that they would not use it.[5]

Resistance also arose from geophysicists and other planetary scientists, who criticized the IAU definition and proposed another in 2017: "a sub-stellar mass body that has never undergone nuclear fusion and that has sufficient self-gravitation to assume a spheroidal shape adequately described by a triaxial ellipsoid regardless of its orbital parameters," which they said amounts roughly to "round objects in space smaller than stars." This definition can apply beyond our own solar system and brings Pluto back into the planetary fold.[6] It is not clear that sharpening application conditions for *planet* has significant scientific consequences, but lots of people found this definitional struggle engaging, with schoolchildren writing the IAU to plead on behalf of the demoted Pluto. If the two sides in this debate persist and find their differing emphases useful for progress in their distinct fields, we may eventually say that, geophysically, Pluto is a planet, but astronomically, it is not.

We often use the adverb *technically* to indicate some aspect in which specialists' usage of a term in the course of their work diverges from that used in other contexts. For example, I might correctly say "Technically, Venus is not a star," implying that there is a use of *star* that is specialized and excludes planets. Technical uses, however, need not drive out more familiar ones. Even an astronomer might say to a child, "The first star you can see at night is usually Venus," using *star* in its everyday sense where it designates all bright objects in the evening sky other than human-produced satellites and the earth's moon.

Different uses – different meanings – can peacefully coexist when they are used in different contexts for pursuit of different interests. But when there are substantive clashes where interests conflict, then there may be struggles over semantic authority, over who's to be "master," as Humpty Dumpty put it. To define is one way to claim semantic authority in at least certain fields.

Courts Authorizing Meanings: *Fruit* and *Marriage*

Many readers know that botanists use the label *fruit* to categorize a tomato. That is, a tomato is a "seed-bearing structure that develops from the ovary of a flowering plant" (livesciences.com). Yet in everyday life people are likely to say that a tomato is a vegetable, not a fruit. The term *vegetable* is a botanical grab bag – parts other than fruits of a plant that might be eaten. This includes leaves like kale and spinach, roots like carrots and parsnips, stalks like celery and fennel, and so on. But for most everyday purposes, vegetables include not only these plant parts but also fruits that are more savory than sweet like the tomato, eggplant/aubergine, and bell pepper/capsicum. The category of vegetable is important from a culinary standpoint, and viewed from that perspective, tomatoes are indeed vegetables. The grocery store stocks tomatoes in the vegetable section, both in fresh and bottled or tinned form. Cookbooks include recipes featuring tomatoes in their vegetable, not their fruit sections. Someone who's agreed to bring vegetables to a buffet may well bring tomatoes. Restaurants list them as vegetables. And so on. Indeed plenty of ordinary speakers do not know that the botanists classify the tomato with the apple rather than with the lettuce. So although 'botanically speaking,' a tomato is a fruit, a tomato is a vegetable 'in culinary terms' and in everyday usage.

Who cares, you might well ask. Most of the time, the botanical definition of tomato is quite irrelevant to what the rest of us do with tomatoes – cooks and botanists simply have different, not competing, interests. But in 1893 the Supreme Court of the United States in the case *Nix v. Hedden* was asked to rule on the question of whether a tomato was a fruit or a vegetable. They unanimously went with cooks and everyday life. The issue arose because an import company wanted the tomatoes they were bringing into the country taxed as fruit rather than as vegetables. Acknowledging that botanically a tomato is indeed a fruit, the court noted that in "ordinary" language, it is a vegetable. Yet the interests endorsed by the court in authorizing the vegetable definition were actually not those of ordinary people or even of chefs, who would probably on this occasion have preferred a different outcome. The court wielded its semantic authority to side with tax collectors: import duty for vegetables was higher than that for fruit.

Sometimes the significance of a court's ruling on the applicability of some term has far more sweeping ramifications. Early in the current century, I began talking and writing about then widespread debates in the US over whether or not a woman should be allowed to marry another woman or a man should be permitted to marry another man. What especially interested me as a semanticist was how often the struggle was framed as a matter of defining *marriage*, especially by those resisting the push to expand the scope of *marriage* to include unions other than the traditional mixed-sex variety. I wrote about that issue in publications appearing almost a decade before the US Supreme Court's historic 2015 ruling, in *Obergefell v. Hodges*, that two people have the right to marry one another anywhere in the US without regard for their gender identity.[7] By the time of the Obergefell decision, a number of other countries, beginning with the Netherlands, had already opened marriage as a legal option for couples beyond those consisting of the traditional pairing of a woman and a man. Whatever word translated the English *marriage* in local languages – in Dutch that was *huwelijk* – now had legal backing for a sense that might include pairing of two people with matching gender identities (or of people outside gender binaries).

In the mid-twentieth century, marriage between people classified as different racially was still illegal in some US jurisdictions. The 2016 movie *Loving* shows the true story behind the case of *Loving v. Virginia*, a case reaching the Supreme Court that challenged Virginia's law against interrracial marriage. In the late 1950s a black woman, Mildred Jeter, and a white man, Richard Loving, were married in the District of Columbia. Their home state of Virginia, however, not only did not recognize their marriage but sentenced them to prison for violating the state's anti-miscegenation law. The Loving couple – who could have asked for a better name? – were persuaded by civil rights activists to take their case to court. The Supreme Court of the State of Virginia ruled against them but the subsequent appeal to the Supreme Court of the United States was successful. In 1967 Earl Warren, then Chief Justice, wrote for the unanimous court:

> Marriage is one of the basic civil rights of man ... The Fourteenth Amendment requires that the freedom of choice to marry not be restricted by invidious racial discrimination. Under our Constitution, the freedom to marry, or not marry, a person of another race resides with the individual and cannot be infringed by the State.[8]

Inspired in part by the growing LGBTQ rights movement and civil rights achievements like the decision in *Loving v. Virginia*, the late twentieth and early twenty-first centuries saw a concerted move to legitimize marriage between people without regard to their gender classification. On the fortieth anniversary of the Loving decision, Mildred Loving issued a statement supporting gender equality in marriage and noting parallels to racial equality. (Her husband and coplaintiff Richard Loving died not many years after the Supreme Court's decision.) The (meta)linguistic debate

over whether the meaning of *marriage* requires that it be con-
tracted between a woman and a man was important in the discussion of marriage equality throughout the decades culminating
in the Supreme Court's 2015 decision. What may surprise some is
that the debate has not ended. The court's decision certainly
carried considerable authority, but it did not end conflict centered
on the meaning of *marriage*. That conflict, of course, was part of
sociocultural conflict over changes in the institution of marriage.
As I pointed out in my 2006 paper, marriage has changed very
significantly in many ways over the centuries, and anthropologists
have found enormous cross-cultural differences. But those resisting recent changes have looked on marriage (and with it *marriage*) as unchanging.

The Defense of Marriage Act (DOMA) passed by the US
Congress and enacted in 1996 included the following definition:
"The word 'marriage' means only a legal union between one man
and one woman as husband and wife, and the word 'spouse'
refers only to a person of the opposite sex who is a husband or a
wife." *Marriage* figures in more than a thousand federal laws, so
that the semantic authority being wielded by lawmakers through
DOMA had a wide range. And of course the word enters in many
ways into governmental practices at other levels than federal.
The word *marriage* and related words also occur in a huge array
of other practices, formal and informal. Insurance, employment
benefits, estate distribution after a death, hospital visitation
rights, inclusion in family events, and much more: to be a spouse
in a marriage has a wealth of consequences. The DOMA definition had its authority removed by the Supreme Court, however,
in their 2013 *Windsor* ruling. In that ruling, they noted that some
states were already allowing couples of the same sex to marry.
The court said that the federal government had to recognize
those marriages.[9] In other words, they rejected the legislative
attempt in DOMA to claim semantic authority over *marriage*.

The *Windsor* decision left open the possibility that individual
states might refuse to allow couples other than those consisting of

a man and a woman to marry. Two years later, however, in *Obergefell v. Hodges*, the Supreme Court declared that the constitutional principles of due process and equal protection render unconstitutional the denial of the right to civil marriage to same-sex couples. So that's it in the US, one might be tempted to say. This particular war over words has been won in favor of a gender-neutral understanding of marriage. But debate continues in some circles.

The Supreme Court's semantic authority to extend the word *marriage* to cover same-sex unions has not been universally accepted by the American public. Lexicographers find themselves still representing distinct and sometimes incompatible usages of the word *marriage*. These distinct usages, of course, arise from the competing social ideologies and practices in which the word figures. They figure in ongoing resistance to the social changes that paved the way for the Supreme Court decision.

The tension is clear in some dictionary definitions. The following is from what I found in October 2018 at the Merriam-Webster website under the general entry for *marriage*.[10]

Definition of *marriage*

1 a *see usage paragraph below*: the state of being united as spouses in a consensual and contractual relationship recognized by law
  b the mutual relation of married persons: wedlock
  c the institution whereby individuals are joined in a marriage
2 an act of marrying or the rite by which the married status is effected; *especially* the wedding ceremony and attendant festivities or formalities

Usage of MARRIAGE

> The definition of the word *marriage* – or, more accurately, the understanding of what the institution of marriage properly consists of – continues to be highly controversial. This is not an issue to be resolved by dictionaries. Ultimately, the controversy involves cultural traditions, religious beliefs, legal rulings, and

ideas about fairness and basic human rights. The principal point of dispute has to do with marriage between two people of the same sex, often referred to as *same-sex marriage* or *gay marriage*. Same-sex marriages are now recognized by law in a growing number of countries and were legally validated throughout the U. S. by the Supreme Court decision in *Obergefell v. Hodges* in 2015. In many other parts of the world, marriage continues to be allowed only between men and women. The definition of *marriage* shown here is intentionally broad enough to encompass the different types of marriage that are currently recognized in varying cultures, places, religions, and systems of law.

Going to Webster's *Student Dictionary*, we find something a little different.[11]

1 **a.** the state of being married: wedlock **b:** the legal relationship into which a man and a woman enter for the purpose of making a home and often raising a family **c:** a relationship between two people of the same sex that is like that of a traditional marriage
2 an act of marrying; *especially*: a wedding ceremony

The Merriam-Webster lexicographers find themselves backed into a corner. When I consulted standard dictionaries in the early 2000s, they all included at least one sense or subsense specifying that a man and a woman were involved, like 1b from the *Student Dictionary*. Most also included something like 1c, which recognized gender-neutral uses but acknowledged that they did not come with a long history of acceptance. The "Usage" note in the general Merriam-Webster acknowledges that there is still controversy among English language users. It also correctly observes that dictionaries will not resolve matters here. What the writers do not acknowledge, however, is that their deliberately sex-neutral definition in the main entry does not inform those consulting the dictionary of the usage of the substantial groups of English speakers who will still only call a union *marriage* if it joins a woman and a man. The "usage note" attempts to address that problem, but it is not completely successful in doing so.

The discussion below, "What is the definition of marriage?," speaks for some but probably not all who still use *marriage* exclusively for 'traditional' marriages – that is, those uniting one woman and one man.[12]

> On June 26, 2015, the United States Supreme Court issued a ruling legalizing gay marriage. Across the Atlantic, in mid-July 2013, the Queen of England signed into law "The Marriage Bill," which allows same-sex couples to marry legally. Around the world, at least fifteen other nations have legalized marriage between same-sex partners. Obviously, the societal definition of marriage is changing. But is it the right of a government to redefine marriage, or has the definition of marriage already been set by a higher authority? . . .
>
> Eden was the scene of the first marriage, ordained by God Himself. The author of Genesis then records the standard by which all future marriages are defined: "A man leaves his father and mother and is united to his wife, and they become one flesh." (Genesis 2:24).
>
> This passage of Scripture gives several points for understanding God's design for marriage. First, marriage involves a man and a woman. The Hebrew word for "wife" is gender-specific; it cannot mean anything other than "a woman."

Semantic authority for the word *marriage* is seen by the writer quoted here as held in divine hands, not human – even if those hands actually belong to humans holding ultimate judicial authority within their community.

There are two important differences between the court's rejection in 1893 of the botanical definition of *tomato* as a *fruit*, on the one hand, and, on the other, its 2013 rejection of the DOMA 'one man–one woman' definition of *marriage* and its extension of that rejection to state regulations in 2015. (1) The *fruit* and the *marriage* cases had vastly different legal consequences. The 1893 ruling on whether tomatoes were fruit had implications only for tax collection and did not in the least restrict botanists in their theorizing. The 2013 and 2015 rulings on *marriage*, in contrast, affected a host of legal provisions at different levels of government. (2) The *fruit* case authorized familiar and long-standing practices and de-authorized nothing of interest to anyone (except the importers who wanted a lower tax bill). The *marriage* case de-authorized some familiar practices and authorized others that were controversial in arenas of great importance to many people.

The bottom line: courts can play an important role in authorizing and de-authorizing meanings, but that judicial exercise of semantic authority may well be questioned when significant numbers of people take their own interests to be threatened.

Inclusive Language Guidelines: Prescribing and Proscribing

Starting in the 1970s, various kinds of US institutions began adopting what were billed as 'nonsexist' language guidelines. Feminist dictionary projects were part, but only a small part, of the general linguistic activism that led to such adoption. These institutions included universities and colleges, publishing houses and newspapers, workplaces, scholarly and professional associations, and social service and governmental agencies. In the late 1990s, linguist Edwin Battistella reviewed a number of these nonsexist language guidelines. "Authorities – the organizations and arbiters of style discussed here – have a common goal in promulgating non-discriminatory usage," he notes. But he finds important differences among them. "The guidelines of various organizations become emblematic of the values and interests of that organization: they reify the values of an organization by establishing not what *is* or what *will be* but *what is expected.* Different authorities represent and speak to different cultures, and the guidelines will reflect such differences."[13] Beginning in the late 1980s and continuing beyond, such guidelines typically were widened beyond the issues of exclusion and derogation raised by feminists to address many other dimensions of social inequality.

The Linguistic Society of America (LSA), to which I belong, finally adopted nonsexist language guidelines in 1995, publishing them online in 1996. The guidelines were drafted by the LSA's Committee on the Status of Women in Linguistics, to which both Ed Battistella and I belonged at the time. The guidelines are written diffidently and with little acknowledgment of gender asymmetry. The document became even weaker after it was revised by the LSA Executive Committee. Twenty years later the LSA expanded the scope of their linguistic guidelines. Here's how the newly articulated guidelines were introduced in 2016:

> Inclusive language acknowledges diversity, conveys respect to all people, is sensitive to differences, and promotes equal opportunities. These guidelines highlight ways in which linguists can both lead the way in proactively writing inclusively and avoid past pitfalls or habits that may unintentionally lead to marginalization, offense, misrepresentation, or the perpetuation of stereotypes. Stereotyping language is often not a matter of intention but of effect.

The guidelines go on to give some examples of potentially problematic ways of writing and speaking and to suggest alternatives. There are also links to other resources: guidelines promulgated by other groups (e.g., the American Psychological Association, MIT Press, the Tasmanian Department of Education), material on implicit bias, an article on dictionaries, and the like.

The LSA guidelines 'nudge.' They suggest general principles rather than offering lists of what's endorsed – what one *should* say– and of what's problematic – what one should *not* say. The guidelines suggest only a mild ethical authority, although they do claim to be based on significant empirical research on language use and its effects. In some institutional guidelines, authority for enforcement is far more apparent – for example, in guidelines issued by schoolbook publishers or governmental authorities. Some of these groups do indeed develop lists of verbal *do*s and *don't*s. Such lists, which typically ignore contexts, can lead to mechanical substitutions of 'good' terminology for 'bad,' but they can be helpful if used judiciously.

It is difficult to determine how much such authority has mattered. It is certainly the case that linguistic practices have shifted significantly over the past few decades. The considerable efforts of reformers who have promoted guidelines have probably had some effect, not least in heightening linguistic awareness. The pronoun *he* is much less often used generically, although it has not vanished. The suffix *-man* (pronounced as if it were spelled '-mun') has given way in many agent nouns to alternative forms. We find *policeman* yielding to *police officer* in many contexts, and *flight attendant* has become significantly more common than the feminized *stewardess*. Indeed *-ess* forms are increasingly rare. Anne Curzan's *Fixing English* has excellent discussion of these matters. So far as I know, however, no one has yet empirically investigated the issue of how much institutionally backed authorizing of 'inclusive' language has contributed to changing linguistic practices. Such authorizing has certainly, however, played some role in drawing attention to matters of language. Sometimes this attention is constructive, but not always, as I will discuss in the following section.

As the discussion of preferred gender pronouns (PGPs) in the preceding chapter suggests, there has been increasing attention in recent years to guidelines that avoid gender binaries. Institutional authorities can mandate listing PGPs in company-internal communications, for example. On July 16, 2019, the City Council of Berkeley, Cal., unanimously adopted a policy to eliminate unnecessary or inappropriate gendered language in the Berkeley Municipal Code. A report attached to the ordinance noted that "broadening societal awareness of transgender and gender nonconforming identities has brought to light the importance of nonbinary gender inclusivity." (Note that these changes have nothing to do with improving the status of women.) The mostly masculine pronouns of the current code will be replaced by *they* (and *them, their,* and *theirs*), *firemen* by *firefighters, manhole* by *maintenance hole, craftsmen* by *craftspeople,* and *brother* or *sister* by *sibling,* with many similar changes made.[14]

As individuals, we wrestle with whether or not to shift linguistic practices that some have identified as problematic, sometimes via institutionally endorsed guidelines. I certainly do. For example, a reader of a draft of this book noted that some might object to my use of *sane* to praise. And in the next chapter I quote a friend's use of *crazy* to deride, and I certainly seem to endorse her implicit view that craziness is bad. Like the friend I quote, I often use the word *crazy* to disparage ideas and behavior that do not seem rationally defensible and *sane* to praise those that do. As my alert reader was aware, such linguistic practices can be (and have been) criticized as insensitive to people living with mental illness. I am well aware that some people's brains function in ways that can on occasion lead others to describe *them* as 'crazy,' as not 'sane,' and that those people are not blameworthy because their brains are misfiring. There are indeed people whom I respect greatly and love deeply for whom this has been the case. Being very close to several people struggling with serious mental health issues, I have come to appreciate that there is greater neural diversity compatible with leading a satisfactory life than I had once realized. I was struck at a NAMI (National Alliance for the Mentally Ill) event I attended some years ago by something the partner of a woman struggling with a very serious and not always controllable mental illness said. "Sometimes Mary [not her real name] acts and talks crazy but that's when the disease has the upper hand rather than her." So I no longer use *crazy* and *sane* to describe people. I continue, however, as both Mary and her partner did, to use them to describe behavior, sometimes behavior for which actors *are* appropriately held accountable, and sometimes for larger-scale social arrangements. Some might describe this choice on my part as "politically incorrect" or "not PC."

Although I continue to use *sane* and *crazy* to express positive and negative evaluations respectively of such things as actions or ideas, I strongly object to blaming mass shootings on "mentally ill monsters." That is what President Trump did in a statement responding to a mass shooting in a Walmart store in El Paso, Tex., on August 3, 2019, and another the next day in a suburb of

Dayton, Ohio. As many pointed out, other countries have roughly the same incidence of mental illness as the US yet far fewer mass shootings. After a gunman in Philadelphia a couple of weeks later fired on and hit six police officers trying to arrest him, Trump returned to proposing that the answer was to force people with mental illness back into detention, back into institutions designed not for healing but for hiding and restraining. Angela Kimball, then acting CEO of NAMI, criticized Trump's name-calling and casting blame for mass shootings on the de-institutionalization of mentally ill people. "Words matter, Mr. President. 'These people' are not 'monsters,' 'the mentally ill,' 'crazy people' – they're us."[15]

Politically Correct (PC): Virtue-Signaling and Mockery

Language guidelines of the sort I've mentioned in the preceding section are prime examples of advocacy for what some call *politically correct* or *PC* modes of language use. Those advancing such guidelines seldom if ever label them PC or even just 'correct' – rather they describe them as 'respectful' or 'polite' or 'inclusive.' The terminology of political correctness actually originated as self-mockery among mid-twentieth-century political leftists, noting and poking fun at the ways in which fallible human beings veered from the ideals they themselves embraced.

Those mocking PC often appeal to George Orwell's account of "Newspeak" in *1984*. They allege that what the would-be reformers advocate is mealy-mouthed at best and often evasively dishonest. Some are infuriated by being told to watch their language and protest that guidelines use institutional authority to deny them free speech. Often there are parodic representations of what guidelines supposedly call for – for example, *vertically challenged* instead of *short*, *personhole* instead of *manhole*, and *nasally disturbing* instead of *smelly*. Almost all reports of the Berkeley legislation mentioned in the preceding section put the elimination of *manhole* in the headlines. This evoked, for older people like me, that 1970s ridiculous *personhole* (never, so far as I can determine, actually seriously proposed by anyone). Not surprisingly, many online comments on the action taken by the Berkeley City Council inveighed against PC run amok. Invented absurdities like *personhole* certainly do scare some away from paying attention to more serious and better grounded proposals for linguistic reform. The actually proposed *maintenance hole* seemed almost as absurd to many.

Sometimes harangues against PC are accompanied by samples of what is described as "telling it like it is," rejecting what these critics present as the PC linguistic straitjacket. In online anti-PC screeds, speaking 'the truth' instead of bowing to PC constraints seems often to involve authorization of racial slurs and other bigoted invectives. Donald Trump's "grab 'em by the pussy" is a relatively mild example. Those who express dismay at such uses of language are dismissed as 'hypersensitive,' too prone to 'take offense.'

Mockery and shaming are not, however, the exclusive province of those resisting proposed linguistic changes. Because issues of terminology have become sites of political contention, websites and pamphlets of many groups now include vocabulary lists. These lists typically identify some forms as 'offensive' or 'outdated' and others as 'preferred' alternatives. Online and face-to-face, some in the vanguard of advocacy for social and accompanying linguistic changes (or wanting to claim affiliation with the reformers) not only themselves scrupulously adopt proposed reforms but also sometimes set themselves up as language 'police.' They may deride someone using a dis-preferred term as 'ignorant' or not 'woke,' or 'bigoted,' or worse. Of course, bigotry may be at play in deliberately discounting widely discussed and widely adopted terminological shifts. In many cases, however, reasoned discussion might be far more effective than derision.

There are many people who are basically noncombatants in these linguistic 'wars' but who get combat reports from all kinds of media, including social media 'friends.' They worry about being on the 'right' side. "What's the PC word for Y?" is a frequent query. Or "I'm not sure if this is the PC way to put it, but . . . "

introduces a comment using terminology that a speaker at least suspects has been questioned by members of a social identity group to which they do not belong. Sometimes the questioning has come from those who are not members but see themselves as allies and advocates for this group. There seems rather little awareness of substantial disagreements on such matters among those who are most directly involved. Where disagreement is noted by outsiders, it is often taken as license for ignoring possible shifts, for sticking with what's familiar.

In the preceding chapter, I examined changes going on in the arena of English gendered personal pronouns and suggested that singular *they* offers a default not only for speaking of individuals whose gender is unknown or irrelevant, but also for those who fall outside gender binaries. Gender binaries are rejected by people who consider themselves somewhere in between the woman–man poles of the gender spectrum or outside that spectrum altogether, perhaps fluctuating somewhat unpredictably. The letter *x* (pronounced like *ex*) is increasingly used to get out of the binary choices. In the next (and final) chapter of this book, "Concluding," I will discuss an 'x-insertion' proposal that has seen some success in the US, namely using *Latinx* instead of *Latina* or *Latino* (or other coinages that aim at gender inclusiveness but still assume that the binary split works). In the UK, *Mx* is widely used as a nonbinary social title. The word *womxn* has been offered by some as indicating trans-inclusiveness (women + trans + nonbinary + queer) yet is denounced by some others as trans-exclusionary (are transgender men really there?) and by yet others as quite unnecessary. When London's Wellcome Collection announced an event for womxn, a storm erupted. Deborah Cameron quoted Caroline Criado-Perez: "I'm fed up with women being just a grab bag of anyone who isn't a proper default human, aka a man." As Cameron points out in a post on her blog, we have not seen *mxn* proposed. There is no fundamental challenge to the traditional picture of men as default humans.

Proposals to make language more trans-inclusive in other contexts (like discussions of unplanned pregnancies or cervical cancer) often erase the words *woman* and *women* completely. As

Cameron has pointed out, joining the traditional feminine terms to others that might include transgender men also potentially affected by the matters being spoken of would be just as inclusive of transgender people but would keep women squarely in the picture. Planned Parenthood could announce health services for "pregnant women and transgender men," for example, rather than for "pregnant people." On his blog, transgender studies scholar and activist Paisley Currah notes that substantially many more millennial Americans, those born between 1980 and 2000, endorse transgender rights (73 percent) than support abortion rights (55 percent, which includes the 22 percent who support abortion in all cases and the 33 percent who support only certain cases). "[W]e need," Currah says, "a transgender feminist approach that is not gender-neutral – that dares to identify *asymmetry* when it sees it."[16] He notes that the move toward gender neutrality in matters like talk of abortion can lead to "los[ing] important historical and analytical frameworks for understanding the restriction and possible ending of abortion as part of a war against women."

Bystanders are sometimes bemused and sometimes outraged. And the conflicts often have a generational flavor, seeming to pit those in their fifties and older, who were part of second-wave feminist efforts, against younger millennials, for whom gender-identity issues, especially nonbinarism, have become central. Perhaps for some, being appropriately linguistically 'inclusive' is like being up on current youth slang. Both 'anti-PC' mockery and 'pro-PC' shaming attempt to de-authorize some words in order to strengthen authorizing of others.

Empowering First-Person Semantic Authority

The primary English sex/gender labels (*female* and *male*, *woman* and *man*) occur frequently in everyday life. And these and related labels have been at the center of struggles over semantic authority. On public restroom doors, they have raised great alarm. Houston proposed equal rights legislation back in 2015 that, if passed, would have allowed transgender people to use whichever public facility they felt (most) comfortable entering. The proposal to allow people to decide this matter themselves was ultimately rejected by voters, especially after advertising proclaimed that men would be enabled to stalk women by falsely claiming to be women (though there is absolutely no evidence this has ever happened). In a postelection analysis, the *Washington Post* quoted Houston retiree Loyce Parker: "Anybody with a penis, I don't want them in the ladies room."[17] (No one, by the way, seemed concerned that women might falsely claim to be men.) This distrust of transgender women was not confined to Houston.

A year earlier Michelle Goldberg wrote in a widely read *New Yorker* article about the refusal of many so-called "radical feminists" to recognize transgender women as women. Sheila Jeffreys, for instance, proclaimed that the label *woman* could not apply to someone having or having had a penis, whether or not that person was now living as a woman. According to Jeffreys and a number of others announcing themselves as feminists, transgender women are not really women at all. Some of those more sympathetic to transgender people have labeled such objectors TERFs – Trans-Excluding Radical Feminists – a term that became quickly adopted to shame those women espousing feminism who denied that transgender girls or women are indeed girls or women. I am a white woman who is not transgender. I am, in other and newer words, *cisgender* or a *ciswoman*. I was labeled *girl* at birth and followed a subsequent constant path through girlhood into womanhood. Having identified as a feminist for decades, I was dismayed to find some feminist-identified people claiming that their semantic authority trumped that of transgender women. Why do they think, I asked myself, that they have the right to police application of *woman* – and especially to do so in the name of 'feminism'?[18] So I strongly disagree with the positions espoused by Sheila Jeffreys and others cited in the *New Yorker* article. The stigmatizing label TERF, however, too readily dismisses anyone who strikes the labeler as not wholly on board with all projects proposed in the name of trans-inclusiveness. Linguistic practices from second-wave feminists like writing *womyn* are often taken as diagnostic of TERF-ness. What is going on here is a very heated debate over semantic authority to apply the label *woman* (and to suppress it in other contexts). There's been far less concern about transgender men and what labels apply to them, which is not to say that their lives are always easy by any means.

Transgender activists have argued for some time that each individual should be authorized to settle the question of their own gender, should have that kind of first-person semantic authority. In trans and trans-friendly communities such first-person authority is widely acknowledged. It generally extends to transgender people whether or not they have taken or plan to take steps to modify their bodies to bring them into closer alignment with the normative bodily configuration of cis people of the same gender. In other words, first-person semantic authority for one's own gender-identity label is not claimed by isolated individuals but in the context of communities that recognize such authority. (An aside: this seems to distinguish first-person authority over gender labels from the first-person authority claimed by Rachel Dolezal, who legally changed her name to Nkechi Amare Diallo in 2016, to be labeled *African American*. There are few if any communities with conventions to support Dolezal's claim to first-person semantic authority in the matter of racial identity, a claim that seems as problematically individualist as Humpty Dumpty's. Of course this may change.) Philosopher Talia Bettcher, herself a transgender woman, argues that a more inclusive semantic convention for *woman* than what predominates in mainstream communities has been developed in a number of communities in which transgender women play a central role.[19] This convention authorizes individuals having the last word in matters of gender identity.

Of course, transgender individuals do not live only in communities that recognize their first-person semantic authority over gender labels. They confront all kinds of institutions, notably including governmental agencies, that demand authority over how they are to be classified. In the absence of any generally agreed-upon semantic authority for assigning gender identity, Lisa Moore and Paisley Currah have observed that "[s]tate actors . . . are forced to choose and monitor a particular criterion for defining sex when assigning legal gender identity":

> In the United States there are state entities with jurisdictional power to define sex [i.e., these entities hold semantic authority]. For example, states, territories, and the federal government each issue all sorts of identification documents – from passports to birth certificates to drivers' licenses to pilots' licenses to Social Security cards. Even state entities that do not issue identity documents but do segregate on the basis of gender make their own rules for gender classification – prisons, hospitals, schools, drug rehabilitation centers, youth service providers, social services. To add yet one more layer of complexity, judges have added to the chaos by finding that one's legal gender for one social function may not hold for others.[20]

There are also nonstate entities like colleges and universities, clubs, and events segregating by sex/gender, each of which makes its own determinations, claims its own semantic authority. Recent years have, for example, seen all of the elite "Seven Sisters" eastern women's colleges open their doors to transgender women, though on slightly different terms and with different policies on people who might have been admitted as women and then transitioned to male status. The Girl Scouts of Western Washington made headlines in the summer of 2015 when they returned a $100,000 gift that came with stipulations that it was not to be used for transgender girls. "We won't exclude ANY girl," they announced, and quickly raised online more than $250,000 from supporters of their trans-inclusionary policies. Increasingly, trans-friendly female-only groups accept someone as a girl or a woman if that is what she says she is – that is, they give semantic authority to the individual whose sex/gender identity is at issue. But others continue to resist, insisting that possession of a penis at some stage of life is absolutely criterial for application of *male*, *boy*, or *man* (and also insisting on "deadnaming"– that is, using pre-transition proper names, most of which are marked as masculine – by, for example, calling a transgender woman "John," the name given at birth, rather than her present name "Joan").

In October of 2018 the US Department of Health and Human Services first made public a proposal to define gender "on a biological basis that is clear, grounded in science, objective and administrable." Genitalia classification at birth was to be the criterion, with chromosomal evidence settling disputed cases. This definition, of course, might be less readily "administrable" than envisioned by the Trump-appointed officials who have proposed it, given that the biology is not always clear. What it would certainly do, if adopted, is resoundingly deny first-person authorizing of gender labels, at least for certain governmental purposes. In a *NY Times* op-ed piece shortly after this news broke, gender theorist and activist Jennifer Finney Boylan responded.[21]

> I just learned on Sunday that I do not exist. This will come as sad news to my children, to whom I've been a mother for over 20 years now. It will come as a shock to my wife, too, to whom I've been married for 30 years. . . . It is so disappointing, then, and more than a little embarrassing, to learn I'm imaginary – a creature no more real than the cyclops, or a hippogriff. . . . I have news for Donald Trump. I do exist. Trans men and women exist. Genderqueer people exist. Redefining us won't make us go away.

So although first-person semantic authority for gender-identity labels has support from a significant group of English speakers, that authority is being challenged by Donald Trump and many others.

Communities Are the Ultimate Semantic Authorities

What Humpty Dumpty did not seem to recognize is that semantic mastery depends on getting some community to which you belong to go along with what you choose your words to mean.

Stipulating that a particular form has a particular meaning can work if a community can be recruited that will use the form with that meaning, develop a conventional linguistic practice supporting that meaning. The early-adopting community may be relatively small and even transient – for example, a classroom taught by the stipulator or the readers of a particular piece of text that launches the stipulation. Small communities operating with the new convention may merge into larger communities, or there may develop overlapping multiple communities of sufficient size and impact to attract attention from dictionary makers.

Communities speaking what is in some sense a single language may authorize somewhat different lexicons with different meanings. They may also have different language ideologies and kinds of communicative practice. Linguist Arthur Spears has argued that African-American communities tend to grant far freer 'semantic license' (his term) than communities whose members are mainly white Americans. That is, he proposes, speakers of African American English tend to be more receptive to creative and innovative usages, licensing speakers to venture into new territory either with new meanings for familiar forms (e.g., *butter* as a general positive evaluation) or new forms that draw from familiar ones (e.g., *emusculation* to speak of the amazing physical attributes of athletes like the legendary "Air" Michael Jordan and "Magic" Johnson of basketball fame). Some, like the new use of *butter*, become widely used and incorporated into the ongoing linguistic practices of a large community. Others are just appreciated and understood in the moment, like *emusculation*, which Spears encountered in an evening with a bunch of men watching basketball. The coinage was noticed but it didn't continue nor, apparently, was there any expectation that it would.

Semantic authorizing is not so straightforward as it might have seemed from Hilary Putnam's picture of recognized experts/epistemic authorities in a community to whom the others in that community defer. Ultimately, authorizing arises within communities as the result of a variety of processes, among which deference to recognized experts is only one. Some draw on institutional authority, others on social hierarchy, others on social pressures, others on informal negotiation when personal interests conflict. Existing hierarchical relations and formal institutions usually help authorize meanings that serve establishment interests. But though the tilt is toward preserving existing power, there is always disruptive potential. Small resistant communities can authorize new linguistic practices that spread. There are no guarantees, but mastery does shift in some ways over time.

Notes

1. See, e.g., Cameron 2012 and earlier in Kramarae and Treichler 1985 and papers in Frank and Treichler 1989, esp. the editors' introduction, Treichler and Frank 1989, and Treichler 1989. Russell 2018 is a more recent contribution.
2. Russell 2018; quotations are from p. 187.
3. For a readable account, see Fred Barbash, "Trump's 'Emoluments' Battle: How a Scholar's Search of 200 Years of Dictionaries Helped Win a Historic Ruling," *Washington Post*, July 27, 2018, www.washingtonpost.com/news/ morning-mix/wp/2018/07/27/trumps-emoluments-battle-how-a-scholars- journey-through-200-years-of-dictionaries-helped-win-a-historic-ruling/. A more detailed account can be found in John Mikhail, "The Definition of 'Emolument' in English Language and Legal Dictionaries, 1523–1806" (June 30, 2017). Available at SSRN: https://ssrn.com/abstract= 2995693 or http://dx.doi.org/10.2139/ssrn.2995693.
4. Putnam 1975.
5. Crane 2016 is a good overview and Britt 2006 expresses a still-relevant skepticism.
6. Runyon et al. 2017 offered this definition; Redd 2017 is an interesting account for the layperson of the issues being raised.
7. McConnell-Ginet 2006a, 2006b.
8. A good place to read about the Loving case is www.oyez.org/cases/1966/395.
9. Amy Howe, "Details on United States v. Windsor: In Plain English," *SCOTUSblog*, June 26, 2013, www.scotusblog.com/2013/06/detail-on-united -states-v-windsor-in-plain-english/.
10. "Marriage," Merriam-Webster, n.d., www.merriam-webster.com/dictionary/ marriage.

11. "Marriage," *Merriam-Webster Student Dictionary*, n.d. www
    .wordcentral.com/cgi-bin/student?book=Student&va=marriage.
12. "What Is the Definition of Marriage?" *Got Questions website*, n.d.,
    www.gotquestions.org/definition-of-marriage.html.
13. Battistella 1997, p. 114.
14. See Maria Alexander, "Berkeley City Council Adopts Gender-Neutral
    Language Policy for Municipal Code," *The Daily Californian*, July 22, 2019,
    www.dailycal.org/2019/07/22/berkeley-city-council-adopts-gender-neutral-
    language-policy-for-municipal-code/ for one of the few accounts that does
    not imply ridicule of the move.
15. "NAMI's Statements Regarding President Trump's Comments on
    Reinstitutionalizing People With Mental Illness," National Alliance on
    Mental Illness (NAMI) website, August 16, 2019, www.nami.org/About-
    NAMI/NAMI-News/2019/NAMI-s-Statement-Regarding-President-
    Trump-s-Comments-on-Reinstitutionalizing-People-with-Mental-Ill.
16. Paisley Currah, "Feminism, Gender Pluralism and Gender Neutrality:
    Maybe it's Time to Bring Back the Binary," *Paisley Currah* (blog), April 26,
    2016.
17. Justin Wm. Moyer, "Why Houston's Gay Rights Ordinance Failed: Fear of
    Men in Women's Bathrooms," *Washington Post*, November 3, 2015, www
    .washingtonpost.com/news/morning-mix/wp/2015/11/03/why-houstons-
    gay-rights-ordinance-failed-bathrooms/.
18. The Goldberg article, "What Is a Woman? The Dispute between Radical
    Feminism and Transgenderism," appeared in the August 4, 2014 issue of the
    New Yorker; it appears online at www.newyorker.com/magazine/2014/08/04/
    woman-2. After I had written this section, Mary Kate McGowan pointed me
    to an excellent and detailed feminist defense of including trans women as
    women. See "'I'm Not Transphobic, But. . .': A Feminist Case against
    the Feminist Case against Trans Inclusivity," *Verso Books Blog*, October 17,
    2018, www.versobooks.com/blogs/4090-i-m-not-transphobic-but-a-feminist-
    case-against-the-feminist-case-against-trans-inclusivity, written by three
    philosophers working in the UK: Lorna Finlayson, Katharine Jenkins, and
    Rosie Worsdale.
19. See Bettcher 2009, 2012.
20. Moore and Currah 2015, p. 64.
21. Jennifer Finney Boylan, "Trump Cannot Define Away My Existence," *The
    New York Times*, October 22, 2018, www.nytimes.com/2018/10/22/opinion/
    trump-transgender-sex-policy.html.

8 Concluding

In this final chapter I highlight some of the lessons I take from thinking and writing about the issues discussed in this book. What I do not do is really conclude. That is true in two senses. As I said in setting the stage for this book, I will not come up with straightforward directives: say this, don't say that, write this, don't write that. Context is too important for such blanket prescriptions. And of course what is best in a particular context is a matter of what's best for particular purposes, what serves particular interests. Rather I point out some general principles that seem important to consider as one engages linguistically in social and civic life. I do not, however, make definitive judgments, draw specific conclusions, about which words to use when. Through sketching many concrete examples of cases where linguistic practices have been important in (re)structuring social relations, including power relations, I hope to illustrate some ways words matter and some ways each of us might think about our own participation in linguistic practices.

I also do not really conclude in the sense of finishing. Though I will (finally) conclude this particular book and send the manuscript off for publication, I will continue to think about the issues it raises, and I hope readers will do so as well. The process of reading, writing, and talking with others during the preparation of this book has opened my eyes and ears to ways that language matters in our lives I had not really considered before. And the media, friends, random people I encounter: all offer access to an unending stream of reports on evolving linguistic practices and attitudes. Every day I notice something new, not necessarily new principles but new particulars that should be explored.

Does It Seem Crazy? Why?

"Are you going to talk about PC gone crazy?" asked a friend. "What do you have in mind?" I retorted. "Oh, you know. Like replacing the label *Cornell Plantations* with *Cornell Botanic Gardens*. I haven't given them any money since that happened."

Intrigued by her clear outrage, I decided to explore the issue further and had an interesting conversation in July 2019 with Christopher Dunn. Dunn became director in 2014 of what was then the Cornell Plantations and in 2016 was renamed the Cornell Botanic Gardens.[1] It proved a fascinating story, one with layers of history and linguistic concerns that I had not expected. Cornell was founded in 1865 as an institution "where any person can find instruction in any subject." The sex-neutral *person* was a considered choice, as founders Ezra Cornell and Andrew Dickson White were at least in principle supportive of higher education for women as well as for people of any racial background. Although the actual experience of women and of people of color at Cornell has often been profoundly problematic, that aspirational inclusivity expressed in the founding statement has proved useful in reform projects over the years. As both a state-supported and privately endowed institution, Cornell is home to a wide range of fields of study and its College of Agriculture and Life Sciences has departments of plant biology, horticulture, and more.

Early on in its history, Cornell maintained extensive gardens near the on-campus home of then President A. D. White and elsewhere on campus, and these were sometimes referred to as *botanical gardens*. As Cornell moved into the twentieth century, there was increasing interest in going beyond flowerbeds to offer a living library of a wide variety of plants, as a resource for education and for sheer enjoyment. In 1928 an *arboretum* was designated and in the mid-1930s noted botanist and horticulturist Liberty Hyde Bailey, who had founded and been the first dean of the College of Agriculture, began pushing to develop a more extensive assemblage of plantings. He apparently said that he wanted to "rehabilitate" the word *plantations*, to rid it of its associations both with single-crop cultivation and with the large single-crop agricultural enterprises of the American south that had depended on the labor of enslaved Africans. There is no record of his exact words on the subject, but he did recommend an institution that would include the arboretum, flower and herb gardens, agricultural test plots, and more – and he wanted the name to cover that wide range. The Cornell Trustees finally launched the Cornell Plantations under that name in 1944.

Enter Christopher Dunn seventy years later. He was puzzled by the name, which still very strongly suggests single-crop plantings, not only the cotton and sugar of the American south but also crops such as coffee and pineapple. He began to explore invest-ment in the name and support for a change among students, staff, and faculty at the Cornell campus, the larger Ithaca community, transplanted Cornellians including alums, and others. The pro-cess might not have received much outside attention, but in November 2015 Cornell's Black Students United (BSU) presented the president and vice-president of the university with a list of demands. The focus of those demands was not language. The students were pressing for courses and training focused on racial issues, increased racial diversity in faculty and other staff, more mental health and other support services for students of color, and regular meetings with those in charge of the university. The final section of their list, however, was devoted to symbols. Renaming the Cornell Plantations was one part of that.

Not surprisingly, however, media coverage often highlighted the name change that the BSU wanted and paid less attention to other matters. At almost the same time both Harvard and Princeton abandoned *master* as the title of heads of colleges, and Yale was seriously considering a similar move.[2] A few months later, Yale also voted to abandon the use of *master*, issuing an interesting account of some of the many discussions that had preceded that decision, the reasons given on both sides.[3] Meanwhile back in Ithaca, on March 2016 an anonymous group of Cornellians calling itself the "Union of White Students" with the aim to "preserve and advance their race" appeared on the scene. They denounced the BSU-advocated retirement of the "Cornell Plantations" label as a "puerile demand." They continued, "We have observed this here at Cornell and are ashamed at the response of the University to placate these delusional minority groups on-campus [by] honoring their demands."[4]

It is by no means only overt white supremacists who deride such moves.[5] One alum dripped sarcasm in commenting on the name change. "You mean it's NOT a slaveholding operation? I had no idea – THANK YOU for changing the name and making that clear to me. (Ridiculous – just ridiculous.)" And another wrote: "A monstrous betrayal of generations of Cornell alumni attached to the Cornell Plantations. And for what? To appease a handful of crybabies who can't read a history book or a map, given that they can't tell the difference between the Cornell Plantations and an agricultural model practiced 150 years ago a thousand miles south of Ithaca. This university administration needs to start standing for something other than appeasement, retreat, and milquetoast nonsense. Can everyone just grow up now? The world doesn't pander, and Cornell shouldn't either." Others, like my friend (if I understand her correctly), just really dislike change in what feels familiar and comfortable. They are particularly annoyed if change seems to them driven primarily by the desire to *appear* enlightened and up-to-date, which is part of what they mean by "politically correct."

Director Dunn approached the whole matter very astutely. Emphasizing his own sense that the old name suggested a narrow focus on a single kind of plant whereas the reality was a wide diversity of species, he was already bringing on board a large portion of those with a direct interest in the matter before the BSU raised its concerns. At least some of the people supporting Dunn's desire for a change would not have done so if they had first seen it as a response to "demands" from a student group concerned about what they experienced as a racist campus climate. Because the way had been paved by Dunn's pointing to confusion about the mission and the nature of the Cornell Plantations, the unwanted suggestion of a single crop, university authorities could readily accede to this "demand" for more racially sensitive language without many ripple effects. In fact, Dunn's first announcement in the Cornell *Daily Sun* in October 2015, which predated the BSU manifesto, deftly tied the two distinct issues together. "There is one key element that all botanic gardens have in common: celebrating, displaying and studying the rich diversity of the world's plants," he wrote. "Yet to be truly effective, this celebration of natural diversity must also embrace human diversity." Of course the botanic diversity Dunn celebrates is driven mainly by the huge stock of different plant species, whereas human diversity, which he also applauds, exists within a single species and has minimal connection to biology. Nonetheless, his marriage of the two issues was rhetorically brilliant.

It is unlikely that any students were confused about the Cornell Plantations in the ways suggested by the comments quoted above. Nor did students at Yale, Harvard, and Princeton think that those designated by *master* were trying to enslave them. In the case of both words, students were pointing to strong historical associations with the experiences of their enslaved ancestors, heavy and disturbing lexical baggage. The vivid and frightening pictures evoked can seem all too real when racist graffiti appear on the door of a black fraternity or a black student is assaulted by white peers yelling racial slurs. These and similar events have indeed happened in recent years on university campuses, including Cornell. The website grammarphobia.com, discussing the proposals for the name change at Cornell, documents a considerable history of the word *plantations* being used to suggest exploitation.[6] Such usages have come primarily but by no means exclusively from African-American speakers.

There is indeed a history that connects this word to the establishments worked by enslaved Africans and to their highly authoritarian, constricting, and outright cruel atmosphere. Of course the word has senses that do not involve farming operations exploiting forced enslaved labor, a fact that some self-appointed 'authorities' point out in criticizing those for whom the associations with slavery cannot be ignored. Both linguists and philosophers often emphasize the sense of words that language users 'intend.' After all, Liberty Hyde Bailey was (purportedly) actually trying to dislodge the old slavery associations of *plantations* when he proposed the name. But we do not control the lexical baggage others attach to our words, and appeals to dictionary senses that would not seem to support that same baggage, while they are sometimes relevant, do not erase the effects those words produce.

It is all too easy for those of us with different life and family histories to underestimate how loaded some language is for others. I have certainly done so myself. I am not suggesting that those who recognize linguistically triggered discomfort and perhaps even feel it themselves will always agree on the best course of action. There is, for example, a strong argument to be made that remembering historical oppression is essential to dismantling current oppressive practices ultimately rooted in that history. This might suggest *not* eliminating all symbols that remind us of past injustice. What I want to do here, however, is encourage readers who do not immediately understand why some other group of people is bothered by some linguistic practice or is suggesting some linguistic change to try to find out more about the issues involved, the background. Don't assume that reactions to language that differ from yours are simply 'crazy,' outside what you consider norms of rationality, or 'uninformed,' explicable as ignorance of what seem to you well-established 'facts' or principles.

Learning more does not guarantee you will agree with would-be linguistic reformers. Nor can it eliminate the sometimes considerable discomfort created by change, especially change in familiar linguistic routines. And there will be instances where even after you have a fuller picture, the proposed changes will continue to seem at best pointless or silly. Still, I recommend inquiry over rage.

Using Language Recommendations to Expand Minds

Several years ago I taught basic mathematics to classes of men at Auburn Correctional Facility, a maximum security prison about 35 miles from my home in Ithaca, NY. These classes were part of the Cornell Prison Education Program, CPEP. CPEP is staffed by faculty and students from Cornell University and offers men accepted into it (via a competitive admissions process) the chance to earn an associate's degree from nearby Cayuga Community College. I actually never discussed labeling preferences with the men in my classes, some of whom I got to know relatively well through having them as students in more than one class.

Well, they did once affirm a label for themselves, though it was offered in jest. One day I handed out pennies when we were doing something on probability. I asked the students to toss them some number of times (20? 50?) and keep track of heads and tails. One man immediately said, "You're not supposed to give us money." I laughed and said, "Well I'll collect it when I'm done." To which another guy responded, "you can't expect to get money back – we're criminals, you know," and we all laughed. The pennies were returned before they left the classroom. And I learned a little more about the many restrictions on how I was supposed to interact with these students. (On another occasion, having failed to clear my plans with the prison authorities, I distributed handwritten holiday cards that were immediately confiscated.)

But somewhere in the early part of this century, the well-known and highly respected prison activist Eddie Ellis issued a statement on labeling people like my math students at Auburn, and those of their cohort no longer behind bars. (I learned about Ellis's linguistic initiative from my friend and Cornell colleague Mary F. Katzenstein, who not only does research and teaching on incarceration in the US but was one of the founders of CPEP and the person who recruited me to work on getting math courses into CPEP's curriculum.) Figure 8.1 is an extract from Eddie Ellis's

When we are not called mad dogs, animals, predators, offenders and other derogatory terms, we are referred to as inmates, convicts, prisoners and felons – all terms devoid of humanness which identify us as "things" rather than as people. These terms are accepted as the "official" language of the media, law enforcement, prison industrial complex and public policy agencies. *However, they are no longer acceptable for us and we are asking people to stop using them.* ...

[T]o assist our transition from prison to our communities as responsible citizens and to create a more positive human image of ourselves, we are asking everyone to stop using these negative terms and to simply refer to us as **PEOPLE.** People currently or formerly incarcerated, **PEOPLE** on parole, **PEOPLE** recently released from prison, **PEOPLE** in prison, **PEOPLE** with criminal convictions, but **PEOPLE.** ...

[C]alling me inmate, convict, prisoner, felon, or offender indicates a lack of understanding of who I am, but more importantly *what I can be.* I can be and am much more than an "ex-con," or an "ex-offender," or an "ex-felon." ...

We believe we have the right to be called by a name we choose, rather than one someone else decides to use. We think that by insisting on being called **"people"** we reaffirm our right to be recognized as human beings, not animals, inmates, prisoners or offenders.

Sent to supportive individuals, institutions, and media sources in 2000 by Eddie Ellis, Founding Director of Center for NuLeadership on Urban Solutions

Posted at https://static1.squarespace.com/static/58eb0522e6f2e1dfce591dee/ t/596e13f48419c2e5a0e95d30/1500386295291/CNUS-language-letter- 2016.pdf

Figure 8.1 An Open Letter to Our Friends on the Question of Language (excerpts)

statement, which has been widely circulated among people involved in prison reform efforts (at least in New York State).[7] At some point, the New York State Department of Corrections (NYS DOC) threw out *prisoner, convict,* and *felon* but mandated that those incarcerated within its walls be labeled *offenders,* which certainly did little to address the issues that Ellis's statement raised. In July 2019, the terms most widely used on official NYS DOC websites and sites to which they linked seemed to be *inmate* and *parolee,* along with *youthful offender.* Many other sources, however, especially those associated with efforts to restructure the system, used such expressions as *people in prison* or *incarcerated people* or just *guys,* where the context made clear that the guys in question were now behind bars or had spent time inside.

Ellis (who died in 2014) clearly recognized that labeling helps create and perpetuate *kinds* of people in part because the labels obscure "what [those labeled] can be," suggesting that their futures are determined by the most problematic aspects of their pasts. Ellis did not use philosopher Ian Hacking's language of *interactive kinds*, which I introduced at the beginning of Chapter 1. What he did was make vivid what Hacking calls the *looping* effects of the labeling so common in speaking of people enmeshed in the system of courts, jails, prisons, parole boards, and the rest. To call people what they prefer to be called is to help them affirm their own chosen identities, to aspire toward becoming the sorts of people they want to be.

In issuing his open letter about language, Eddie Ellis was hoping not only to change labeling practices in ways that would be helpful to incarcerated or formerly incarcerated people. He was also challenging allies and potential allies to examine their own assumptions about those who had been convicted of crimes and sentenced to spend time (in most cases, many years, sometimes a lifetime) in prisons. The challenge reached a largely receptive audience. In part this was because Ellis himself was widely respected in the community of prison activists: he was taken seriously. And in part this was because thinking about the labeling questions led many to recognize problematic self-limiting assumptions that the incarcerated or formerly incarcerated people with whom they were working continued to make. It was also because many activists working to support people in prisons or on parole came to recognize that they themselves often continued to hold limiting assumptions about the potential of those whose transformative efforts they were trying to support.

Kyung-Ji Rhee, Deputy Director of the Center for NuLeadership on Urban Solutions, a think tank and action-oriented organization founded by Eddie Ellis, spoke with me in July 2019 about the impact of Ellis's language initiative. Although the Center has lacked resources to document testimonials and other evidence of Ellis's influence in this area, she told me about some typical cases. For example, the NY Public Library in 2005–2006 issued a booklet subtitled "A guide for *ex-inmates* on information sources in New York City" (italics added), focused on "The Job Search." In 2012, the cover of what looks to be an essentially identical booklet has replaced "ex-inmates" by "formerly incarcerated people." A *New York Times* editorial in the *Sunday Review* section of May 7, 2016, is titled "Labels Like 'Felon' Are an Unfair Life Sentence." It lauds the Obama Department of Justice, which included people who had worked with Eddie Ellis, for moving away from those familiar labels and following Ellis's recommendations to "humanize" talk about those currently or formerly incarcerated.

Throughout our conversation Rhee repeatedly spoke of the linguistic manifesto as a 'portal,' of importance less in itself than in opening people's minds to broader understanding of the 'system' and its corrosive impacts not just on those incarcerated but on their families and communities. Noting that the Center is deeply committed to young people and the issues that dominate their experience, she suggested that they may issue an addendum addressing such growing concerns as gender and, more generally, intersectionality of identities. But she wanted to emphasize that Eddie Ellis's call is for more than "humanizing" language. It is ultimately, she suggested, about stimulating reflection on how labeling practices help "generate, validate, and perpetuate" meanings with built-in assumptions that prop up the structural *in*justices on which the so-called criminal justice system rests. (Michelle Alexander's 2010 book, *The New Jim Crow: Mass Incarceration in the Age of Colorblindness*, details a host of ways in which US policing, courts, and prisons are deeply unjust and profoundly racist.)

Have words like *prisoner, felon,* and *convict* disappeared? Of course not. But Eddie Ellis's letter was an important linguistic intervention that led many, including incarcerated or formerly incarcerated people, to see wider ranges of possibility for rehabilitative justice. It is not that those words themselves had prevented recognition of possibilities for positive change. But having attention drawn to their 'essentializing' and 'dehumanizing' tendencies both for those so designated and for others working with them helped increase not only the resolve but the effectiveness of programs like CPEP and the Center for NuLeadership on Urban Solutions and many others.

Naming Frontiers

In the past decade or so, the term *Latinx* has become increasingly used for designating Americans from Latin America or with Latin American heritage. I have mentioned it briefly at several earlier points in the book, but I now want to discuss this relatively recent label in fuller detail. For many, *Latinx* is successor to *Latina/o*. The conventional assumption of Spanish speakers is that the same form *Latino* indicates both individuals who identify as masculine and groups of people of both the standard gender identities. But, as in other contexts, many women, including transgender women, have felt excluded by these so-called masculine generics. By the late twentieth century we began to see *Latino/a* and then, to up feminine visibility, *Latina/o*. The next development was graphic combination of the feminine *-a* and the masculine *-o* prefixes with the 'at' symbol @ to indicate a fusion of the Spanish feminine *-a* and masculine *-o* endings. *Latin@*, I've been told, is to be pronounced as if it were *Latinao*, but for neither Spanish nor American-English speakers does this sequence of vowels roll off the tongue very readily. The written form *Latin@* is used without comment, for example, in the third edition of Michael Omi and Howard Winant's classic *Racial Formation in the United States*, substantially revised in 2015 from the 1986 and 1994 versions, which used *Latino*.

As 2020 approached, however, there was a widespread shift, at least among young people and some older academics and other writers who see themselves as politically progressive, to *Latinx*. The publication in late 2018 of *Latinx: The New Force in American Politics and Culture* by Ed Morales, who teaches at Columbia, highlights this shift.

> By titling this book *Latinx*, I'm attempting, like the mostly young folks that are embracing this label, to engage with several

threads of thinking about identity and naming, recognizing and evaluating the potential of such a label's elasticity and ability to evade categorization. I'm drawing attention to the Latinx people as one of the primary destabilizers of American – and by extension, Western, identity. Often erased from America's founding narrative Latinx – in all our previous guises – have always been present as a crucial counter-narrative, a people that live in a world of many worlds, possessing an identity of multiple identities.[8]

He continues:

For all of *Latinx*'s space-age quirkiness, the term has a technocratic emptiness to it that can make it hard to warm up to. It feels like a mathematician's null set, and many are unsure of how to pronounce it. But even amid ongoing debate around the term on campuses and in the media, the growing movement to embrace *Latinx* highlights how it dispenses with the problem of prioritizing male or female by negating that binary. The real power of the term and its true meaning erupt with its final syllable. After years of Latin looks, Latin music, and Latin America, the word describes something that is not as much Latin – a word originally coined by the French to brand non-English- and Dutch-speaking colonies with a different flavor – as it is an alternative America, the unexpected X factor in America's race debate.

And how should *Latinx* be pronounced? According to most of its promoters, as if the word were *LaTEENex*, with stress on the middle syllable just as in *Latina* or *Latino*. The syllable *-ex* should be thought of as replacing either *-a* or *-o*, with no other change. But I have heard *Latinx* pronounced *LAtin-ex* as if it were the English word *Latin* with an *-ex* suffix attached. (In the UK the title *Mx* has gained considerable traction; here too the *-x* is supposed to signal inclusion of those who might reject both traditional gender labels – the title 'Mx,' however, is pronounced like 'mix' rather than like 'mex.' And recall the hullabaloo in the UK around *womxn* that I mentioned in the preceding chapter.)

In mid-September of 2018, shortly after Merriam-Webster added *Latinx* to its dictionary, the *Washington Post* had an article that looked at responses to the word from several of those who might be designated by it.[9] Sandra Velez was indignant about *Latinx* as an anglicization of Spanish. "Do they hate or revile their Hispanic/Latino ancestry so much they are willing (unwitting?) accomplices in erasing their own heritage? Because that's exactly what's happening." More ambivalently, transgender activist Ruby Corado, who speaks both Spanish and English fluently, noted her own attachment to the traditional gendered terminology. "I grew up fighting for my gender to be recognized as Latina. That's something that's not going to change, but [Latinx] is something I'm adapting to as I'm doing work with millennials. I come from the old school, so I actually like the term 'Latina.' But I embrace that term [Latinx] as well. You have to understand, I came from a time when everything was gender-based." Finally, there's a much less equivocal endorsement of *Latinx* from Brooklyn College professor of psychology María R. Scharrón-del Río, who embraces the *they* paradigm for others to use in referring to them (i.e., to Professor Scharrón-del Río). Scharrón-del Río offers some useful background. "The term was coined within queer Internet groups. That was where it was used first and foremost." And they continue:

> We need to see more and that's part of what the 'x' does – it makes visible the fact that [some] people aren't included within the 'a' or the 'o.' And it's really a linguistic intervention. Just knowing that there is an 'x' makes you think about what that means and makes you question what you often take for granted.

Commentators' views on the *Post* piece were mixed, some advocating for just *Latin*, a suggestion I've seen in a number of places, or the neologism *Latine*, and others ready to get on board with *Latinx*.

Though *Latinx* is widespread on college campuses in lectures and classrooms, it has barely infiltrated official usage at universities and colleges as I write in the summer of 2019. What used to be the Cornell *Latino* Studies Program is now called the *Latina/o* Studies Program, and the graduate concentration is still called *Latino* Studies. But the text in Figure 8.2 was posted on January

The former Latina/o/x Student Success Office (LSSO) is officially changing its name to employ the gender-inclusive term "Latinx."

Inspired by other organizations and student services offices across the nation that have adopted the term, LSSO is choosing to use Latinx as a gender-neutral and non-binary alternative to Latina/o or Latin@. Examples abound of "Latinx" being used in a higher education student services context across the country, such as the Center for Chicanx and Latinx Academic and Student Success at University of California-Davis.

The "Latinx" term has been rising in popularity since 2004, mainly among students, scholars and activists. It has been specifically embraced by members of the LGBTQ+ community who identify themselves outside of the male/female binary. As terms evolve to become more inclusive, LSSO continues to evolve as well.

Gender inclusivity has always been one of LSSO's commitments. In 2005, LSSO opened as the first office on campus to include "Latina/o" in its name. This set a precedent that the Latina/o Studies Program (previously Latino Studies Program) eventually followed. As a student services office, LSSO endeavors to offer an affirming space for students with respect for their own evolving ways of identifying. The name change aligns with the recent university statement citing Cornell's ongoing commitment to equal education opportunity for community members of all gender identities and expressions. Incorporating Latinx into LSSO's name was supported by a majority of students and alumni in a recent community survey.

Latinx is not the perfect solution, and will not satisfy everyone. However, it is a step toward maintaining a welcoming and inclusive environment to better serve students of Latin American descent.

This article was written by Karen Loya '19 and posted on January 15, 2019 and is used with permission of the author and of Prof. Debra A. Castillo, Director of Cornell's Latina/o Studies Program in the academic year 2019–20. The article is accessible at https://latino.cornell.edu/content/latinaox-student-success-office-changes-its-name-latinx-student-success-office

Figure 8.2 Cornell's Latina/o/x Student Success Office Name Change

15, 2019, announcing that *Latinx* had won out over the previous *Latina/o/x* in the name of an affiliated student services group. That is among the few examples I found in the summer of 2019 of *Latinx* as an official designator. Berkeley still has a *Chicana/o and Latina/o* Studies Program. Princeton's is still just *Latino* Studies, with the (Spanish) masculine form used generically (and I noticed several very recent references to the Berkeley program as just *Chicano and Latino*). The University of Texas has *Mexican*

American and Latina/o Studies, though there are references on their site to their group as *Latino* Studies. Yet Hunter College of the City University of New York (CUNY) is home to the Centro de Estudios *Puertorriqueños*, retaining the traditional masculine generic. The Hunter unit is, however, known informally as the Centro or by its English name, the Center for *Puerto Rican* Studies, both gender-neutral labels. Lehman College in the Bronx, also part of CUNY, offers a major in *Latino/Puerto Rican* Studies and a minor not only in that but also in *Mexican and Mexican American* Studies. At the University of Arizona, the *Mexican American* Studies department offers a course in *Chicana/Latina* Studies and another course title includes mention of *Latina/Latino* identities. And Florida's University of Miami offers *Cuban* and *Cuban American* Studies.

I avoided using *Latinx* earlier in this book for two reasons. The first is its novelty. Many readers, especially those born before the 1980s, will not have encountered it. Even if they have, they may be perplexed by it linguistically, given the pronunciation challenges it presents to both English and Spanish speakers. Most readers, however, will have seen and heard *Hispanic* or *Latino* or both. This is why those terms figure in the discussion in Chapter 1 on the rich historical background for thinking about labeling this panethnic group. The Trump-led assault on would-be asylum-seekers and other immigrants trying to cross the southern border of the US is just a part of the current historical context that will profoundly affect the future of the Latino/Hispanic population of the US. My second reason for avoiding *Latinx* was that it falls into the category Geoff Nunberg dubbed *prejudicial* expressions, immediately conveying a message about the politics of one who deploys it.[10] In this case what I might well convey is something like, "I want you to recognize that I am allying myself with trendy young Latinos and Latinas in embracing gender inclusivity and welcoming all people of Latin American heritage, including those outside the gender binary – I too reject transphobia." Although I strongly support transgender inclusivity, I do not want to suggest that not using *Latinx* manifests transphobia or at least being "out of it."

What does the future hold for these ongoing identity and naming struggles? Sociologist Eduardo Bonilla-Silva in the fifth edition of his *Racism without Racists: Color-Blind Racism and the Persistence of Racial Inequality in America* predicts that the emerging prominence of this group will be an important factor in establishing Latin American–style racism in the US. He expects that a triracial system will oust the old black–white dichotomy: white, 'honorary white,' and black. This middle group, Bonilla-Silva suggests, would include light-skinned Latinos as well as Chinese, Korean, and Japanese Americans along with, perhaps, Middle Eastern and Indian (i.e., Asian Indian) Americans and most 'mixed-race' Americans. (The term *mixed race*, as Bonilla-Silva points out, is itself problematic, since it seems to presuppose the existence of 'pure' races to be mixed.) As in Latin America, 'whitening' would be a goal and there would be a 'pigmentocracy' or color-based hierarchy. The illusion of colorblindness would grow even stronger, Bonilla-Silva suggests, and would continue to reinforce racism.

In *Latinx*, Morales offers a much more positive, almost utopian, vision of the future in which people with Latin American roots become a cohesive and politically powerful group in the US.

> Latinx was coined so as not to privilege gender, and is perhaps the first time an ethno-racial group has chosen to rename itself for such a reason. ... The Latin X factor – the product of a race made up of all races, genders, sensibilities, proclivities – is something that remains partially untapped and has the ability to draw from multiple human traditions and work between them. ... [W]hat Latinx can claim is the ability to imagine multiple others within one awareness, allowing otherness to fade as it becomes part of an internal conversation. ... The Latin X factor ... is a continuing, eternal process of translation, in which the next analogy is fruit for a new conversation, a new beginning.[11]

Morales plays with the 'x' of *Latinx* and uses it to fashion his gloriously optimistic multiracial future. He does not consider possible alliances of Latinx people with other identity groups such as

Asian Americans, one of the possible coalitions discussed by philosopher Linda Alcoff over a decade ago in her very insightful critique of the black–white dichotomy that has tended to dominate racial discourse in the US.[12] He does, however, move beyond a pigment-ocracy.

There will inevitably be further developments for people now labeled *Latinx* and their descendants, whether racism and racial divisions worsen or become less significant. And whether *Latinx* will have a long shelf life is very much an open question.

Typographical Distinctions: Boundary-Policing and Dog-Whistling

Typographical matters are seldom discussed by those of us focused on matters of meaning, but they can be important. Indeed, *Latinx* and, even more dramatically, *Latin@*, only really do their thing as envisioned when encountered visually. Not surprisingly, both emerged online. And, as I noted above, whether or not someone uses these innovative labels is sometimes used to categorize them as ally (or not), as 'woke' to matters of social justice or shamefully ignorant of current linguistic norms. (The word *woke* in such uses is now being abandoned, I should add.[13])

The first typographical issue I want to discuss, however, pre-dates the internet. It's using the contrast between capital and lowercase letters to draw boundaries. In her excellent 2010 book, *The Everyday Language of White Racism*, linguistic anthropologist Jane H. Hill includes the following statement on her treatment of racial category labels. "I prefer to capitalize Black and White, but this is almost never seen in newspapers or magazines. In fact, I have had copy-editors for scholarly journals who were preparing my work for publication correct this usage, changing these words to lower case."[14] What she leaves unsaid is that capitalization of *black* has been far more common than capitalization of *white*, a typographical indicator of the 'unmarked' status of whiteness. Her consistent capitalization of both labels is one way of announcing her challenge to the still widespread presumption that whiteness can "go without saying," be taken as the normative state of humanity. When I began writing this book, I planned to follow her example (and that of many other racially progressive writers in the late twentieth and early twenty-first centuries). But as I read more widely in very recent writings, especially by black thinkers I particularly admire, I noticed what seemed a trend to use lower-case for both words so I have followed that example instead.

My decision not to capitalize *black* and *white* as labels of racialized groups in the US has not seemed to bother any of my readers. Some, however, have been made uncomfortable by my not writing *Deaf* to designate those deaf people who identify with a culture centered on sign language (in the US context, ASL) and on the experiences of people with little or no hearing. In abandoning the conventional *Deaf/deaf* distinction, I was influenced by the following statement from three sign-language scholars, two of whom are themselves deaf: Jami Fisher, Gene Mirus, and Donna Jo Napoli.

> For decades, people in Deaf Studies and a large majority of members in deaf communities used a capital "D" to indicate a sociological affiliation and a lower-case "d" to indicate audiological status only. The sociological affiliation is commonly – and perhaps too loosely – termed Deaf culture. To avoid misunderstanding, we do not use the term *culture*. Like some others in our field, we choose to break from the "d/D" convention to avoid being mired in identity politics and marginalization of deaf people who might not fit squarely into these arbitrary boundaries. Doing so is not a rejection or minimization of the socio-cultural tendencies of those in what we refer to below as deaf communities, but rather, is meant to be inclusive of the various and individual ways of being deaf.[15]

Tribes, a play by English playwright Nina Raines, explores deafness and Deaf culture in the sense of a social life among a community of signing deaf people.[16] Billy, the central character, is in his twenties, born deaf into a hearing and non-signing family.

Sylvia is around the same age, born hearing into a deaf and signing family. She is highly fluent both in BSL (British Sign Language), and in English, having acquired them both in very early childhood. She is, however, becoming progressively deaf and will soon lose even the small amount of residual hearing she has at the time the play begins. Billy's family has not exposed him to signing but has worked hard to help him learn to lip-read, something at which Sylvia is not very good, and to speak English comprehensibly. Billy's family do not, however, realize at all that much of what goes on in family dinner-table exchanges, for example, passes him by.

In Billy's first encounter with Sylvia at an event celebrating a deaf artist, we see his thrill at beginning to learn from her the expressive possibilities of signing. He has asked her to show him some sign, and she signs "F-L-O-W-E-R," speaking the letters as she finger-spells using motion to show blossoming, followed by wilting, and says "Sign poem." "Wow," says Billy. When he finally introduces her to his family we learn of his father Christopher's active hostility to activism among deaf people and of the whole family's ignorance about sign languages and their fear that Sylvia will take Billy, whom they all love deeply, from them. (Daniel is Billy's brother, Beth is his mother, Ruth his sister.) Before Sylvia arrives, Daniel mentions that she is 'making' Billy learn to sign, to which Christopher responds, "Next thing we know, he'll be banging on about the bloody deaf community." And then, to the shock of Beth and Ruth, Christopher says, "He [Billy] is not [deaf]. He's been brought up in a hearing family, he's been protected from all that shit! I'm talking about the hardliners, capital D deaf, people who call us Audists." Sylvia arrives and later in the scene, responding to Christopher's questions, she expresses her own frustration with processes of exclusion she sees operating in the local "Deaf Community" to which Billy is becoming increasingly attached. "It's hierarchical," she says. Billy, she notes, gets points by being born deaf, an 'asset' she does not have, but he loses them by not being able to sign. Her status is helped by her having grown up in a very deaf family and becoming natively fluent in BSL. And, finally, we see the increasing fear Sylvia experiences that she will soon essentially be confined to deaf-only spaces. Near the end of the play, she expresses her frustrations with the "community" to Billy. "There's no empathy. 'You're going deaf – so what? We're all deaf.' You're not allowed to be depressed about it." The capital *D* vs lowercase *d* can bring such issues into sharp relief. (I first saw *Tribes* in London in 2010 or 2011, and was pulled back into its world when the Ithaca-based Kitchen Theatre Company staged it in June 2019.)

A far more deliberately vicious typographical distinction is what's sometimes called the *echo* or the *anti-Semitic triple parentheses*. The account available on the Anti-Defamation League's website suggests that this particular practice actually originated in an auditory phenomenon, an echo effect used in a 2014 alt-right podcast to mark Jewish names specially and quite audibly with this slight acoustic manipulation.[17] The acoustic echo was translated into a typographic convention used on platforms like Twitter. Typically, triple parentheses (or brackets) encased a proper name or some descriptive label in order to signal to others in the know that the particular person named was Jewish or that the kind of person or phenomenon was to be understood as Jewish. So, for example, you might see *(((George Soros)))* or *(((banker)))* or *[[[internationalism]]]*. The echo functions as a *dog whistle*, a term used for 'coded' signals of racism, expressions like *welfare* that do not literally convey anything about race but can serve to express and activate racist sentiments when directed toward an audience that shares such attitudes.[18] Like a whistle that only dogs hear, the echo typographic practice was initially comprehensible only to those in anti-Semitic alt-right online networks. The typographic echo drew wider attention when members of such networks began using it in replying to or retweeting messages of Jewish journalists.[19] Once it was noticed in late spring of 2016, a wide range of people countered by 'echoing' their own names, some of them Jewish people reappropriating those triple parentheses defiantly, and others allies showing their support of those targeted by the echoes. Once noticed, the echoes had less force. The visible echo may still, however, offer a certain 'deniability' to its user – after all, just as *welfare queen* doesn't have blackness as part of its literal meaning, so this typo-graphic practice does not overtly denote anti-Semitism (unlike, for example, sticking a Star of David symbol by someone's name or picture). By this stage, however, given considerable awareness of the practice, the dog-whistling triple parentheses have probably become a (sometimes deniable) slur used in deliberate defiance of widespread norms against explicitly racist speech.

As I said at the beginning of this book, I will not go down the rabbit hole of language use on the internet. There are all sorts of evolving uses of typographic devices to do the kind of work that is done face-to-face by stuff we hear ('tone of voice,' pauses, rhythms and tempo, accented syllables, variations in pronunciation, laugh-ter, and much more) and by nonverbal stuff we see (raised eyebrows, smiles and frowns, rolled eyes, gaze direction, bodily postures, and more). And everything changes very rapidly. This is in part because younger generations play a central role in shaping these resources and in part because there are no real 'authorities' insisting on particular ways of doing things. Philosophers of language and linguists are increasingly dealing with online com-munication and its implications for power relations. Linguist Gretchen McCulloch's *Because Internet: The New Rules of Language*, published in the summer of 2019, is good for orienting relative newbies to evolving online linguistic conventions. And philosopher Karen Frost-Arnold's forthcoming *Who Should We Be Online? A Social Epistemology for the Internet* should prove very useful for considering matters of reliability and accountabil-ity and exploring phenomena, like communicative 'silos,' that can amplify misinformation and erode trust. And I have several times mentioned the Dangerous Speech Project (at dangerousspeech .org), which offers considerable insight into online dangerous speech and strategies for effective online counterspeech.

There is much that is distinctive about digital communication, but there are also many commonalities with longer-established forms of linguistic practice. The short bursts of words that keep emerging in the early mornings and throughout the day from

Donald J. Trump, the president of the US as I write this, do not typically draw much from linguistically novel resources. All too often, they are just like language that has been encountered for many years by Americans who do not look like normative fully 'white' Americans, especially if the targets have dared to be critical in any way of American institutions or social arrangements. The immense power held by their source, however, heightens their potential for endangerment.

"Why Don't You Go Back Where You Came From?"

On Sunday, July 14, 2019, Donald J. Trump, Tweeter-in-Chief, sent out this message, the ellipsis marks noting the break between three successive tweets.

> So interesting to see "Progressive" Democrat Congresswomen, who originally came from countries whose governments are a complete and total catastrophe, the worst, most corrupt and inept anywhere in the world, now loudly ... and viciously telling the people of the United States, the greatest and most powerful Nation on earth, how our government is to be run. Why don't they go back and help fix the totally broken and crime infested places from which they came. Then come back and show us how ... it is done. These places need your help badly, you can't leave fast enough. I'm sure Nancy Pelosi will be very happy to quickly work out free travel arrangements!

The women about whom Trump was tweeting, from his perch at the top of the US executive branch, have been dubbed *the squad*. They are all relatively young, politically progressive, and were first elected to the House of Representatives in November 2018, beginning their initial terms in January 2019. They are Alexandria Ocasio-Cortez of New York, Ilhan Omar of Minnesota, Ayanna S. Pressley of Massachusetts, and Rashida Tlaib of Michigan. Rep. Ocasio-Cortez was born in the Bronx to Puerto Rican parents; Rep. Pressley, who is black, was born in Cincinnati and grew up in Chicago; Rep. Tlaib was born in Detroit to parents who had emigrated from Palestine. Only Rep. Omar is not US-born; she was born in Somalia, and came to the US from Kenya as a child with her family, becoming a citizen in 2000.

The Congresswomen themselves quickly responded, pointing out not only that they were US citizens but also that criticism of governmental policies and practices is not unpatriotic. But neither the president nor his supporters bought into that. A day after the initial tweets South Carolina Senator Lindsay Graham appeared on *Fox and Friends*, a conservative talk show. Although he said Trump should "aim higher," he launched into the kind of rhetoric that characterized the Red Scare and the infamous McCarthy hearings of the 1950s. "We all know that [Rep. Alexandria Ocasio-Cortez] and this crowd are a bunch of communists, they hate Israel, they hate our own country, they're calling the guards along our border – the Border Patrol agents – concentration camp guards," Graham declared. "They accuse people who support Israel as doing it for the benjamins, they are anti-Semitic, they are anti-America."[20]

The "anti-Semitic" charge seemed especially ironic in light of the profoundly anti-Semitic foundation of the 1950s McCarthy-led investigations of "un-American" activities as detailed in Joseph Litvak's 2009 book, *The Un-Americans: Jews, the Blacklist, and Stoolpigeon Culture*. Litvak argues that there is an ongoing price demanded for assimilation as (fully white) Americans, namely, a willingness to become vigilante enforcers. To 'name names' of those who might criticize dominant interests or institutions is to solidify claims of 'true' patriotism. As Litvak shows, 'naming names' often meant disclosure of pre-Americanized personal names in order to underscore Jewish heritage. Rep. John Rankin of South Carolina, who chaired HUAC (the House Un-American Activities Committee) temporarily, made a great show of revealing the "real names" of a number of celebrities, none of them actually communists, who had signed a statement criticizing the dangers to free speech of the investigations being conducted by the committee.

> One of the names is June Havoc. We found out from the
> motion-picture almanac that her real name is June Hovick.
> Another one was Danny Kaye, and we found out that his real
> name was David Daniel Kaminsky. Another one here is John
> Beal, whose real name is J. Alexander Bliedung. Another one is
> Cy Bartlett, whose real name is Sacha Baraniev. Another one is
> Eddie Cantor, whose real name is Edward Iskowitz. There is one
> who calls himself Edward Robinson. His real name is Emmanuel
> Goldenberg. There is another one here who calls himself Melvyn
> Douglas, whose real name is Melvyn Hesselberg.[21]

Rankin's use of 'real name' strongly suggests that one who 'calls himself' something other than their 'real name' is deceiving the public. The message, conveyed clearly albeit implicitly, was that the Jewish heritage signaled by the earlier name indicated something shameful and un-American.

Two days after Trump's initial string of tweets, the House passed a resolution "condemning President Trump's racist comments directed at Members of Congress." The full text of the resolution can be found online.[22] Note it was Trump's comments and not Trump himself that the resolution labeled "racist." This was to avoid the resolution's running afoul of Congressional rules of 'decorum' that prohibit impugning the motives of the president or of other members of Congress. Predictably, the vote was along party lines, with only four Republicans and one Independent (who had very recently left the Republican party) joining the 182 House Democrats in voting for the resolution.

Almost as soon as those first "go back" tweets went out, hosts of people told their own stories about hearing "go back where you came from" or variants like "go back to China" or "go back to Africa" in their own lives.[23] And there were well-documented reports that many physical assaults, including hate-fueled killings, were accompanied by some version of this white nationalist trope.[24] (These "go back" messages clearly constitute *dangerous speech* as discussed in Chapter 5, and such reports in response to the anti-immigrant tweets and chants are important instances of the *counterspeech* urged by the Dangerous Speech Project as an alternative to censorship.) Among the particularly telling stories in this genre were those from Native Americans. Trump supporters outside the Arizona state legislature in January 2018 were challenging darker-skinned people about their immigration status and told several to "go home." A Navajo legislator, Rep. Eric Descheenie, replied "Don't ask that question" to the immigration-status question and later noted to reporters "I'm indigenous. My ancestors fought and died on these lands."[25] A week after Trump's initial tweets, Native American congresswoman Deb Haaland wrote an opinion piece for the *New York Times*.

> I question the standing of anyone who would call to send my sisters and colleagues – Congresswomen Ilhan Omar, Alexandria Ocasio-Cortez, Ayanna Pressley, Rashida Tlaib – or any other American 'back.' As a 35th-generation New Mexican and a descendant of the original inhabitants of this continent, I say that the promise of our country is for everyone to find success, pursue happiness and live lives of equality. This is the Pueblo way. It's the American way.[26]

But even those of indigenous descent who might in principle endorse Rep. Haaland's generous inclusivity may, when provoked, indulge themselves in something less welcoming. I heard a story some years ago, perhaps invented, about a woman in a supermarket line in New Mexico who overheard someone speaking in a language she did not understand. The English-speaking 'patriot' proclaimed loudly. "We speak English here in America. Why don't you go back where you came from?" The response came quickly. "I was speaking Navajo. Why don't you go back?" In 2002, Sherman Alexie, noted Native American author, recounted the following similar story from his own experience.

> Soon after 9/11, I walked out of my health club in downtown Seattle, and a white man in a BIG truck with a BIG American flag, stopped at the crosswalk, leaned out his window, and yelled "Why don't you go back to your own country?" Doubled over with laughter, it took me several seconds before I could stand up and yell back, "You first!"[27]

In a similar vein, there are T-shirts carrying the message "Fighting Terrorism Since 1492" widely available on the web (with varied accompanying images). Such retorts illustrate effective counterspeech.

Trump's comments did not create immigrant-phobia but, coming from the president of the US, they licensed overt expression of such fears and the hatred they feed. A few days after the initial tweets, Trump spoke to an overflow crowd of supporters in Greenville, NC, home of East Carolina University.[28] They apparently came primed. There were T-shirts for sale with messages like "Love It or Leave It," "Let Me Help You Pack," "Build The Wall Deport Them All," and, apparently very popular, "Fuck Off We're Full." And people waiting in line had comments like these. "I feel like, 'Hey, man. You hate the country, you don't like it, you trash the country – get out of the country! Move on!' … Everybody's tweeting crazy things. Everybody is! Why point the finger at him?" Another offered similar comments.

> [Trump's tweets were] only about the systems of government from where they're from. These wenches [!]. These disrespectful wenches criticize our country incessantly. Well, Ilhan Omar, go back to some Middle Eastern country where you'd be afraid to live under Sharia law! I don't care what color the skin is … You don't like America? Go back to where your ancestors are from and then try to make that country better.

There were vanishingly few dissenters in that crowd. Those critical of Trump, said one attendee, "make us want to support him more." Given all that, it was unsurprising that when about fifteen minutes into his speech Trump began speaking about the "squad" and particularly Rep. Omar, a loud voice was heard shouting "Treason" followed by another "Traitor." And then, unscripted and spontaneous, came the trisyllabic chant "SEND HER BACK," which continued for fifteen full seconds while Trump stood beaming. A day later Trump claimed, after some muted criticism from other Republican leaders, to have tried to stop the chant and that he did not agree with it. (Videos make clear that he said nothing, just stood and smiled.) After another 24 hours, however, he pronounced the chanters "patriots," apparently relieved that his base really was fully on board. The 2019 "SEND HER BACK" cries evoked the chants of "LOCK HER UP" targeting Democratic candidate Hillary Clinton during the 2016 election campaign. Clinton's subsequent labeling of those chanters as *deplorables* failed as effective counterspeech by completely closing off the possibility of any mutually respectful exchange.

Trump repeatedly insists, "I don't have a racist bone in my body." When he did that shortly after his initial tweets began drawing criticism, Rep. Ocasio-Cortez responded with her own tweet. "You're right, Mr. President – you don't have a racist bone in your body," she tweeted. "You have a racist mind in your head, and a racist heart in your chest. That's why you violate the rights of children and tell the Congresswoman who represents your home borough, to 'go back to my country.'"[29] It may indeed be Trump's mind and heart that led to his racist actions and words but the actions and words and their clear effects can be more reliably assessed. Writing on the changing meanings of *racist* a little over a week later, linguist John McWhorter suggested that Trump may indeed not have been harboring racially inflected views of the four women, noting that some uses of *racist* do make such views criterial for applying the term.[30] And indeed one of the few black people in the crowds waiting to attend the NC rally, a realtor and retired air force officer, seemed to think that race had to have been mentioned for the remarks to qualify as racist. "He didn't say anything in his comments about race ... [The Congresswomen] happen to have views that are toxic, especially for members of Congress. They lie to advance their cause." Trump, I and others have suggested, may be less a liar about such matters as his motives than a bullshitter.[31] He does not care how he is evaluated by what McWhorter dubs the punditocracy: he cares primarily about cultivating the attention and adulation of his nearly (but not completely) all-white fan base. He also cares, however, about expanding his authority, his already enormous power to damage not only individuals' lives but also institutions and practices critical to social well-being. And there are many supporting him in order to advance their own projects.

Philosopher Jennifer Saul has introduced the useful notion of *racial figleaves*[32] in discussing Trump's use in his 2016 campaign of claims about Mexicans being rapists and his proposal to ban Muslims or people from certain countries from entering the US. The "figleaves" were utterances used to obscure racism, to deflect the idea that what was said was racist. Why? Because, as she correctly observes, the vast majority of Americans, including Trump and the bulk of his supporters, do not want to be so labeled and, often quite sincerely, do not believe themselves to be racist. Figleaves include, for example, denials ("I don't have a racist bone in my body") and what Saul dubs *friendship affirmations* ("Some of my best friends are black/Muslim/ ... "). These two figleaves are among what sociologist Eduardo Bonilla-Silva calls *semantic moves* designed to shield a speaker from accusations of racism. And there are others. Trump, for example, occasionally qualifies or hedges – "Not all Mexicans – some of them are probably good people". Perhaps the most capacious of figleaves is not to mention race or social identity at all, to claim that what one is talking about is not race but something else altogether. As I already noted and as his black supporter in NC observed, the tweets attacking the Congresswomen made no mention of their race at all. Rather Trump slammed their lack of "Americanism," "love of country," or "patriotism."

What were once dog whistles, 'code' words for racial matters, may have some rhetorical effectiveness in shielding their users (and those who approve of what is being said) from having to label themselves *racist*. This effectiveness persists in the ingroup (note the comments of Trump supporters) even after there is clear evidence that such ways of talking are disproportionately aimed at black and brown people and are strongly associated with violence toward them. Indeed, the 'colorblind' and 'post-racial' ideologies now so predominant have led many to take mentions of race as inherently racist.

Do the evolving and competing meanings of *racist*, which I discussed earlier in the book, imply that the word has been drained of useful meaning? Though he does not say so explicitly, that is what I take to be McWhorter's position. I strongly disagree. *Racist* has clearly established senses that emphasize effects rather than motives, and its strong negative evaluative punch can be useful. The label does, however, have to be applied sparingly and strategically. Censuring Trump's tweets as racist was an important symbolic move because it publicly resisted his expansion of what Saul calls, drawing on work by philosopher Mary Kate McGowan, the "boundaries of permissibility" in relations among racialized social groups. POTUS is, after all, at the top of a political hierarchy in a country which still controls a disproportionately large share of the world's resources and continues to exert colonial power. (The term is no longer 'colonies' but 'territories' – American Samoa, Guam, Northern Mariana Islands, Puerto Rico, and the US Virgin Islands.) What he says – or tweets – reaches millions of people across the globe and is attended to by international actors of many kinds. Those who may have been silently thinking "America should be kept for us (white) Americans" were given presidential permission to yell "Send them home" about those they see as having 'invaded' the country they claim as their own. The censurers tried to retract that permission.

At the same time, censurers as well as those of us among the American public who approved of the censure of Trump's tweets by the House of Representatives should beware of taking this public labeling as evidence of their/our general moral superiority on matters of racial justice. What Trump is doing is not just attacking people of color, immigrants, and would-be immigrants. He certainly does that, and the resolution was rightly highly critical of such attacks. But there is much more that is wrong with the tweets.

In criticizing the four Congresswomen, the forty-fifth president of the US continues to attack *dissent*, just as he did with Colin Kaepernick. Kaepernick is an African-American professional football player who first "took a knee" in 2016 during the playing of the American national anthem before the beginning of a game in which he was playing for the San Francisco '49ers. Others soon followed, kneeling rather than standing as the anthem played. They did so to protest police brutality, especially the killing of unarmed black men. Then candidate Trump exploded, describing these actions as "disgraceful," Kaepernick was essentially black-listed, and in May 2018 NFL team owners adopted a policy requiring all players on the field to stand during the playing of the anthem. Trump applauded their action but said on *Fox and Friends* that it didn't go far enough. "Well, I think that's good," he said in response to being told of the decision. Then he continued, "I don't think people should be staying in locker rooms. But still, I think it's good. You have to stand proudly for the national anthem, or you shouldn't be playing, you shouldn't be there. Maybe you shouldn't be in the country."[33] Again, the suggestion is that criticism of the US is not to be tolerated, that dissenters "maybe" "shouldn't be in the country."

Unfortunately, the congressional resolution was silent about Trump's ongoing assaults on freedom of speech and other symbolic actions. Without continuing dissent of various kinds, including symbolic, racism can only worsen.

Framing the Free Speech Debate

The clauses that prohibit the United States government from infringing on freedom of speech or of the press in the first amendment of the Bill of Rights are there to protect the kind of political dissent that President Trump and his chanting chorus threaten. Somehow, however, the political right has managed to present itself as the defenders of free speech, claiming that it's the advocates of what they call PC or 'political correctness' who limit what others are allowed to say. It's "crybabies" and "oversensitive" members of historically oppressed groups who are reining in free speech. Cries of *fake news* and "go back" are far more threatening to free speech and freedom of the press than any excesses of 'political correctness' (which do indeed exist). When the president of the US suggests that "maybe" you should be deported because of protesting police violence against black men, you face a powerful threat to your right to dissent. Students of color pushing for dominant white communities to pay more attention to their experiences and sometimes to rethink how they speak (don't call the head of the college *master*, for example) have little more than moral power to wield. Sometimes, however, they do get institutional support.

Some current students at Cornell were dismayed in February 2019 when an eighty-eight-year-old white alumnus being honored by the Cornell Alumni Association spoke at a student–alum conference about his admiration for the "Negro" baseball player Satchel Paige and followed that up, perhaps sensing some discomfort in his audience, with the comment, "Now they call them blacks." Students, especially but not only black students, expressed their shock to organizers of the event. To their credit, without being asked to do so, the organizers arranged an impromptu "talk-back" immediately after the event at which students and others had a lengthy discussion about what had happened. For some the word *Negro* itself triggered associations with the Jim Crow era. For others the "they call them blacks" comment was more disturbing. It was not only the "otherizing" effects of *they* but the speaker's apparent unawareness that *Negro* is outdated except in names for long-lived institutions like the United Negro College Fund. Where, they wondered, was this man during the civil rights struggles of the 1960s and the decades that have followed? What media does he see or hear? Who does he talk with? The next day the speaker apologized, saying that he was "devastated to hear how my words hurt members of the Cornell community." In a later conversation reported by the *Chronicle of Higher Education*, he tried to explain. "I didn't understand that some people took exception to the word 'Negro.' I didn't know what else to call him; I mean, he was in the Negro Baseball League. That's history." Then he continued. "People interpret things in different ways, and sometimes you don't say things in the right way. Most of the time you don't have to worry about it because people know who you are. The world is very different now." As the head of Cornell's Black Alumni Association commented, no one ascribed malicious intentions to this elderly speaker but the point was the effect.[34]

This particular incident was a powerful reminder especially to black students at Cornell that for very few of them is it true that other Cornellians "know who you are." Their borderline status as Cornellians, not fully insiders and yet also not outsiders, seemed underscored. And it was a reminder to many of us that, as the speaker remarked, "the world is very different now." I'm married to someone just a couple of years younger than the speaker, and I myself am less than a decade younger. Having to think about saying things "in the right way" has indeed become more an issue than it was when I was a college student. And "the right way" changes, as I have emphasized throughout this book. Martin Luther King, Jr., used *Negro*. And I recently confirmed that my (not yet) husband used it in a letter to me in November 1959. He was writing about having signed a faculty petition at Ohio State urging the university not to approve off-campus housing if there was evidence that the landlord practiced racial or religious discrimination (not, readers will notice, going so far as to refuse approval unless positive evidence of nondiscriminatory practices was forthcoming). Evidence from "a Negro student" (and others), he wrote, that there was indeed discrimination by landlords had prompted the faculty action. In 1959 *Negro* (capitalized!) was indeed the 'polite' form, and it was used by blacks and by whites trying to speak respectfully. In other correspondence between us from 1959 to 1960 I also find I called my twentysomething female peers *girls* but never *women* and our male peers *guys*, *boys*, or occasionally, *men*. (The idea of being neither female nor male, of being "beyond the binary," was not in the air at all back then, at least not in the circles in which I moved.) And I used the label *feminist* to disparage rather than to speak approvingly of someone. Changing those particular practices has been easy. In the final section I'll note briefly the much greater challenges posed by some other linguistic changes I have decided that I should make.

Let me reiterate that I do not endorse every linguistic reform advanced in the name of respectfulness or sensitivity to others' feelings. And I do not think there is always one 'correct' way to speak for someone wanting in general to respect others. Sometimes there seem to be knee-jerk emotionally charged reactions without enough analytic thinking behind them. And on occasion there are what strike me as overblown and out-of-proportion responses to speech (or sometimes actions) experienced as problematic. Shaming 'friends' on social media because of something they have said or done does happen. Labeling them racist (or sexist or transphobic or against some other identity group) is usually part of the shaming. And shaming labels may be applied by those who do not themselves belong to the group whose well-being they present themselves as protecting. Such practices strike me as counterproductive at best.

Hypocrisy can come into play when these helpful enforcers of symbolic reforms to benefit some oppressed group manage themselves to continue other practices that materially sustain that oppression. I have indeed sometimes witnessed academics displaying their feminist commitments by using feminine generics, but then ignoring the intellectual achievements of their female students while promoting the careers of no-more-distinguished male students. This is of course empty 'virtue-signaling.' I don't think it's common, but it does happen.

So linguistic reform gets a bad name on the basis of occasional insincerity or mean-spiritedness. Such 'abuses' generally pale, however, compared to the vitriolic language frequently encountered online attacking those with views on political or so-called 'cultural' issues different from the attacker's own. Embarrassing someone else is hardly in a class with overtly threatening them or hurling racial slurs or other highly charged terms. Apart from Trump's tweets, I see such attacks mainly in "comments" sections or at sites like *Urban Dictionary* (urbandictionary.com), but I know from others' accounts that vicious words are far more widespread, and can include physical threats. This is not to say that abusive language is confined to one position on the political spectrum. But "send her back" *presidential* tweets and crowd chants show the considerable power behind efforts to paint those critical of American institutions, standard current practices, and the distortions of its history promulgated in textbooks as unpatriotic traitors who should be silenced.

Like the founders of the Dangerous Speech Project, I think that censorship is seldom effective. It is naïve of course to think that there is some kind of fair and open marketplace of ideas in which the true and the good will ultimately prevail. At the same time it is also naïve to think that society can be protected from dangerous speech through legislation or similar steps, that we can count on authority to promote the true and the good. Counterspeech, though, does not have to be limited to individual on-the-spot responses. Alliances can be useful, strategizing, enlisting others to resist. It is *because* words matter that freedom of speech matters.

Linguistic Change Can Be Painful

How things are said marks social identity, regional origins, education, and much more. Elite status is inconsistent with using anything other than what is sometimes (somewhat misleadingly) called "correct grammar, pronunciation, and spelling," a somewhat mythical 'standard' in speech and in writing. People, among them myself at a younger age and probably many readers of this book, often make fun of 'errors' in the speech or writing of others. I no longer 'mock' others over such matters – I am, after all, a linguist, and I do now know something of the sometimes shameful history of how linguistic 'standards' arise and are promulgated as a device for indicating and preserving social hierarchy. But even those who were nicer than I am and never commented snidely on the linguistic practices of others were probably like me in taking some pride in their own conformity to those standards. All this was inculcated in some of us at very young ages. No matter how clearly we recognize the arbitrariness of most of this and the pernicious social stratification 'standard' norms help enforce, we still at some gut emotional level feel the force of those 'grammatical rules.' We "had to be carefully taught" some of these rules because even the well educated and the 'best' authors did not always adhere to them: for example, that *each child* and *every person* were singular expressions and thus could/should only be linked to a singular pronoun. It is, or at least has been for me, much easier to shake off the religious beliefs and practices of parents or teachers than to abandon their linguistic 'purism.' No 'intelligent' person – and being seen as intelligent was very important – would fail to follow these rules, my parents and teachers seemed to think, unless they were so unfortunate as not to have gotten a good education.

And language is evaluated aesthetically – the words ring out beautifully or sound ugly. Familiarity matters as well, especially for language that is repeated in religious rituals. For many Christians, formulas like "In the name of God the Father, Son, and Holy Ghost" do not translate well into gender-neutral or even gender-inclusive renderings.

Anne Fadiman, daughter of writers Annalee Jacoby and Clifton Fadiman, was reared by the purest of purists. Neither she nor her brother disappointed their parents by 'grammatical' heresy. She has an elegant essay on her struggles with 'sexist' language and especially the generic masculine pronoun in her collected essays on books and words, *Ex Libris: Confessions of a Common Reader*, a short but delightful collection for lovers of books and of words.[35] Like many who came of age before the 1990s, Anne Fadiman struggled to reconcile her own growing understanding of historically robust sexist practices with her 'purist' instincts, honed over a lifetime. But then while reading a passage from E. B. White about 'the essayist,' a discussion he brought to life with a putatively generic 'he,' she suddenly feels a door shut. She has realized that White simply was not thinking of women like her who might be essayists. But good substitutes for those generic masculines are not always readily available.

> My reactionary self ... prevails when I hear someone attempt to purge the bias from "to each his own" by substituting "to each their own." The disagreement between pronoun and antecedent is more than I can bear. To understand how I feel about grammar, you need to remember that I come from the sort of family in which, at the age of ten, I was told I must always say *hoi polloi*, never 'the *hoi polloi*', because *hoi* meant "the," and two "the's" were redundant – indeed something only hoi polloi would say ... I call the "to each his own" quandary the "His'er Problem," after a solution originally proposed by Chicago School superintendent Ella Young in 1912: "To each his'er own." I'm sorry. I just can't. My reactionary self has aesthetic as well as grammatical standards and *his'er* is hideous.

She concludes:

> What I am saying here is very simple. Changing our language to make men and women equal has a cost. That doesn't mean it shouldn't be done. High prices are attached to many things that are on the whole worth doing. It does mean that the loss of our heedless grace should be mourned, and then accepted with all the civility we can muster by every writer worth his'er salt.

Anne Fadiman's 'his'er' problem preceded the age of searching for words that do not presume a gender binary. Nowadays, singular *they* recommends itself even more forcefully to those sympathetic to such concerns. It is easy to abandon familiar expressions like "to each his own" but finding antecedents in such authors as Shakespeare and Jane Austen can ease the discomfort of nonagreement of *they* with words like *each* and *every*.[36] Here's Austen's Emma Woodhouse speaking. "Every body was punctual, every body in **their** best looks." Notice that Emma still treats 'every body' as grammatically singular: she says "Every body **was** punctual" and not "Every body **were** punctual," with a singular verb to agree with the subject. Jane Austen not only used singular *they* with expressions like *each* and *every*, which one can argue are 'notionally' plural. She also has Emma use it in speaking of an unknown person. "Who is in love with her [Harriet Smith]? Who makes you **their** confidant?" Such cases may soften up some to accept such uses as this. "Someone seems to have left **their** computer here." And perhaps pointing to a figure far off in the distance, "It looks like they are [not *is* for purists] going to fall from that spot." As the last example suggests, thinking of semantically singular *they* as parallel to semantically singular *you* can be helpful, especially for those who, like Anne Fadiman, inhaled ideas about grammatical 'propriety' early in childhood. On that model, even when used to refer to one individual, *they* remains grammatically plural so far as verb agreement goes ('they are' just like 'you are') but takes a singular form in the reflexive ('themself' just like 'yourself').

But many of us still find it very hard to use *they* to speak of some individual identified by name or in some other way specified. Consider a sequence like this. "Lee is so secretive. They refuse to tell me where they were born." It would be very hard to interpret those *they*s as referring to some plurality of people – clearly all that makes sense is to identify *Lee* as antecedent of *they*. But this still 'feels funny' to many of us older folks. I am myself trying to beat down that feeling and go ahead and use *they* to speak of individuals whom I know prefer that, because I think it is the right thing to do. Readers may have noticed my doing this in the *Latinx* section above when I use *them* and later *they* to refer to Professor María R. Scharrón-del Río, who has publicly said they prefer such usage. I confess that it still feels somewhat odd, and I find myself considering alternatives. But I have come to think that the funny feeling may have little to do with my lingering grammatical conservatism. After all, singular *they* is a phenomenon I deal with relatively easily these days. My persisting hang-up here may have more to do with a gender conservatism that, while finding changes in people's affirmed gender identities relatively easy to accommodate, is still caught in the binary.

Words are not lifeless symbols. They live in us and in the social worlds they allow us to create and transform. They do show their histories, and it is often easier to say what fits with existing dominant views and social arrangements. But words can be recruited for new and resistant purposes. Audre Lorde famously said, "The master's tools will never dismantle the master's house." Language, however, is not fully under the master's control. Resisters can launch new ways of understanding familiar words, and they/we can create new words and arrangements of words – and, maybe, eventually new worlds.

Notes

1. One account that discusses other similar cases around the country is at Scott Jaschik, "Cornell Will Drop 'Plantations' Name," *Inside Higher Ed*, August 29, 2016, www.insidehighered.com/news/2016/08/29/cornell-plans-drop-plantations-name-its-gardens.
2. David Shimer and Victor Wang, "Harvard, Princeton Abolish 'Master,'" *Yale News*, December 2, 2015, https://yaledailynews.com/blog/2015/12/02/harvard-princeton-abolish-master/.
3. "Decisions on Residential College Names and 'Master' Title," Statements, Office of the President, Yale University website, https://president.yale.edu/speeches-writings/statements/decisions (see April 27, 2016).
4. Phoebe Keller, "Union of White Students Forms at Cornell, Aims to 'Advance Their Race,'" *The Cornell Daily Sun*, March 3, 2016, https://cornellsun.com/2016/03/03/union-of-white-students-forms-at-cornell-aims-to-advance-their-race/.
5. Quotes from alums appear in Jaschik, "Cornell Will Drop 'Plantations' Name."
6. "Plantation Mentality," *Grammarphobia* blog, November 13, 2015, www.grammarphobia.com/blog/2015/11/plantation.html.
7. There are a number of resources for following and expanding on Ellis's advice at "Resources for Humanizing Language," The Osborne Association website, n.d., www.osborneny.org/resources/resources-for-humanizing-language/. That advice even had impact at the federal level during the late years of the Obama administration as noted in an admiring *NYT* editorial: "Labels Like 'Felon' Are an Unfair Life Sentence," *The New York Times*, May 7, 2016, www.nytimes.com/2016/05/08/opinion/sunday/labels-like-felon-are-an-unfair-life-sentence.html.
8. This quote is from p. 3 of Morales 2018, the next is from p. 4.
9. Rachel Hatzipanagos, "Latinx: An Offense to the Spanish Language Or a Nod to Inclusion?," *Washington Post*, September 14, 2019, www.washingtonpost

.com/news/post-nation/wp/2018/09/14/latinx-an-offense-to-the-spanish-language-or-a-nod-to-inclusion/?utm_term=.53b9f8bf0f7b

10. See the mention of Geoff Nunberg's idea of prejudicials in the Chapter 5 discussion of the N-word.

11. Morales 2018, pp. 306 and 307 (last two sentences).

12. Alcoff 2007.

13. See, e.g., Sam Sanders, "It's Time to Put 'Woke' to Sleep," *NPR*, December 30, 2018, www.npr.org/2018/12/30/680899262/opinion-its-time-to-put-woke-to-sleep.

14. Hill 2010, n. 7 to ch. 1, p. 185.

15. Fisher, Mirus, and Napoli 2019, n. 2.

16. The script of *Tribes* (2010) is available both from Dramatists' Play Service at dramatists.com (www.dramatists.com/cgi-bin/db/single.asp?key=4542) and from the NHB Modern Plays series, published in the UK by Nick Hearn Books (www.dramaonlinelibrary.com/plays/tribes-iid-153990).

17. "Echo," Hate Symbols, Anti-Defamation League website, n.d., www.adl .org/education/references/hate-symbols/echo.

18. This is what Saul 2018 calls an intentional overt dog whistle. Stanley 2015 treats examples like *welfare* as dog whistles though, unlike Saul, he seems to suggest that the context in which they are used does not affect their functioning as dog whistles.

19. Matthew Yglesias, "The (((Echo))), Explained," *Vox*, June 6, 2016, www .vox.com/2016/6/6/11860796/echo-explained-parentheses-twitter.

20. Graham's comments can be found at Justin Baragona, "Lindsey Graham Backs Trump's Racist Tweets on "Fox & Friends": The Squad Are "Communists" Who Hate America," *The Daily Beast*, July 15, 2019, www.thedailybeast.com /lindsey-graham-backs-trump-on-fox-and-friends-the-squad-are-communists-who-hate-america.

21. Litvak 2009, p. 4.

22. "Read the House Resolution Condemning Trump's Racist Comments Directed at Members of Congress," *The New York Times*, July 16, 2019, www .nytimes.com/2019/07/16/us/politics/house-resolution-trump.html.

23. Some of these stories can be found at Tanya Chen, "Americans Are Sharing What It's Like to Be Told to 'Go Back to Your Country' After Trump's Racist Attack,' *BuzzFeed News*, July 15, 2019, www.buzzfeednews.com/article/ tanyachen/trump-go-back-country-racist-comments-stories.

24. See, e.g., Christopher Mathias, "Have You Been Told to Go Back to Your Country?" *HuffPost,* July 22, 2019, www.huffpost.com/entry/go-back-to-your-own-country-database-huffpost-propublica_n_5d35cd58e4b020cd99470021 and also Michael Luo, "Trump's Racist Tweets, and the Question of Who Belongs in America," *The New Yorker*, July 15, 2019, www.newyorker.com/

news/our-columnists/trumps-racist-tweets-and-the-question-of-who-belongs-in-america.

25. Ben Giles and Paulina Pineda, "Legislative Staffers Say Pro-Trump Supporters Called them 'Illegal' for Being Dark-Skinned," *Arizona Capital Times*, January 26, 2018, https://azcapitoltimes.com/news/2018/01/26/arizona-capitol-eric-descheenie-cesar-chavez-lisette-flores-selianna-robles-katie-hobbs-tomas-robles-trump-supports-yell-illegal/.

26. Deb Haaland, "Trump Wants Immigrants to 'Go Back.' Native Americans Don't," *The New York Times*, July 22, 2019, www.nytimes.com/2019/07/22/opinion/trump-immigration-native-americans.html.

27. Lisa Ginet, my daughter, mentioned Sherman Alexie's story to me; I found it as an epigraph to Tellefsen 2005.

28. Some accounts of the NC rally are at Peter Nicholas, "It Makes Us Want to Support Him More," *The Atlantic*, July 18, 2019, www.theatlantic.com/politics/archive/2019/07/send-her-back-trump-supporters-his-nc-rally/594268/, Michael Kruse, "Trump's North Carolina Supporters Were Ready to Unload," *Politico Magazine*, July 18, 2019, www.politico.com/magazine/story/2019/07/18/donald-trump-north-carolina-rally-227403, and "The Real Meaning of 'Send Her Back!,'" *The New York Times*, July 18, 2019, www.nytimes.com/2019/07/18/opinion/trump-rally-send-her-back.html. The quotes from attendees all come from the Atlantic article.

29. Tod Perry, "AOC Responds to Trump's Claim He 'Doesn't Have a Racist Bone in His Body,'" *Good*, July 16, 2019, www.good.is/articles/aoc-responds-to-trump-saying-hes-not-racist.

30. John McWhorter, "Racist Is a Tough Little Word," *The Atlantic*, July 24, 2019, www.theatlantic.com/ideas/archive/2019/07/racism-concept-change/594526/.

31. McConnell-Ginet 2018a.

32. Saul 2017b.

33. Adam Edelman, "Trump Says NFL Players Who Kneel During National Anthem 'Maybe Shouldn't Be in the Country,'" *NBC News*, May 24, 2018, www.nbcnews.com/politics/donald-trump/trump-says-nfl-players-who-kneel-during-national-anthem-maybe-n876996

34. Nicholas Bogel-Burroughs, "Cornell Gave an Alumnus an Award. While Accepting It, He Called Satchel Paige a 'Negro,' Prompting Swift Backlash," *The Cornell Daily Sun*, February 13, 2019, https://cornellsun.com/2019/02/13/cornell-gave-an-alumnus-an-award-in-his-acceptance-speech-he-called-satchel-paige-a-negro-prompting-swift-backlash/. See also Marjorie Valbrun, "When an Alumnus with a Mike Says Something Offensive," *Inside Higher Ed*, February 14, 2019, www.insidehighered.com/news/2019/02/14/speaker-cornell-alumni-event-offends-audience-and-college-quickly-responds.

35. Fadiman 1998. Quotations from pp. 74–75 and 77–78.
36. Examples abound. I first found many of these at https://pemberley.com/
janeinfo/austheir.html. Linguist Geoff Pullum quotes a wide array of well-
respected authors using the pronoun *they* with a grammatically singular
noun phrase as its antecedent at www.lel.ed.ac.uk/~gpullum/grammar/
sing_they_sli.pdf.

References

Adams, Michael. (2008). Nicknames, Interpellation, and Dubya's Theory of the State. *Names*, 56(4), 206–220.

Adams, Michael. (2009). Power, Politeness, and the Pragmatics of Nicknames. *Names*, 57(2), 81–91.

Alber, Alex. (2019). Tutoyer Son Chef. Entre Rapports Sociaux et Logique Managériale. *Sociologie du Travail*, 61(1), 1–29.

Alcoff, Linda. (2003). Latino/as, Asian Americans, and the Black-White Binary. *The Journal of Ethics*. Special Issue: *Race, Racism, and Reparations* 7(1), 5–27.

Alim, H. Samy. (2016). Who's Afraid of the Transracial Subject? Raciolinguistics and Transracialization. In Alim, Rickford, and Ball, eds. 2016, pp. 33–50.

Alim, H. Samy, John R. Rickford, and Arnetha F. Ball, eds., (2016). *Raciolinguistics: How Language Shapes Our Ideas about Race*. Oxford University Press.

Alim, H. Samy and Geneva Smitherman. (2012). *Articulate while Black: Barack Obama, Language, and Race in the US*. Oxford University Press.

Allan, Keith. (2015). When Is a Slur Not a Slur? The Use of *Nigger* in "Pulp Fiction." *Language Sciences*, 52(1), 187–199.

Allan, Keith. ed. (2018). *The Oxford Handbook of Taboo Words and Language*. Oxford Handbooks in Linguistics. Oxford University Press.

Allan, Keith and Kate Burridge. (1991). *Euphemism & Dysphemism: Language Used as a Shield and Weapon*. Oxford University Press.

Allan, Keith and Kate Burridge. (2006). *Forbidden Words: Taboo and the Censoring of Language*. Cambridge University Press.

Anderson, Benedict. (1983). *Imagined Communities: Reflections on the Origins and Spread of Nationalism*. Verso.

Anderson, Luvell. (2018). Calling, Addressing, and Appropriation. In D. Sosa, ed., *Bad Words*. Oxford University Press, pp. 6–28.

Anderson, Luvell and Ernie Lepore. (2013a). Slurring Words, *Nous* 47 (1), 25–48.

Anderson, Luvell and Ernie Lepore. (2013b). What Did You Call Me? Slurs as Prohibited Words. *Analytic Philosophy*, 54(3), 350–363.

Anolli, Luigi, Valentino Zurloni, and Giuseppe Riva. (2006). Linguistic Intergroup Bias in Political Communication. *The Journal of General Psychology*, 133(3), 237–255.

Antony, Louise M. (2016). Bias: Friend or Foe? In Michael Brownstein and Jennifer Saul, eds., *Implicit Bias and Philosophy, vol. 1: Metaphysics and Epistemology*. Oxford University Press, pp. 157–190.

Apfelbaum, Evan P., Kristen Pauker, Samuel R. Sommers, and Nalini Ambady. (2010). In Blind Pursuit of Racial Equality? *Psychological Science*, 21, 1587–1592.

Appiah, Kwame Anthony. (1996). Race, Culture, Identity: Misunderstood Connections. In Kwame Anthony Appiah and Amy Gutmann, *Color Conscious: The Political Morality of Race*. Princeton University Press.

Appiah, Kwame Anthony. (2005). *The Ethics of Identity*. Princeton University Press.

Appiah, Kwame Anthony. (2018). *The Lies that Bind: Rethinking Identity/Creed, Country, Color, Class, Culture*. Liveright Publishing Corporation: A Division of WW Norton & Co.

Asher, Nicholas, Soumya Paul, and Antoine Venant. (2017). Message Exchange Games in Strategic Contexts. *Journal of Philosophical Logic*, 46(4), 355–404.

Asim, Jabari. (2007). *The N Word: Who Can Say It, Who Shouldn't, and Why*. Houghton Mifflin.

Austin, J. L. (1975 [1962]). *How to Do Things with Words*, 2nd ed. Edited by J. O. Urmson and Marina Sbisà. Harvard University Press.

Bailey, Moya and Trudy. (2018). On Misogynoir: Citation, Erasure, and Plagiarism. *Feminist Media Studies*, 18(4), 762–768. DOI:10.1080/14680777.2018.1447395.

Baker, Robert. (1975). "Pricks" and "Chicks": A Plea for "Persons." In Robert Baker and Frederick Elliston, eds., *Philosophy and Sex*. Prometheus Books, pp. 45–64.

Baron, Dennis. (2020). *What's Your Pronoun? Beyond He and She*. Liveright.

Battistella, Edwin. (1997). Guidelines for Nonsexist Usage. *SECOL Review*, 21(1), 104–125.

Beardsley, Elizabeth L. (1973). Referential Genderization. *Philosophical Forum*, 5, 285–293.

Beaver, David and Jason Stanley. (2019). Toward a Non-Ideal Philosophy of Language. *Graduate Faculty Philosophy Journal*, 39(2), 503–547.

Beeghly, Erin. (2015). What is a Stereotype? What is Stereotyping? *Hypatia*, 30(4), 675–691.

Beeghly, Erin. (2018). Failing to Treat Persons as Individuals. *Ergo: An Open Journal of Philosophy*, 5(26), 687–711.

Beeghly, Erin and Alex Madva. (2020). *An Introduction to Implicit Bias: Knowledge, Justice, and the Social Mind*. Routledge.

Bem, Sandra. (1983). Gender Schema Theory and its Implications for Child Development: Raising Gender-Aschematic Children in a Gender Schematic Society. *Signs: Journal of Women in Culture and Society*, 8, 598–616.

Bem, Sandra Lipsitz. (1993). *The Lenses of Gender*. Yale University Press.

Benaji, Mahzarin R. and Susan A. Gelman, eds. (2013). *Navigating the Social World: What Infants, Children, and Other Species Can Teach Us*. Oxford University Press.

Benesch, Susan, Cathy Buerger, Tonei Glavinic, and Sean Manion. (2018, December 31). Dangerous Speech: A Practical Guide. *Dangerous Speech Project*; https://dangerousspeech.org/guide/.

Bennett, Lerone, Jr. (1967). What's in a Name? Negro vs. Afro-American vs. Black. *Ebony* 23 (November 1967), 46–48, 50–52, 54.

Bergman, Bear. (2013). *Blood, Marriage, Wine and Glitter*. Arsenal Pulp Press.

Bettcher, Talia. (2009). Trans Identities and First Person Authority. In Laurie Shrage, ed., *"You've Changed": Sex Reassignment and Personal Identity*. Oxford University Press, pp. 98–120.

Bettcher, Talia Mae. (2012). Transwomen and the Meaning of "Woman." In Nicholas Power, Raja Halwani, and Alan Soble, eds., *The Philosophy of Sex: Contemporary Readings*, 6th ed. Rowman & Littlefield, pp. 233–250.

Beukeboom, Camiel J. (2014). Mechanisms of Linguistic Bias: How Words Reflect and Maintain Stereotypic Expectancies. In J. Forgas, O. Vincze, and J. Laszlo, eds., *Social Cognition and Communication*. Psychology Press. pp. 313–330.

Blake, Renée. (2016). Toward Heterogeneity: A Sociolinguistic Perspective on the Classification of Black People in the Twenty-First Century. In Alim, Rickford, and Ball, eds. 2016, pp. 153–169.

Blum, Lawrence. (2002). *"I'm Not a Racist, But . . .": The Moral Quandary of Race.* Cornell University Press.

Blum, Lawrence. (2010). Racialized Groups: The Sociohistorical Consensus. *The Monist*, 93(2), 298–320.

Bodine, Ann. (1975). Androcentrism in Prescriptive Grammar: Singular "They," Sex-Indefinite "He," and "He Or She." *Language in Society*, 4, 129–146.

Bolinger, Dwight. (1980). *Language: The Loaded Weapon; The Use and Abuse of Language Today.* Longman.

Bonilla-Silva, Eduardo. (2018). *Racism without Racists: Color-Blind Racism and the Persistence of Racial Inequality in America*, 5th ed. Rowman & Littlefield. (First published 2003.)

Brison, Susan J. (1998). Speech, Harm, and the Mind-Body Problem in First Amendment Jurisprudence. *Legal Theory*, 4(1), 39–61.

Britt, Robert Roy. (2006, November 21). Why Planets Will Never Be Defined. *Space.com*, www.space.com/3142-planets-defined.html.

Brown, Roger and Albert Gilman. (1960). The Pronouns of Power and Solidarity. In Thomas R. Sebeok, ed., *Style in Language*. MIT Press, pp. 253–276.

Brownmiller, Susan. (1975). *Against Our Will: Men, Women, and Rape.* Simon & Schuster.

Brownstein, Michael. (2019). Implicit Bias. *The Stanford Encyclopedia of Philosophy* (Fall 2019 Edition). Edited by Edward N. Zalta. https://plato.stanford.edu/archives/fall2019/entries/implicit-bias/.

Burnett, Heather. (2019a). *A Formal Perspective on Social Meaning and Identity Construction through Language.* HDR thesis. Université de Paris.

Burnett, Heather. (2019b). Signalling Games, Sociolinguistic Variation and the Construction of Style. *Linguistics & Philosophy*, 42, 419–450.

Burnett, Heather. (2020). A Persona-Based Semantics for Slurs. In B. Cepollaro and D. Zeman, eds., *Grazer Philosophische Studien*, 97(1), 31–62.

Cameron, Deborah. (2012). *Verbal Hygiene*, 2nd ed. Routledge.

Camp, Elisabeth. (2013). Slurring Perspectives. *Analytic Philosophy*, 54 (3), 330–349.

Camp, Elisabeth. (2017). Why Metaphors Make Good Insults: Perspectives, Presupposition, and Pragmatics. *Philosophical Studies*, 174(1), 47–64.

Cappelen, Herman. (2018). *Fixing Language: An Essay on Conceptual Engineering*. Oxford University Press.

Citron, Danielle Keats. (2014). *Hate Crimes in Cyberspace*. Harvard University Press.

Coates, Ta-Nehisi. (2015). *Between the World and Me*. Random House, Spiegel and Grau.

Collins, Patricia Hill. (1998). *Fighting Words: Black Women and the Search for Justice*. University of Minnesota Press.

Collins, Patricia Hill and Sirma Bilge. (2016). *Intersectionality*. Key Concepts Series. Polity Press.

Connell, R. W. (1987). *Gender and Power: Society, the Person and Sexual Politics*. Stanford University Press.

Crane, Leah. (2016, April 4). Wandering Stars: A Brief History of Defining "Planet." *Physical Science* 9. www.lateralmag.com/articles/issue-9/wandering-stars-a-brief-history-of-defining-planet.

Crenshaw, Kimberlé. (1989). Demarginalizing the Intersection of Race and Sex: A Black Feminist Critique of Antidiscrimination Doctrine, Feminist Theory and Antiracist Politics. *University of Chicago Legal Forum*, 1, 139–167.

Curzan, Anne. (2014). *Fixing English: Prescriptivism and Language History*. Cambridge University Press.

Dembroff, Robin. (2018, January 30). The Nonbinary Gender Trap. *New York Review of Books*. www.nybooks.com/daily/2018/01/30/the-nonbinary-gender-trap/.

Denizet-Lewis, Benoit. (2009). *American Anonymous: Eight Addicts in Search of a Life*. Simon & Schuster.

DiAngelo, Robin. (2018). *White Fragility: Why It's So Hard for White People to Talk About Racism*. Beacon Press.

Dodson, Howard. (2007). What's at Stake: Redefining African American. *Logos*, 6(3) (Summer 2007). www.logosjournal.com/issue_6.3/dodson.htm.

Du Bois, W. E. B. (1999 [1903]). *The Souls of Black Folk*. Norton Critical Edition. Edited by Henry Louis Gates, Jr. and Terri Hume-Oliver. Norton. (The original is available free at gutenberg.org in various electronic formats, as well as in audio format.)

Dunbar-Ortiz, Roxanne and Dina Gilio-Whitaker (2016). Native Americans Can't Agree on What to Be Called. In Dunbar-Ortiz and Gilio-Whitaker, *"All the Real Indians Died Off" and 20 Other Myths About Native Americans*. Beacon Press, pp. 145–149.

Eberhardt, Jennifer L. (2019). *Biased: Uncovering the Hidden Prejudice That Shapes What We See, Think and Do*. Viking: An Imprint of Penguin Random House.

Eckert, Penelope. (1989). *Jocks and Burnouts: Social Categories and Identity in the High School*. Teachers College Press.

Eckert, Penelope. (2000). *Language Variation as Social Practice: The Linguistic Construction of Identity in Belten High*. Wiley-Blackwell.

Eckert, Penelope and Sally McConnell-Ginet. (1992). Think Practically and Look Locally: Language and Gender as Community-Based Practice. *Annual Review of Anthropology*, 21, 461–490. (Reprinted in C. Roman, S. Juhasz, and C. Miller 1994, *The Woman and Language Debate: A Coursebook*. Rutgers University Press, pp. 432–460.)

Eckert, Penelope and Sally McConnell-Ginet. (1995). Constructing Meaning, Constructing Selves: Snapshots of Language, Gender, and Class from Belten High. In Kira Hall and Mary Bucholtz, eds., *Gender Articulated: Language and the Socially Constructed Self*. Routledge, pp. 469–507. (Reprinted in McConnell-Ginet 2011, 129–163.)

Eckert, Penelope and Sally McConnell-Ginet. (2013). *Language and Gender*. 2nd ed. Cambridge University Press.

Ehrlich, Susan. (2001). *Representing Rape: Language and Sexual Consent*. Routledge.

Ehrlich, Susan. (2007). Legal Discourse and the Cultural Intelligibility of Gendered Meanings. *Journal of Sociolinguistics*, 11(4), 452–477.

Embrick, David G., and Kasey Henricks. (2013). Discursive Colorlines at Work: How Epithets and Stereotypes are Racially Unequal. *Symbolic Interaction*, 36(2), 197–215.

Fadiman, Anne. (1998). *Ex Libris: Confessions of a Common Reader*. Farrar, Straus, and Giroux.

Faucher, Luc and Edouard Machery. (2009). Racism: Against Jorge Garcia's Moral and Psychological Monism. *Philosophy of the Social Sciences*, 39(1), 41–62.

Fausto-Sterling, Anne. (2000). *Sexing the Body: Gender, Politics and the Construction of Sexuality*. Basic Books.

Fausto-Sterling, Anne. (2017). Against Dichotomy. *Evolutionary Studies in Imaginative Culture*, 1(1), 63–66.

Ferrara, America. (2018). *Americans Like Me*. Gallery Books, Imprint of Simon & Schuster.

Fine, Cordelia. (2010). *Delusions of Gender: How Our Minds, Society, and Neurosexism Create Difference*. W. W. Norton.

Fisher, Jami, Gene Mirus and Donna Jo Napoli. (2019). STICKY: Taboo Topics in Deaf Communities. In Keith Allan, ed., *The Oxford Handbook of Taboo Words and Language*. Oxford University Press, pp. 160–179.

Fogal, Daniel, Daniel W. Harris, and Matt Moss, eds. (2018). *New Work on Speech Acts*. Oxford University Press.

Frank, Francine Wattman and Paula A. Treichler, eds. (1989). *Language, Gender, and Professional Writing: Theoretical Approaches and Guidelines for Nonsexist Use*. Modern Language Association.

Freedman, Estelle B. (2013). *Redefining Rape: Sexual Violence in the Era of Suffrage and Segregation*. Harvard University Press.

Fricker, Miranda. (2007). *Epistemic Injustice: Power and the Ethics of Knowing*. Oxford University Press.

Friedan, Betty. (1963). *The Feminine Mystique*. W.W. Norton & Company.

Gates, Henry Louis, Jr. (1989). What's in a Name? *Dissent* (Fall, 1989), 487–496.

Garcia, Jorge L. A. (1996). The Heart of Racism. *Journal of Social Philosophy* 27, 5–45

Garcia, Jorge L. A. (1999). Philosophical Analysis and the Moral Concept of Racism. *Philosophy and Social Criticism*, 25(5), 1–32.

Gelman, Susan A. (2003). *The Essential Child: Origins of Essentialism in Everyday Thought*. Oxford University Press.

Glick, Peter and Susan T. Fiske. (1996). The Ambivalent Sexism Inventory: Differentiating Hostile and Benevolent Sexism. *Journal of Personality and Social Psychology*, 70(3), 491–512.

Glick, Peter and Susan T. Fiske. (2001). An Ambivalent Alliance: Hostile and Benevolent Sexism as Complementary Justifications of Gender Inequality. *American Psychologist*, 56, 109–118.

Goffman, Erving. (1967). On Facework. In Erving Goffman, *Interaction Ritual: Essays on Face-to-Face Behavior*. Doubleday, pp. 5–45.

Gould, Stephen Jay. (1981). *The Mismeasure of Man.* W. W. Norton.

Gracia, Jorge J. E. (2008). *Latinos in America: Philosophy and Social Identity.* Blackwell.

Greenberg, Jeff, and Tom Pyszczynski. (1985). The Effects of an Overheard Ethnic Slur on Evaluations of the Target: How to Spread a Social Disease. *Journal of Experimental Social Psychology,* 21(1), 61–72.

Greenberg, Joseph H. (2005) [1956]. *Language Universals: With Special Reference to Feature Hierarchies.* De Gruyter.

Grice, H. Paul. (1989). *Ways of Words.* Harvard University Press.

Gutiérrez, Ramón A. (2016). What's in a Name? The History and Politics of Hispanic and Latino Panethnicities. In Ramón A. Gutiérrez and Tomás Almaguer, eds., *The New Latino Studies Reader: A Twenty-First Century Perspective.* University of California Press, ch. 1, pp. 19–53.

Hacking, Ian. (1999). *The Social Construction of What?* Harvard University Press.

Hancock, Ange-Marie. (2016). *Intersectionality: An Intellectual History.* Oxford University Press.

Haslanger, Sally. (2012) [2000]. Gender and Race: (What) Are They? (What) Do We Want Them to Be? In Sally Haslanger, *Resisting Reality: Social Construction and Social Critique.* Oxford University Press, pp. 221–247.

Haslanger, Sally. (2012) [2010]. Language, Politics, and "The Folk": Looking for "The Meaning" of "Race." In Sally Haslanger, ed., *Resisting Reality: Social Construction and Social Critique.* Oxford University Press, pp. 429–445.

Hill, Jane H. (2008). *The Everyday Language of White Racism.* Wiley-Blackwell.

Horn, Laurence. (1984). Toward a New Taxonomy for Pragmatic Inference: Q-Based and R-Based Implicature. In Deborah Schiffrin, ed., *Meaning, Form, and Use in Context: Linguistic Applications.* Georgetown University Press, pp. 11–42.

Hull, Akasha (Gloria T.), Patricia Bell Scott, and Barbara Smith, eds. (2016) [1982]. *All the Women Are White, All the Blacks Are Men, But Some of Us Are Brave. Black Women's Studies,* 2nd ed. City University of New York. (First published by Feminist Press, Old Westbury, NY.)

Hulse, Carl. (2019). *Confirmation Bias: Inside Washington's War over the Supreme Court from Scalia's Death to Justice Kavanaugh.* Harper Collins.

Jeshion, Robin. (2013). Expressivism and the Offensiveness of Slurs. *Philosophical Perspectives*, 27, 232–259.

Jones, Karen. (2002). The Politics of Credibility. In Louise M. Antony and Charlotte Witt, eds., *A Mind of One's Own: Feminist Essays on Reason and Objectivity.* Westview (Taylor & Francis), pp. 154–176.

Kennedy, Randall. (2003). *Nigger: The Strange History of a Troublesome Word.* Vintage Books.

King, Thomas. (2013). *The Inconvenient Indian: A Curious Account of Native People in North America.* The University of Minnesota Press. (Originally published 2012, Doubleday Canada; 2nd ed., 2017.)

Kramarae, Cheris and Paula Treichler, eds. (1985). *A Feminist Dictionary.* Pandora.

Kraus, Michael W., Xanni Brown, and Hannah Swoboda. (2019). Dog Whistle Mascots: Native American Mascots as Normative Expressions of Prejudice. *Journal of Experimental and Social Psychology*, 84, 103810. https://doi.org/10.1016/j.jesp.2019.04.008.

Kukla, Rebecca. (2014). Performative Force, Convention, and Discursive Injustice. *Hypatia*, 29(2), 440–457.

Kukla, Rebecca and Mark Lance. (2009). *'Yo!' and 'Lo!': The Topography of the Space of Reasons.* Harvard University Press. (See esp. ch. 6, "Vocatives, Acknowledgments, and the Pragmatics of Recognition," ch. 7, "The Essential Second Person," [on communication and calling] and ch. 8, "Sharing a World" [interpellation].)

Lacour, Claudia Brodsky (1992). Doing Things with Words: Racism as Speech Act and the Undoing of Justice. In Toni Morrison, ed., *Racing Justice, En-gender-ing Power: Essays on Anita Hill, Clarence Thomas, and the Construction of Social Reality.* Pantheon Books, pp. 127–158.

Lakoff, Robin. (1973). *Language and Woman's Place.* Harper and Row.

Langton, Rae, Sally Haslanger, and Luvell Anderson. (2012). Language and Race. In Gillian Russell and Delia Graff Fara, eds., *The Routledge Companion to the Philosophy of Language.* Routledge, pp. 753–767.

Langton, Rae. (2018). Blocking as Counter-Speech. In Fogal, Harris, and Moss, eds. 2018, pp. 144–164.

Lee, Erika. (2015). *The Making of Asian America: A History*. Simon & Schuster.

Leslie, Sarah-Jane. (2017). The Original Sin of Cognition: Fear, Prejudice and Generalization. *The Journal of Philosophy*, 114(8), 1–29.

Leslie, Sarah-Jane, and Susan A. Gelman. (2012). Quantified Statements Are Recalled as Generics: Evidence from Preschool Children and Adults. *Cognitive Psychology*, 64(3), 186–214.

Leslie, Sarah-Jane and Adam Lerner. (2016). Generic Generalizations. In E. Zalta, ed., *Stanford Encyclopedia of Philosophy*. http://plato .stanford.edu/entries/generics.

Lewontin, R. C. (1972). The Apportionment of Human Diversity. In Theodosius Dobzhansky, Max K. Hecht, and William C. Steere, eds., *Evolutionary Biology*, Vol. 6. Meredith Publishing Company, pp. 381–398). DOI:https://doi.org/10.1007/978-1-4684-9063-3_14.

Litvak, Joseph. (2009). *The Un-Americans: Jews, the Blacklist, and Stoolpigeon Culture*. Duke University Press.

Maas, Anne, Daniela Salvi, Luciano Arcuri, and Gün Semin. (1989). Language Use in Intergroup Contexts: The Linguistic Intergroup Bias. *Journal of Personality and Social Psychology* 57(6), 981–993.

Madva, Alex and Michael Brownstein. (2018). Stereotypes, Prejudice, and the Taxonomy of the Implicit Social Mind. *Noûs*, 53(2), 611–644

Manne, Kate. (2016). Humanism: A Critique. *Social Theory and Practice*, 42(2) (April 2016), 389–415.

Maparyan, Layli Phillips, ed. (2011). *The Womanist Idea*. Routledge.

Martin, Ben L. (1991). From Negro to Black to African American: The Power of Names and Naming. *Political Science Quarterly*, 106(1), 83–107.

Matsuda, Mari J. (1989). Public Response for Racist Speech: Considering the Victim's Story. *Michigan Law Review* 87 (August 1989). (Reprinted in Matsuda et al., eds. 1993, pp. 17–52.)

Matsuda, Mari J., Charles R. Lawrence III, Richard Delgado, and Kimberlè Williams Crenshaw, eds. (1993). *Words that Wound: Critical Race Theory, Assaultive Speech, and the First Amendment*. Westview Press.

McConnell-Ginet, Sally. (1989). The Sexual (Re)Production of Meaning: A Discourse-Based Theory. In Francine H. Frank and Paula A. Treichler, eds., *Language, Gender, and Professional Writing: Theoretical Approaches and Guidelines for Nonsexist Usage*. Modern

Language Association. (Reprinted with slight changes in Cameron, ed. 1998 and with additional comments in McConnell-Ginet 2011).

McConnell-Ginet, Sally. (2003). 'What's in a Name?': Social Labeling and Gender Practices. In J. Holmes and M. Meyerhoff, eds., *The Handbook of Language and Gender*. Blackwell, pp. 69–97.

McConnell-Ginet, Sally. (2006a). Why Defining is Seldom "Just Semantics'": Marriage, "Marriage," and Other Minefields. In B. Birner and G. Ward, eds., *Drawing the Boundaries of Meaning: Neo-Gricean Studies in Pragmatics and Semantics in Honor of Laurence R. Horn*. John Benjamins, pp. 223–246.

McConnell-Ginet, Sally. (2006b). Why Defining is Seldom "Just Semantics": Marriage, "Marriage," and Other Minefields. Shortened version of McConnell-Ginet (2006a), anthologized in D. Cameron and D. Kulick, eds., *Language and Sexuality: A Reader*. Routledge, pp. 227–240.

McConnell-Ginet, Sally. (2008). Words in the World: How and Why Meanings Can Matter. *Language*, 84(3), 497–527.

McConnell-Ginet, Sally. (2011). *Gender, Sexuality, and Meaning: Linguistic Practice and Politics*. Oxford University Press.

McConnell-Ginet, Sally. (2012). Generic Predication and Interest Relativity. *Canadian Journal of Linguistics*, 57(2), 261–287.

McConnell-Ginet, Sally. (2014). Gender and Its Relation to Sex: The Myth of Natural Gender. In Greville Corbett, ed., *The Expression of Gender*. DeGruyter, pp. 3–38.

McConnell-Ginet, Sally. (2018a). Truth, Trust and Trumpery. *The Southern Journal of Philosophy*, 56 (Special Supplement), 33–49.

McConnell-Ginet, Sally. (2018b). Semantics and Pragmatics: Blurring Boundaries and Constructing Contexts. In Kira Hall and Rusty Barrett, eds., *Oxford Handbook of Language and Sexuality*. Oxford University Press. www.oxfordhandbooks.com/view/10.1093/oxfordhb/9780190212926.001.0001/oxfordhb-9780190212926-e-6.

McGowan, Mary Kate. (2012). On "Whites Only" Signs and Racist Hate Speech. In Ishani Maitra and Mary Kate McGowan, eds., *Speech and Harm: Controversies over Free Speech*. Oxford University Press, pp. 121–147.

McWhorter, John. (2016). Stop Policing the N-Word. *Time*. May 3, 2016. https://time.com/4316322/larry-wilmore-obama-n-word/.

McWhorter, John. (2018). Trump and the N Word. *The Atlantic*. August 15, 2018. www.theatlantic.com/ideas/archive/2018/08/trumps-racism-isnt-new/567700/.

Mills, Charles W. (2003). "Heart Attack": A Critique of Jorge Garcia's Volitional Conception of Racism. *The Journal of Ethics*. Special Issue: *Race, Racism, and Reparations* 7 (1), 29–62.

Mills, Charles. (2007). White Ignorance. In Shannon Sullivan and Nancy Tuana, eds., *Race and Epistemologies of Ignorance*. SUNY Press, pp. 11–38.

Mills, Charles W. (2017). *Black Rights/White Wrongs: The Critique of Racial Liberalism*. Oxford University Press.

Mirus, Gene, Jamie Fisher, and Donna Jo Napoli. (2019). (Sub)lexical Changes in Iconic Signs to Realign with Community Sensibilities and Experiences. *Language in Society*, 49(2), 283–309. DOI:10.1017/S0047404519000745.

Moore, Lisa Jean and Paisley Currah. (2015). Legally Sexed: Birth Certificates and Transgender Citizens. In Rachel E. Dubrofsky and Shoshana Amielle Magnet, eds., *Feminist Surveillance Studies*. Duke University Press, pp. 58–78.

Morales, Ed. (2018). *Latinx: The New Force in American Politics and Culture*. Verso.

Most, Andrea. (2000). "You've Got to be Carefully Taught": The Politics of Race in Rodgers and Hammerstein's "South Pacific." *Theatre Journal*, 52(3), 307–337.

Nickel, Bernhard. (2016). *Between Logic and the World: An Integrated Theory of Generics*. Oxford University Press.

Nunberg, Geoff. (2012). *Ascent of the Asshole: The First 60 Years*. PublicAffairs.

Nunberg, Geoff. (2018). The Social Life of Slurs. In Fogal, Harris, and Moss, eds. 2018, pp. 296–316.

Omi, Michael and Howard Winant. (2015). *Racial Formation in the United States*, 3rd ed. Routledge. (First published 1986.)

Painter, Nell Irvin. (2010). *The History of White People*. W.W. Norton.

Parrott, Lilli. (2010). Vocatives and Other Direct Address Forms: A Contrastive Study. In A. Grønn and I. Marijanovic, eds., Russian in Contrast, Oslo Studies in Language, 2(1), 211–229. ISSN 1890–9639. https://journals.uio.no/index.php/osla/article/view/68.

Payne, B. K., Vuletich, H. A., and K.B. Lundberg, K. B. (2017). The Bias of Crowds: How Implicit Bias Bridges Personal and Systemic Prejudice. *Psychological Inquiry*, 28, 233–248.

Phillips, Layli (Maparyan), ed. (2006). *The Womanist Reader: The First Quarter Century of Womanist Thought.* Routledge.

Pinker, Steven. (2002). *The Stuff of Thought: Language as a Window into Human Nature.* Viking.

Pollock, Mica. (2004). *Colormute: Racetalk Dilemmas in an American School.* Princeton University Press.

Poussaint, Alvin F. (1991) [1967]. A Negro Psychiatrist Explains the Negro Psyche. Reprinted in August Meier, John Bracey, Jr. and the late Elliott Rudwick, *Black Protest in the Sixties*, 2nd ed. Markus Wiener Publishing. (Originally published in *The New York Times Sunday Magazine*, August 20, 1967, pp. 52+).

Putnam, Hilary. (1975). The Meaning of *Meaning*. In K. Gunderson, ed., *Language, Mind, and Knowledge.* University of Minnesota Press, pp. 131–193.

Raymond, Chase Wesley. (2016). Linguistic Reference in the Negotiation of Identity and Action: Revisiting the T/V Distinction. *Language*, 92(3), 636–667.

Redd, Nola Taylor. (2017). Planet Again? Pluto, Most Moons Count Under Proposed Definition. *Space.com*, 25 March 2017. www.space .com/36214-planet-definition-includes-pluto-most-moons.html.

Reich, David. (2018). *Who We Are and How We Got Here: Ancient DNA and the New Science of the Human Past.* Oxford University Press.

Rhodes, Marjorie, Sarah-Jane Leslie, Lydia Bianchi, and Lisa Chalik. (2018). The Role of Generic Language in the Early Development of Social Categorization. *Child Development*, 89(1), 148–155.

Rickford, John R. (2016). Language and Linguistics on Trial: Hearing Rachel Jeantel and Other Vernacular Speakers in the Courtroom and Beyond. *Language*, 92(4), 948–988.

Ritchie, Kate. (2019). Should We Use Racial and Gender Generics? *Thought: A Journal of Philosophy*, 8(1), 33–41.

Roberts, Craige. (2015). Accommodation in a Language Game. In Barry Loewer and Jonathan Schaffer, eds., *The Blackwell Companion to David Lewis.* Blackwell., pp. 345–366.

Rosch, Eleanor. (1973). On the Internal Structure of Perceptual and Semantic Categories. In T. E. Moore, ed., *Cognitive Development and the Acquisition of Language*. Academic Press, pp. 111–44.

Rosch, Eleanor. (1975). Cognitive Representations of Semantic Categories, *Journal of Experimental Psychology: General*, 104, 192–233.

Runyon, Kirby D., S. A. Stern, T. R. Lauer, W. Grundy, M. E. Summer, and K. N. Singer. (2017). A Geophysical Planet Definition. *Lunar and Planetary Science* XLVIII, 1448. /www.hou.usra.edu/meetings/lpsc2017/pdf/1448.pdf.

Russell, Diana E. H. (1990). *Rape in Marriage*. Indiana University Press.

Russell, Lindsay Rose. (2018). *Women and Dictionary Making: Gender, Genre, and English Language Lexicography*. Cambridge University Press.

Saul, Jennifer. (2017a). Are Generics Especially Pernicious? *Inquiry*, 1–18. DOI:https://doi.org/10.1080/0020174X.2017.1285995.

Saul, Jennifer. (2017b). Racial Figleaves, the Shifting Boundaries of the Permissible, and the Rise of Donald Trump. *Philosophical Topics*, 45(2), 97–116.

Saul, Jennifer. (2018). Dogwhistles, Political Manipulation, and Philosophy of Language. In Fogal, Harris, and Moss, eds. 2018, pp. 360–383.

Schabas, William. (2000). Hate Speech in Rwanda: The Road to Genocide. *McGill Law Journal*, 46, 141–171.

Schnake, Sherry B. and Janet B. Ruscher. (1998). Modern Racism as a Predictor of the Linguistic Intergroup Bias. *Journal of Language and Social Psychology* 17(4), 484–491.

Schulz, Muriel. (1975). The Semantic Derogation of Women. In Barrie Thorne and Nancy Henley, eds., *Language and Sex: Difference and Dominance*. Newbury House, pp. 64–75.

Serano, Julia. (2007). *Whipping Girl: A Transsexual Woman on Sexism and the Scapegoating of Femininity*. Seal Press.

Serano, Julia. (2013). *Excluded: Making Feminist and Queer Movements More Inclusive*. Seal Press.

Shapiro, Fred R. (1985). Historical Notes on the Vocabulary of the Women's Movement. *American Speech*, 60(1) (Spring 1985), 3–16.

Shelby, Tommie. (2002). Is Racism in the "Heart"? *Journal of Social Philosophy* 33(3), 411–420.

Shields, Matthew. (2019). *The Pragmatics and Epistemology of Conceptual Disagreement*. PhD Dissertation, Department of Philosophy, Georgetown University.

Sibomana, André. (1999). *Hope for Rwanda: Conversations with Laure Guilbert and Hervé Deguine*. Pluto Press.

Smitherman, Geneva. (2000 (revised)) [1994]. *Black Talk: Words and Phrases from the Hood to the Amen Corner*. Houghton Mifflin.

Smitherman, Geneva. (2006). *Word from the Mother: Language and African Americans*. Routledge.

Sosa, David, ed. (2018). *Bad Words*. Oxford University Press.

Spears, Arthur K. (2006). Perspectives: A View of the "N-Word" from Sociolinguistics. *Diverse Issues in Higher Education*. Published online July 13, 2006. https://diverseeducation.com/article/6114/.

Spears, Arthur K. (2007). African American Communicative Practices: Improvisation, Semantic License, and Augmentation. In H. Samy Alim and John Baugh, eds., *Talking Black Talk: Language, Education, and Social Change*, Teachers College Press, Multicultural Education Series, pp. 100–111.

Spires, Derrick R. (2020). *The Practice of Citizenship: Black Politics and Print Culture in the Early United States*. University of Pennsylvania Press.

Stannard, Una. (1977). *Mrs Man*. Germainbooks.

Stanley, Julia P. (1977). Paradigmatic Woman: The Prostitute. In D. L. Shores and C. P. Hines, eds., *Papers in Language Variation*. University of Alabama Press, pp. 303–321.

Stanley, Jason. (2015). *How Propaganda Works*. Princeton University Press.

Steele, Claude. (2010). *Whistling Vivaldi: How Stereotypes Affect Us and What We Can Do*. W. W. Norton.

Swanson, Eric. (2021). Slurs and Ideologies. In Robin Celikates, Sally Haslanger, and Jason Stanley, eds., *Analyzing Ideology: New Essays*. Oxford University Press.

Taylor, John R. (2003). *Linguistic Categorization*, 3rd ed. Oxford University Press.

Tellefsen, Blythe. (2005). America Is a Diet Pepsi: Sherman Alexie's *Reservation Blues*. *Western American Literature*, 40(2), 125–147.

Tirrell, Lynne. (2012). Genocidal Language Games. In Ishani Maitra and Mary Kate McGowan, eds., *Speech and Harm: Controversies over Free Speech*. Oxford University Press, pp. 174–221.

Treichler, Paula. (1989). From Discourse to Dictionary: How Sexist Meanings Are Authorized. In Frank and Treichler, eds., 1989, pp. 51–79.

Treichler, Paula and Francine Wattman Frank. (1989). Introduction: Scholarship, Feminism, and Language Change. In Frank and Treichler, eds., 1989, pp. 1–32.

Veilleux, Fred. (1995). Indians Are a People, Not Mascots. In Laura J. Lederer and Richard Delgado, eds., *The Price We Pay: The Case against Racist Speech, Hate Propaganda, and Pornography*. Hill and Wang, pp. 45–54.

Voigt, Rob, Nicholas P. Camp, Vinodkumar Prabhakaran, William L. Hamilton, Rebecca C. Hetey, Camilla M. Griffith, David Jurgens, Dan Jurafsky, and Jennifer Eberhardt. (2017). Language from Police Body Camera Footage Shows Racial Disparities in Officer Report. *Proceedings of National Academy of Sciences*. 114(25) (June 20, 2017), 6521–6526.

von der Malsburg, Titus, Till Poppels, and Roger P. Levy. (2020). Implicit Gender Bias in Linguistic Descriptions for Expected Events: The Cases of the 2016 US and 2017 UK Elections. *Psychological Science*, 31(2), https://doi.org/10.1177/0956797619890619.

von Hippel, Willem, Denise Sekaquaptewa, and Patrick Vargas. (1997). The Linguistic Intergroup Bias as an Implicit Indicator of Prejudice. *Journal of Experimental Social Psychology*, 33, 490–509.

Wales, K. F. (1983). Modern English: Brown and Gilman Re-appraised. *Studia Linguistica*, 37(2), 107–25.

Watson, Peter. (1960). On the Failure to Eliminate Hypotheses in a Conceptual Task. *Quarterly Journal of Experimental Psychology*, 12(3), 129–140.

Wierzbicka, Anna. (1986). What's in a Noun? (Or: How Do Nouns Differ in Meaning from Adjectives?). *Studies in Language*, 10, 253–389. (Reprinted in Anna Wierzbicka, 1988, *The Semantics of Grammar*. John Benjamins, pp. 463–497.)

Wigboldus, Daniël H. J., Gün R. Semin, and Russell Spears (2000). How Do We Communicate Stereotypes? Linguistic Biases and Inferential Consequences. *Journal of Personality and Social Psychology*, 28(1), 5–18

Williams, Raymond. (1983). *Keywords: A Vocabulary of Culture and Society*. Revised ed., Oxford University Press. (This version first published in 1983 in UK by Fontana Paperbacks.)

Wittgenstein, Ludwig. (1958). *Philosophical Investigations*. 3rd ed. Translated by G. E. M. Anscombe. Macmillan. (German and English on facing pages.)

Index

Asian American, 23–24, 59–60, 61–62, 80, 93

ASL. *See* American Sign Language

asshole, 163–164

Atrocities Documentation Survey, 145

Auburn Correctional Facility, 252

audism, 177–179

changes in ASL sign for, 211

Austen, Jane, 199, 281–282

Austin, John, 190, *See also* speech act

Aztec (language). *See* Nahuatl

Aztec (people), 18

Bailey, Liberty Hyde, 247–248, 251

Bailey, Mona, 181

Baltic languages, 110

Baraniev, Sacha. *See* Bartlett, Cy

Barnett, Sonya, 159

Barr, Roseanne, 142

Bartlett, Cy, 269

Battistella, Edwin (Ed), 231–232

Beal, John, 269

Beale, Fran, 160

Beardsley, Elizabeth, 51

Beaver, David, 80

Beeghly, Erin, 81. *See also* Madva, Alex

Belten High, 67–71

Bem, Sandra Lipsitz, 37, 176

Benesch, Susan, 136

benevolent sexism, 180

Bennett, Lerone Jr., 25–27. *See Ebony*

Bettcher, Talia, 240

biases, cognitive, 97–101

Bill of Rights, US, 275

Bird, Carolyn, 176

birth certificate

marking sex/gender on, 33–36

bitch, 161

black feminism/feminist. See womanism

Black is Beautiful, 3, 26

Black Lives Matter, 90–92

willfully misinterpreted as 'only black' rather than 'black also,' 92

Black Panther, The (newspaper), 21

Black Panthers, The, 21, 27

Black Power, 26

Black Students United (BSU), Cornell, 248

Black/black, 25–30, 88, 209. *See also* African American, *colo(u)red (people)*, *Negro/negro*

self-labeling connected to political activism, 26, 27

Blackwell, Henry, 192, 195

Blake, Renée, 28–29

BLM. *See* Black Lives Matter

Blum, Lawrence, 13–14. *See racialized group*

Bodine, Ann, 112

Bolinger, Dwight

on nouns vs adjectives, 42–44

Bonilla-Silva, Eduardo, 90, 185, 261, 273

Botanic Gardens, Cornell, 247–251. *See* Plantations, Cornell

Boylan, Jennifer Finney, 242

"Boys don't cry," 104

Brison, Susan, 196

British Sign Language (BSL), 264

Brooks, Richard, 145

Brown, Michael, 91. *See also* Black Lives Matter

Brown, Roger, 110, 111–112. *See also* Gilman, Albert

Brownmiller, Susan, 194

Brownstein, Michael, 81

BSL. *See* British Sign Language (BSL)

Burnett, Heather, 165–166

Burridge, Kate, 208

Bush, George W., 128–129

Butler, Robert C., 177

Caesar, Julius, 74, 109

Cameron, Deborah, 57–58, 197–198, 218–219, 237–238

gender (and racial) limitations in
definitions of litigated, 225–228
SCOTUS elimination of racial
restrictions on, 226
Marriage Bill, The, 230
Martin, Tracy, 91. *See* Martin, Trayvon
Martin, Trayvon, 90–92
Maryapan, Layli, 180
mascots, 153–158
masculine. *See* gender identity vs gender
expression
master
Harvard, Princeton, and Yale's
abandonment of as title, 248
Matal v. Tam, 156
McCarthy, John, 268–269
McCulloch, Gretchen, 266
McGowan, Mary Kate, 47, 274
McVeigh, Timothy, 102–103
McWhorter, John, 272–273
Me Too. *See* #MeToo
Meng, Grace, 24
mental illness, 234–235
metaphor, nonhuman, 138–143, 144
Mexican, 20. *See* Latino/Hispanic
Mills, Charles, 89, 184, 187
Miqmaq, 205
Mirus, Gene, 209–212, 263
misogynoir, 181
misogyny. *See* sexism
Mock Spanish, 186
Moore, Lisa, 240–241
Mora, Cristina, 21–22
Morales, Ed, 256–257, 261–262
Morrison, Toni, 189
Mosley, Walter, 152–153
Most, Andrea, 100

NAACP. *See* National Association for
the Advancement of Colored
People
Nahuatl, 205

name. *See also* nickname
alternative forms of and bearer's
preferences, 127–128
bestowing to dominate vs changing
for self-affirmation, 126
'real' of Jewish origin revealed by
HUAC, 268–269
sexual politics of, 126–127
unequal power to bestow, 122
name-calling
as language game, 144–145
as recruiting allies to harm those
'named,' 144, 145
by blacks targeting whites, 149
demonizing people with mental
health challenges, 234–235
not targeting identity groups,
162–163
NAMI. *See* National Alliance for the
Mentally Ill
naming, 125–130. *See also* epistemic
injustice
as giving analytical and political access
to phenomena (e.g., *date rape*,
sexual harassment), 182
family names, 126
sexual politics, 126
Napoli, Donna Jo, 209–212, 263
National Alliance for the Mentally Ill
(NAMI), 234, 235
National Association for the
Advancement of Colored People
(NAACP), 26
National Collegiate Athletic Association
(NCAA), 155
National Football League (NFL), 146,
153, 274–275
National Geographic, article on race, 11
National Memorial for Peace and
Justice, 117
Native American Indian Studies, 41. *See*
Indigenous Peoples Studies

CPSIA information can be obtained
at www.ICGtesting.com
Printed in the USA
LVHW011201210820
663744LV00014B/436

9 781108 445900